The Representational Theory of Mind

The Representational Theory of Mind

An Introduction

Kim Sterelny

Basil Blackwell

First published 1990
First published in USA 1991

Basil Blackwell Ltd
108 Cowley Road, Oxford, OX4 1JF, UK

Basil Blackwell, Inc.
3 Cambridge Center
Cambridge, Massachusetts 02142, USA

British Library Cataloguing in Publication Data

A CIP catalogue record for this book is available from the British Libriary.

Library of Congress Cataloging in Publication Data

Sterelny, Kim.
The representational theory of mind: an introduction / Kim
Sterelny.
   p.   cm.
Includes bibliographical references.
ISBN 0-631-15884-7   ISBN 0-631-16498-7 (pbk.)
1. Representation (Philosophy) 2. Mind and body. 3. Mental
representation. 4. Knowledge, Theory of. I. Title.
B105.R4S73 1991   90-35273
128'.2—dc20   CIP

Typeset in 10½ on 12pt Ehrhardt
by Best-set Typesetters Ltd, Hong Kong
Printed in Great Britain by
T. J. Press Ltd, Padstow, Cornwall

Contents

Preface

In Australia a few years ago there was a vogue for beginning papers with an account of what they were not about; perhaps this preface may begin a similar fashion. For this book is not a conventional introduction to the philosophy of mind. Those books are normally directed at an ontological question. Are human minds physical entities, and do they have only physical properties? Keith Campbell's *Body and Mind* (1970), to take one excellent example of this genre, both tries to clarify these questions and to answer them. This book is not primarily a contribution to the dualist–physicalist debate, for I regard that debate as essentially settled. Of course, I know that there are many who disagree, but I will assume throughout that we need to give some kind of physicalist theory of the mind. Those sympathetic to dualism will take it that I have set myself an impossible task; they will expect the theories considered hereafter to be impoverished, or flawed in some other deep way. They might find chapter 10 cheering. To the extent that this book argues for physicalism, the argument is indirect. It's a demonstration, contrary to dualist expectation, that we can construct physicalist theories of important aspects of our mental life. But I have not concerned myself with the phenomenon (or perhaps phenomena) that has generated most of the recent heat in the ontological debate, consciousness and the subjective nature of experience. I do not ignore the introspected life because I think it is uninteresting, or because no problems about the nature of introspection and experience remain. Rather, I do so because I have nothing to say on that topic that has not already been said. Bill Lycan's *Consciousness* (1987) is a fine materialist tract on experience written from on overall theoretical stance very similar to mine. I haven't much to add to what he has said. Moreover, the facts of experience have not played much role in the construction of empirically grounded theories of thinking; it's those theories that are the focus of this book.

My brief is not inner experience but sentience. My aim is to explain and defend a physicalist theory of intelligence against its rivals. Moreover, I want to defend a theory of our intelligence that is compatible not just with physicalism but with our pretheoretic view of ourself. On that view, we are agents. Our actions, sometimes, are caused by our beliefs and desires; more generally, by our thoughts. In my view, it is literally true that we sometimes do something because we want to. Many contemporary physicalists take their physicalism to have radical consequences. Some think it is just plain false that we have beliefs and desires; if so, belief and desire could hardly explain behaviour. Many more think that talk of belief and desire is in some way second rate. While it may, in some sense, be true that I think well of Australian red wines and for that reason often drink them, this truth does not have the same status of, say, the truth that I am an evolved animal. Humans have their evolutionary history independently of anyone's views or interests on the matter. Our evolutionary history is objective. Not so, according to some, is our intentional profile. Whether a creature has thoughts, and what those thoughts are, depends somehow on the person describing them. The theory defended in this book is conservative, not radical; I think we are both organisms and agents.

The book falls roughly into two. The first six chapters consist of an exposition, elaboration and defence of one of the main contemporary theories of human (but not only human) sentience. I defend a functionalist theory of mind. The essential characteristic of a mental state, or of a mental device, is its function; the job it does in the ongoing mental life. So, for instance, on this view, the essential characteristic of pain is its role in the detection of current bodily damage, and the avoidance of future damage. The design of a device by natural selection determines its function or functions. The job of the retina is to register the intensity of the light that strikes the eye, because evolution has designed the retina for that purpose. Similarly, the complex set of pathways, neurotransmitters, hormones and the like on which our experience of pain is based exists because natural selection has favoured a complex system of damage detection and avoidance. That is why the function of pain is detection and avoidance.

More specifically, I defend a version of the language of thought hypothesis. The point of this hypothesis is to explain how internal states can simultaneously have the function of representing the world, and of directing behaviour in ways that make sense given their representational content. Very roughly, according to this hypothesis, thoughts are sentences in the head. They represent or misrepresent the world, in virtue of causal relations of some kind between chunks of these sentences and individuals and types of individual in the world. When you think about beer, you have within your head a mental sentence with a mentalese expression for beer in it. It's an expression for beer because it stands in some kind of causal relationship with the stuff. Thoughts are language-like representations of the world. But thoughts also direct behaviour, and an account of how they do that links the representational theory of the mind to computational theorizing about the mind. There are plenty of uselessly loose analogies between minds and computers around, but in my view that model does real work in explaining how internal representational structures can direct behaviour.

Probably all this seems hopelessly vague, or hopelessly cryptic. I hope by the end of chapter 6, it will seem clear and intuitively plausible; a compelling vision of sentience. Sad to say, it has not seemed so to many in a position to know better. The final four chapters consider rivals and objections.

There is a widespread view that a mentalese theory of intelligence is 'unbiological', that it is physicalist in name only. It fails sufficiently to take into account the fact that we humans, and all other sentient creatures of which we know, do our thinking with brains. Brains are very different from standard computers; neurons, the elements from which they are constructed, are simple and slow. But there are huge numbers of them, and they are densely connected; a single neuron can be directly connected to as many as 10,000 others. Moreover, the pattern of skill varies sharply between minds and computers. As we all know, computers are calculating prodigies; they are fast and accurate. But it is very difficult to get them to recognize patterns. It would be hard to make one do well in a 'What's that tune?' contest. These contrasts make many suspect that if we want to understand human mental processing, there is no point in looking to artificial intelligence. Since the language of thought hypothesis does look to computational theories for its account of process, it is threatened by these suspicions. In chapters 7–10, I try to alleviate these suspicions, and consider some of the theories they have given rise to.

Of course, the division of the book into the exposition and defence of one theory, and the examination of its rivals cannot be sharp. There is critical material in the first chunk; in particular, the fifth chapter is largely devoted to arguing against sceptics who deny that our thoughts represent (or misrepresent) our world. Moreover, the defence of the representational theory of mind against its rivals requires its constructive development.

My approach is not just physicalist, it is naturalist. 'Naturalism' is a term in philosophy so vague that it is in danger of becoming merely honorific. As I shall use it (or perhaps preempt it), it has a methodological as well as an ontological dimension. Naturalists are physicalists, though our stricter comrades (for instance the Churchlands) think some of us are nonpractising physicalists. I prefer to think that we are small 'p' physicalists (see chapter 9 for the dispute). But naturalists have methodological views about philosophy as well; we think philosophy is continuous with the natural sciences. On this view, philosophical theories are conjectures whose fate is ultimately determined by empirical investigation, though obviously they are vastly less well developed than the paradigms of natural science; consequently their ties to the data are much looser. An alternative is to see philosophy as an investigation into conceptual truths proceeding by thought experiments that probe the way we understand our own concepts. Colin McGinn's *The Character of Mind* (1983) is a recent introduction to the philosophy of mind written from this perspective. I certainly agree that unravelling complex concepts is part of the philosophical enterprise, but I do not think it is possible to segment the investigation of thinking into a purely conceptual chunk that is independent of the empirical world, and an empirical chunk. For example, I do not believe an account of the nature of mental representation divides into conceptual truths about representation in general, and empirical facts about how our heads work. There very likely are 'conceptual truths'; truths that depend only on the way we understand concepts and thus depend not at all on how the world is. But I doubt that there are any very interesting conceptual truths about the mind, or about thinking.

So this book is one of a considerable number of recent attempts to show that philosophical and empirical investigations can be synthesized to the benefit of both. It is meant to introduce people to this approach to philosophy by exemplifying it. Thus, I have produced a manifesto, or at least an advertisement, as well as a text. It is certainly not just a summary, or report on the existing literature; I have tried to advance the debate as well as explain it.

The validity of this enterprise is best established by doing it, rather than preaching its virtues and pouring forth polemics against its rivals, though readers of my earlier book with Michael Devitt will know that I have not previously been shy as either preacher or polemicist. This book has fewer philosophers wearing black hats in it than *Language and Reality* (Devitt and Sterelny, 1987), though this gentleness of style is also caused by the great difficulty, even obscurity, of many of the issues I discuss. I don't dare to be dogmatic, much as I would have liked to be. But one, perhaps unfortunate, consequence of a non-polemical approach is that the partisans of one understanding of the philosophy of mind may find that their views have been given too little consideration. I have really written only on empirical approaches to the philosophy of mind and psychology. There is an otherwise diverse group who think there are important truths about the mind that, for one reason or another, are inaccessible to the natural sciences. Putnam in his recent moods, Peacocke, those who write on Kripke, Wittgenstein and the Kripgenstein paradox all fall in their different ways into this category. I have had largely to ignore this group, the constraints on time, energy and space being what they are. I hope those who do not share my approach will at least find this book useful as a good synopsis of what they do not like, and perhaps, as an exemplary instance of what to avoid.

I do not primarily intend this as a first book in philosophy of mind. There already exist fine elementary texts; for instance, Campbell's *Body and Mind* (1970), and Churchland's *Matter and Consciousness* (1988a). I have not attempted to produce a rival to these, but rather a bridge between introductory works and contemporary debate. So the basic use I have in mind is for an upper level undergraduate course, or perhaps for a graduate course. That is how I have used drafts. I have, however, tried to make this work as accessible as possible to those with not much philosophical background. To that end, I have explained technical vocabulary as I have introduced it. I have also provided a short glossary, for I would like it to be readable and useful to those with a background in one or other of the cognitive sciences. That, I hope, is enough of explanation and apology.

To the despair of authors, books don't write themselves. They don't grow like mould in the back of a drawer, however much they resemble fungi in other ways. Nor are they produced entirely by their authors. Michael Devitt, Peter Godfrey-Smith, Frank Jackson, Karen Neander, Philip Pettit and Bill Ramsey wrote comments on various chunks of draft, and I would like to express my thanks to them all. But in addition to formal commentary, I have discussed the issues herein with them many many times, and that help may well have been even more valuable. I have also had this type of informal feedback from Nick Agar, Kathy Akins, David Braddon-Mitchell, Fiona Cowie, John Fitzpatrick, Bill Lycan, Andrew Milne, Norbert Hornstein and Steve Stich. My thanks and apologies to those I have forgotten to mention. I began this book while at the Australian National University's Institute for Advanced Study, which is a wonderful place to work; I was able to return there for a month at the beginning of 1989, thanks to the Automated Reasoning Project. But most of it was written at the Victoria University of Wellington; the philosophy department here has proved to be a very comfortable and easy place to work. It also gave me the opportunity to inflict rough versions of this book on advanced undergraduates in 1988 and 1989. Let me put on record my thanks to these guinea pigs, who were good to teach and surprisingly un-complaining. Every effort has been made to trace the copyright holder for figures 4 and 5 and I should like to thank MIT Press and W. H. Freeman for their help in this as yet unsuccessful search.

Let me finish with a few words on terminology and style. In this field, terminology is anything but uniform. Positions and ideas go by many names. Instead of selecting a name and using it consistently, I have mostly chosen to reflect this diversity. I hope thereby to make terminology used in follow-up reading familiar from use. The exception is where I regard an existing terminology as downright confusing; I have noted these occasions in the text. The 'Suggested Reading' is, of course, very selective. It has been constrained both by space and my own knowledge; I know that many fine books and papers have been excluded. Finally, a remark on pronouns: using 'he' when gender is not determined by context grates on many. Using 'he or she' repeatedly is intolerably clumsy, so I have compromised by juggling more or less at random between 'he' and 'she'.

1

A Functionalist Theory of the Mind

1.1 Materialism and Functionalism

Philosophy is an integrative discipline. The sciences, history, our own and others' experience inform us about aspects of reality. They are pieces of a puzzle. Philosophers try to build an overall picture of the world and our place in it from these pieces. That task is not easy. Some pieces are missing, and others are incomplete. There is much we do not know. But there is a more serious problem yet: sometimes the parts seem incompatible. This book is concerned with such a case.

There are two very different pictures of what we are. One is derived from immersion in our own culture. According to this picture, we are conscious rational agents. We live in, and thus experience, a physical and social world. As a result, we have hopes and fears, plans, expectations, beliefs. Our actions reflect, and are explained by, these mental facts. Thus, Skidnose Harris voted for Thatcher because Skidnose feared street crime, and believed Thatcher would reduce it. We can relate behaviour to our mental life this way even when we are sceptical about the wants and beliefs involved. Thus we can explain Zoltan's eating garlic sandwiches by appeal to Zoltan's fearing vampires and believing garlicky breath to be a vampire repellent. We do so despite our justified scepticism about vampires. In brief, and grandiosely, we are conscious, self-directed beings. Our actions have intentional or belief-desire explanations. We are intentional agents. Our actions reflect our thoughts. This is the picture of *folk psychology*.

There is an alternative *physicalist* picture which emphasizes our continuity with nature. Humans are organisms. We do not differ, except perhaps in complexity, from the rest of the biological world. The biological world, in turn, is just a part of the physical world. The message of the last 300 years of science is that ultimately we – and all else – are nothing but swarms of particles.

If we are particle swarms, could we be conscious, thinking beings as well? This book will develop and discuss a compatibilist position; I hope to show that we are physical thinkers. I shall assume, rather than argue, that human beings are physical entities. If the folk picture and the scientific picture were to prove incompatible, one option is to abandon the scientific picture. It has been thought that no sentient being, or no conscious being, could be just a physical object. So, since we are sentient and conscious, we are not mere physical systems. That is not my view. The doctrine of 'the ghost in the machine' is not only inconsistent with all we know from physiology, neurophysiology and human evolution, it's as well wracked with internal problems. None of its defenders have ever shown how our physical and our nonphysical elements could interact. So I shall make the still controversial assumption that dualism won't do.

We cannot reject the scientific image of ourselves, so we must try to reconcile it with what we know of ourselves from our common experience. What makes a mental state the distinctive mental state it is; for example, what makes anger anger? It is often supposed that the distinctive feature of that mental state – the feature that makes it anger – is its introspective, experiential quality. Being angry feels a certain special way. Though initially tempting, there are many difficulties with this idea. First, the introspectible qualities of anger sometimes simply seem absent; a person can be angry without being able to tell that fact about themselves. Second, it's not obvious that the experiential sensations of anger are different from other emotional states of great arousal; fear, excitement. Third, anger seems to have a cognitive component: to involve (like jealousy) special types of belief and desire. For example, the desire to do violence. But cognitive states need not be conscious. Nor are they distinguished from one another by their experiential quality.

These objections may not be fatal to the view that to be angry is to have an inner experience of a special sort. But there is an alternative, *functionalist* account of anger. The central thesis of all the many forms of functionalism is this: the essential feature of any mental state is its causal role. So, according to the functionalist, the distinctive or essential characteristic of anger is its causal role. Anger has distinctive causes that typically involve the belief that wrong has been done, and distinctive mental, behavioural and physiological consequences. The same is said of other mental states as well: their essential or constitutive feature is their causal role.

The functionalist story attempts to reconcile the common sense and the scientific picture. Functionalism reveals how two descriptions of the same state may both be appropriate and insightful. Anger is anger, functionalists say, in virtue of its causal role. But they do not deny that the occupier of that causal role is a physiological state: most probably a complex of hormonal activity and arousal of aspects of the nervous system. A physical state *realizes* the functional state. Arousal of the nervous system realizes anger. So human mental life can be described in two different, but complementary, ways. It is a mental life in virtue of its functional description. A complete functional description specifies the causal roles of the full range of human psychological states. But that mental life has a physical description as well: a description which specifies the physical nature of the occupiers or realizers of those causal roles. Strictly speaking, a functionalist need not be a physicalist. There is no contradiction in saying that the essential feature of anger is its causal role, and then going on to assert that the occupier of that role is some nonphysical entity. But to the best of my knowledge, no functionalist has ever taken that line. For a crucial attraction of functionalism as a theory of mind is that it reconciles physicalism, the view that there is nothing but physical systems, with folk psychology.

The distinction between role and occupant will repeatedly reappear in the rest of this book, so it is important to see that it is not mysterious. We can make the same distinction in politics; between, say, the President of the US and the particular person who occupies that role. We can ask questions about that role; about the legal, constitutional and political powers the president has simply by virtue of being president. We can ask questions about the occupier: about his/her political background and skills; about size, sex or birth place. We can make the same distinction in biology. For instance, zoologists think about the causal role echo location plays in the life of the bat. In doing so, they determine the discriminatory capacities and range of the system, test its role in courtship and mating, and so on. But they might also investigate the physical systems that occupy that causal role in the bat. To do that, they work out how the bat produces its high pitched noises without deafening itself, how it detects the echoes and uses the information in them, and trace the nervous pathways through which that information is expressed in action.

This distinction, therefore, is important and pervasive. It goes by a number of names. I have so far talked of the distinction between causal or functional role, and the occupant of that role. Often, I will instead talk of the realization or implementation of states playing a functional role.

Many functionalists take folk psychology to provide a partial, and only partially correct, functional description of the mind. Only partial: there is much in human psychology on which our inherited self-description is silent: how perception works; the organization and operation of memory; and much else. Only partially correct: no doubt the folk have many of the details wrong. The task of theoretical psychology is to extend, systematize and correct the view that we are thinking agents. But our theory is compatibilist if the essential features of folk psychology make their way into the full functional specification of the human mind. We will consider in chapter 7 the the view that we are not agents. There are those that think that intentional psychology is wrong, root and branch, not just in a few details.

In the next sections I discuss more specific forms of functionalism. But before moving on to those, I want to emphasize two general features of functionalist positions.

First, the availability of double descriptions is not restricted to psychology. Functionalists often draw an analogy with computer science. We have two different descriptions of computers. An engineer can provide us with a hardware description of the silicon beast. That description will specify the layout, circuitry and interconnections of the device: it will be a description in the language of the engineer. But we can also describe the computer through its information flow. A flow chart specifies the flow of information through a computer and the task it carries out at each point. A data base specifies that information, the contents of its memory. We can give a description of the machine's operation by specifying the flow of symbols through the machine and its operations on those symbols.

For us, this talk of double descriptions is mostly an unfulfilled promise. There is much about our mental life we do not understand, and the physical description of that life remains sketchy. What is the physical realization of my capacity to play chess, or of my ability to recognize an Australian Cabernet Sauvignon? Functionalism outlines a program, not an achievement. We should not be too worried by this, for we have been here before. Until Crick and Watson's discovery of the structure of DNA in 1953, population geneticists used a functionally specified notion of a gene without knowing its physical realization.

Genes were identified by their causal role in inheritance and development. A flourishing science of population genetics waited some while for a physical description of the entities playing a distinctive role in the resemblance between offspring and parents.

The example of the gene is important. For it points to a relative independence of the theory of function from the theory of physical realization; the first can be developed independently of the second. (I will return to this example in section 9.3). One important feature of functionalism is that the theory of the mind is relatively independent of the theory of the brain, even though brain states realize mental states. The existence, extent and nature of this independence is very controversial, and is the special focus of chapter 9.

Second, the relationship between functional kinds and their physical realizations is complex. Two different people can be in the same mental state. They can both believe the Bomb is dangerous. Psychological kinds like this can be *multiply realized*. The same mental state can have different physical realizations in different people, or in the same person at different times. Both Kasparov and Karpov remember the last game of their last match. A functional description specifying a certain causal role is true of them both. But the physical realizations of that role may well be quite different. For the neural organization of our central memory is flexible and shows a good deal of individual variation. So, though Karpov and Kasparov remember the game, there may be no consequent neural description true of them both. Remembering the last game might be realized differently in each grandmaster.

Humans and other animals can be in the same psychological state – fear, for instance – despite the differences between our and their brains. Furthermore, if there are intelligent aliens or robots, then there are systems whose intelligence has a very different physical basis from ours. If so, the one mental state might have wildly varied physical realizations. Remembering the last game of the match might be realized by silicon chips as well as by neurons. Once more, it is important to notice that multiple realization is not an obscure peculiarity of psychology. Valves, transistors and new semiconductors realize the same functions of controlling current flow in electrical devices. Gizzards (in birds) and rumens (in ruminants) play the same role of breaking down and rendering digestible tough vegetation, despite their very different constructions.

Psychological kinds are realized by neural kinds in complex and varied ways. So the natural kinds of psychology are not identical to the natural kinds of the physical basis of the mind. Hence, despite the fact that we are nothing but complex physical systems, functionalists claim that psychology is an autonomous discipline. It is relatively independent of the sciences of the brain.

The functionalism that I have sketched is crude and oversimplified. Many crucial issues have not yet been touched upon. But three main ideas have been introduced. First, the core idea of functionalism: mental kinds, or mental properties, are identified by what they do, or what they are for, not what they are made of. Second, though functionalists are physicalists, functionalism does not tie psychological theory closely to the physical details of the brain. It leaves open the possibility that other beings might be sentient in the way we are without being built of the same stuff. Third, functionalism is a compatibilist view of the mind, attempting to show that we are both intentional agents and complex physical systems.

1.2 Functionalism and Teleology

If functionalists are right, minds are a type of functional system. Suppose that it is so. What is a functional system? Which kinds of functional systems are minds? I will mostly leave the second of these questions to the next chapter, but will attempt to answer the first now.

Once one accepts the basic functionalist premise, it is natural to try to answer both these questions by drawing from computer science. We design and build computers, so we understand them. Since they seem to have some of the same capacities that intelligent creatures have, perhaps we can understand our intelligence by understanding theirs. This is an idea particularly attractive to functionalists. Computers, like minds, have two distinct and complementary descriptions, and both seem to be symbol-using devices. Perhaps minds and computers are the same kind of functional system. So 'machine functionalists' suggested that cognitive processing might be a special case of running a program. Cognitive states would then be states of the machine on which the mind-program was running.

Computational processes have typically been explored through Turing machines. A Turing machine is an amazingly simple device, yet one which is, in principle, extraordinarily powerful. It consists of a long tape divided into regions passing through a reader. On the tape are printed symbols from a finite alphabet. The reader views one region at a time, and may carry out the following operations: (a) it may erase the symbol on the region it is viewing and replace it with another from the list, and (b) it may move the tape one region left or right. Turing machines are not good devices for practical purposes, for they are slow and difficult to program. But they can, given time, compute anything that *any* mechanical device can compute, and their simplicity of structure makes their operations easy to describe.

We fully describe a Turing machine by providing for it a *machine table*. Such a description specifies the symbols the machine can recognize: the alphabet it reads. So the possible inputs to the machine are the various messages or instructions that can be stated in this alphabet. What the machine does depends partly on the message, and partly on the state it is already in. So a full description of the machine lists all the possible pairings of messages and states, and specifies its new state and its output. A machine table looks like this:

	1	2	3	4	5	6	7
Y	_L1	_L1	YL4	YR5	YR6	YR6	_R7
_	_L1	YR2	halt	YR5	YL3	AL3	YR6
1	1L2	AR2	AL3	1L7	AR5	AR6	1R6
A	1L1	YR6	1L4	1L4	1R5	1R6	_R2

This is, in fact, a quite famous table; it is the simplest known 'universal machine' (of which, more in section 10.1). The table reads as follows. The leftmost column specifies the possible inputs to the machine; as you can see there are only four. The machine will be in one of seven states, so its behaviour is completely described by this matrix of 28 cells. Except for the cell which switches the machine off, the first two symbols in the cell describe the output. The machine prints a symbol on a tape, then scans right or left on that tape to the next symbol which becomes the new input in the next machine cycle. The final symbol in the cell directs the machine into its new machine state. So, for example, if the machine is in state 2, and its input is 'A', it prints 'Y', scans one square to the right, and changes state to state 6.

A machine table delineates a function from input and internal state to new internal state and output. It thus defines the causal roles of the Turing machine's states, the states of the computational device. If cognitive states are machine states, our (vastly more complex) machine table will specify the functional role of our mental states. But how do machine tables relate to the physical world? How do we recognize a Turing machine when we see one? Suppose you came across an alien artifact. Lights flicker when you shout at it. It turns out to emit strange noises, wriggle in odd ways, and gives birth to curiously marked bits of paper, perhaps as a result of its experiences. What would you need to find out to know whether the device was thinking?

To this question there is a standard answer, but one that generates lots of problems. A physical device realizes a machine table and hence is a functional system, it was thought, if (1) there is a one–one correlation between (a) inputs on the machine table and the types of physical events that causally influence the device; (b) physical states of the device and central states of the table; (c) physical reactions of the device and outputs in the table; (2) the transitions specified by the machine table correspond to causal relations between the physical states that realize the machine states. So, for example, column 7 of the table says that if the machine is in S7 and receives Y it stays in S7, prints '_' and scans right. A physical realization of this table must have the realizations of Y and S7 cause a realization of '_' and a realization of a right-scan.

Anything whose behaviour fits a machine table is a functional system. For it is then a Turing machine, a symbol processing device. So, at least, it was supposed. But this was a bad idea, for it caused functionalists to fall into two quite different bogs.

First, one–one correlations are cheap: there are lots and lots of them. If one–one correlations between machine table states and physical states suffice to make a physical entity a computing functional system, then *functional descriptions are too cheap*. A number of critics (P. M. Churchland, 1981; Block, 1978) concluded that making a functional claim about the mind is to make no substantial claim. Block and Hinckfuss pointed out that all sorts of very surprising entities will turn out to be information processing systems, maybe even the very same kind that we are, if you only have to correlate physical events in them with the inputs, states and outputs of a machine table. Functional claims (they suggest) are trivial, but the claim that something is sentient is far from trivial, so the essence of sentience cannot consist in being a functional system. Block pointed out that the Brazilian economy might qualify; Hinckfuss that a pail of water in the sun might. For if a *vast* number of activities are going on, there is a good chance of establishing the required correlations. So this notion of a functional system is much too weak; the existence of entirely accidental correlations between physical states and symbols on a table is not nearly enough for something to be *any* kind of functional system, let alone our kind. For of course the Block–Hinckfuss point does not depend on there *probably* being a one–one correlation between physical processes in a bucket of water and the states of the machine table that describes the human mind. The *possibility* of such a correlation suffices. For if there were such a correlation, even if that requires a vastly unlikely coincidence, the bucket of water still would not be a conscious thinking being. A bucket of water is not a functional system at all, still less an intelligent one. So the idea that the human mind might be a Turing machine leads to a much too weak conception of functional systems and functional properties. We need a robust conception of functional properties.

Secondly, the Turing machine picture of mentality, and its associated notion of realization, induced in the literature much muddle about physical realization. What gets realized? As I told the story in Section 1.1, and will continue telling the story, natural kinds are realized by more physically fundamental natural kinds. A blood pump in humans is realized by a four-chambered, valved muscle; in reptiles by an organ with different structure. I think this is the only sensible picture: theories in psychology, biology and physiology identify natural kinds and express laws and generalizations about those kinds. But they also enquire as to how those kinds relate to more physically fundamental ones. Unfortunately, talk of Turing machines has promoted the idea that physical realization is a relation between a mathematical description and a physical object. The relation is between a *mathematical object*, namely the mathematical function the machine table specifies, and a *physical device*. Needless to say, a relationship like that is a somewhat mysterious one. But it's the idea of realization used in Putnam's early functionalist papers, and most of the secondary literature on those papers. I take realization to be a relation between natural kinds. In the literature on 'machine functionalism', the ideas of multiple realization of the functional by the physical, and the consequent relative autonomy of psychology, were for the first time clearly expressed. But unfortunately these ideas were mixed in with more dubious notions.

So a functional system is more than just any old collection of causally interrelated activities. If a functional system is just an entity whose behaviour can be described in terms of a set of inputs, internal states and outputs, then the solar system would be one. For we could say that planets take as input gravitational and inertial information (their own mass and velocity detect these inputs) and produce as output an orbit. But this is surely wrong. Planets are not gigantic instruments whose function is the detection of the mass of the sun and the orbital display of that information; the solar system is not a 3D graphic display *about* astrophysics; it's an *instance* of astrophysics. But exactly what has gone wrong here? What does the solar system lack that functional systems have? The functionalist still owes us an account of the nature of functional systems in general, and sentient ones in particular.

It does not seem to be a matter of complexity. We can imagine discovering that the solar system is a laboratory instrument without changing our astrophysics. Science fiction is full of large scale engineering projects. Furthermore, a thermostat is a functional system, yet it is physically very simple. It just consists of a bimetallic strip that flexes and cools; at certain curvatures, it completes an electric circuit. Thermostats are physically much less complex than a bucket of river water warming in the sun. Such buckets teem with activity; microorganisms will be gobbling up inorganic chemicals and each other; there will be eddies and flows as convection shifts the water around; water will be evaporating off; oxygen will be dissolving in. A mad frenetic whirl, but a bucket of water warming in the sun is not a functional system at all, despite the complexity of the causal transactions within it.

Functional systems have a design. Humans and other naturally occurring sentient creatures are not the result of conscious design. But they are the result of a process that bears some striking similarities to design, namely natural selection. We are complex physical structures, with internal elements intricately interrelated. That is because we are evolved organisms, and, in virtue of our evolutionary history, our organs are designed to carry out various tasks. Evolutionary history enables us to distinguish between functional role and mere causal effect. Human hearts pump blood and make noises. Their biological purpose is to pump blood. The explanation of our having hearts at all is that we spring from ancestors whose reproductive prospects were enhanced by their having protohearts that pumped blood. Doubtless those protohearts made noises too, but those noises were selectively irrelevant. They did not increase fitness.

Functional systems are systems whose existence and structure have a teleological explanation. Neither the interrelations within the solar system nor in the bucket have such an explanation. Our body clearly does have such an explanation, as do its components. The exquisite design of the eye, for instance, has been much chewed over. It's a functional system within a functional system, for it is composed of parts functionally, not just causally, interrelated: lens, retina, focusing mechanism, light meter, shield, plus lubrication, maintenance and movement subsystems. I think the functionalist should hold that the mind too is a functional system within a larger one. What are its components? That is a difficult empirical question. The mind stores information. We remember, sometimes, what we want to. But do we have one memory or many? Perhaps long- and short-term memory are distinct components. We remember facts and we remember how to do things: one component or two? We perceive the world, and come to have beliefs about it. But are there distinct perceptual systems, or are perception and cognition integrated? Discovering the functional organization of the mind is one of psychology's hard tasks.

In endorsing a functional theory of the mind, and a teleological account of functional systems, I am committing myself to the view that the mind has a design; I assume from natural selection rather than conscious planning. It has an internal organization designed to carry out various perceptual, cognitive and action-guiding tasks. It has that organization and those purposes in virtue of its evolutionary history. When I talk of mental functions, the notion of function is biological; it is the same sense in which the function of the kidney is excretion and water regulation.

1.3 Homuncular Functionalism

In 1.1, I argued that psychological properties are functional properties. The essential feature of fear, for instance, is not its subjective, experiential character, but its functional role. Consequently, we have available two relatively independent descriptions of the human mind: a functional theory, detailing and explaining those roles, and a physical theory explaining how those roles are realized in an intelligent agent.

This is a very important idea. But it is also an oversimplification. For it is not true that there is a single functional, and a single physical, theory. Psychological kinds differ dramatically in the extent to which they are tied to a particular physical realization. Some psychological kinds are very abstract, i.e. very independent of their physical implementation. Consider thoughts, that is, beliefs, desires, fears, suppositions and the like. What kind of creature is capable of having thoughts; in Dennett's terminology, what kind of creatures are intentional systems? Many kinds. Notice, first, that one's particular array of perceptual organs does not matter. Helen Keller had a seriously impoverished collection compared to the rest of us. Some think that dolphins are intelligent; if so, their beliefs are formed from very different sense experiences than ours. If there are intelligent creatures anywhere whose perceptual equipment is batlike, they too would form beliefs from a perceptual world utterly different from our own. Electric eels are doubtless too dumb to have beliefs and desires in anything like our sense, but they sense their environment via distortions it causes in electric fields they generate. Post-Bomb big-brained mutant eels might well be intentional systems, notwithstanding their unusual sensory array and fishy physiology. Nor need thought control behaviour in the way thought controls ours: bats and dolphins don't act like people. We need not suppose that intentional systems have to be built using the same biochemistry as we find in the human mind. There are minor biochemical differences (and large anatomical differences) between human and animal brains. There are neurotransmitters (chemicals that link one neuron to the next) found in some animals but not in us, and vice versa. Much larger differences are easy to imagine. Current computers are hardly sophisticated or complex enough to count as intentional systems. Only Searle, of whom more later, and a few others are prepared to bet that nothing like a Hal 2000, the rogue computer of *2001*, could ever be made. If microcircuits can be the physical basis of an intentional system, then thinking certainly is not tied to any specific biochemistry.

So what is essential to being an intentional agent, a being that acts on its beliefs and goals? That is a matter of some controversy. In particular, there is an ongoing debate about (1) the degree of rationality required, and (2) the need for some perceptionlike flow of information from the external world to the mind. But, as a first approximation, let's say that an intentional system must (a) have perceptual systems of some kind, so there is a flow of information from the world into the system, (b) have a reasonably rich system of internal representation; thermostats aren't intentional systems in part because they represent only temperature, (c) have cognitive mechanisms that enable it to use perceptual information to update and modify its internal representations of the world, and (d) have mechanisms that translate its internal representations into behaviour that is adaptive if those representations fit the world.

If this is a reasonable approximation, then intentional systems could be *psychologically* very different indeed. Creatures of varying sense organs, creatures with memories of distinct organization and capacity, language users, and nonlanguage users can all be intentional systems.

Contrast belief with a psychological state like human sexual desire. Of course, many nonhuman animals have sexual urges. But there is good reason to suppose that sexual desire in humans is a state very different from that of any other animal. The biology is quirky: in women, ovulation is concealed, as practitioners of the rhythm method well know, and there is no breeding season. Women are almost unique amongst female animals in being capable of orgasm. (As far as I know, pigmy chimps are the only other contenders.) The sexual bond between humans is strong and psychologically important; in this, we are unusual amongst the mammals. It's plausible to suppose that our sexual psychology is deeply tied to our *particular* psychological and physical nature, perhaps especially to our sense of smell and touch. Try to imagine your sexual desires were you to be equipped with echo location, or the olfactory sensitivity of a bloodhound. You are imagining, surely, a very different state.

So there are not two theories of the mind, a functional theory and a physical theory. For psychological states vary in the degree to which they are independent of their physical realization, and in the extent to which they are tied to particular psychological organization. We need a theory of mind which recognizes these facts, as simple functionalism does not. So simple functionalism needs to be replaced by *homuncular functionalism*.

Homuncular functionalism has three elements. The first is the idea of functionalism itself: the essence of a mental state is what it does, not what it is. The second element is the view that the mind is modular. Minds are ensembles. Our general and flexible intelligence emerges out of the interactions of lesser and more specialized intelligences that compose us. Dim because monomaniac homunculi cooperate to form clever ones. A complex function like visual perception is broken into interacting less complex ones. We will see in section 2.4 that one advantage of the computational theory of the mind is that it makes precise the idea of the analysis of complex skills into simpler ones. The third, and vital, element is to apply the first two ideas recursively. That is, each homunculus is in turn seen as an ensemble of more specialized and hence simpler homunculi. And so on until we reach a level where the tasks the homunculi must carry out are so simple that they are psychologically primitive. For example, in theories of visual perception perhaps the detection of a shape's edge on the retinal image might be primitive. To explain that, we need to go to neurobiology, not psychology.

This idea is probably best explained through examples. I have argued that intentional systems have a multiplicity of psychological structures. That is partly because the ground plan of an intentional system is simple. It might look as shown in figure 1.

Now, if my earlier remarks are right, any sentient being (a) whose perception–cognition–action information flow has this organization, (b) whose information states meet fairly modest conditions on revisability and rationality, and (c) whose actions reduce the gap between goals and information when the latter fit the world is an intentional system. Many different psychologies meet these conditions, because our ground plan abstracts away from an enormous amount of detail. On this view, it does not matter if there are other homunculi in the system; for instance, a language homunculus. Further, the components can have enormously differing organizations and still be a perceptual system, an information store, or a goal store. How *these* homunculi are organized is genuinely a

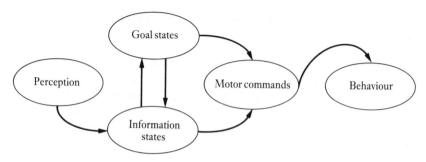

Figure 1

matter for psychology. But it's not relevant to the question: are we confronted with a believer-desirer?

Let's consider another example. Dennett was (and is) interested in the problem of consciousness. What is special about the cognitive plan of a conscious agent? His answer was provocative and controversial: he argued that introspective consciousness is essentially tied to language. We are conscious of that we can say. So Dennett's ground plan of a conscious agent varies from the one above essentially in requiring a language homunculus. We are introspectively aware only of the instructions to the speech centre. The addition of that module makes the conditions on being a conscious agent more restrictive than the conditions on merely being an intentional agent. Still, Dennett has abstracted away from many psychological details, for nothing about the inner workings of these homunculi is relevant to the question: are we faced with a conscious sentience?

Let's focus now not on overall maps of a mind, but on a component. How might visual imagination work? Over the last ten years or so, this has been the subject of much debate, and a substantive, if very controversial, theory has evolved. Stephen Kosslyn (1980, 1983) has been most responsible for this. He is particularly impressed by two features of mental imagery. One is a striking parallel between vision and imagination; for example, both visual and imaginative representation looses 'grain' (i.e. becomes less detailed, and less rich informationally) as one moves from the focus of attention. Second, Kosslyn thinks that the representations constructed in visual imagination are syntactically and semantically pictorial, rather than linguaform. For instance, he thinks every part of an image represents part of what is imaged. This is a characteristic of pictures but not words: in a generic sketch of a woman, every chunk stands for part of a woman, but, in the word 'woman', 'wom' represents nothing.

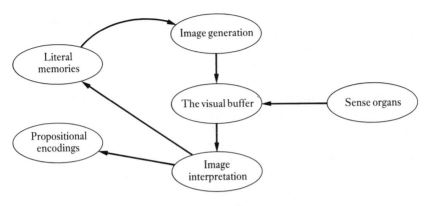

Figure 2

Kosslyn has argued that visual imagination has something like the organization shown in figure 2.

Again, this map of the flow of representation abstracts away from many psychological details. Literal memory is an information store from which the geometric shape of an image is recalled by an image generation unit which then activates a pattern on a buffer (the buffer is thought of as analogous to a VDU unit). There are many ways such information might be organized. In Kosslyn's actual simulation of this process, the information was (a) divided into a file–subfile system; thus an image of a women might be broken into subfiles for her head, torso and so on. (b) The subfiles' information was stored as 'polar coordinates', i.e. as a set of points in which each point is defined by its angle and distance from a point of origin. From this data, the generator could draw lines on the buffer. But these details are not crucial to Kosslyn's theory of the nature of imagination. If he is right, *somehow or other* such data has to be stored, retrieved, used. But a theory of the necessary conditions for a visual imagination abstracts away from those details, for *they* are *not* necessary.

The two key developers and defenders of homuncular functionalism are Dennett and Lycan, though Simon (1981) defends similar ideas. Face recognition is a favourite example of them both. Face recognition is extremely important to social creatures like ourselves, and we probably have a cognitive mechanism specialized for it. For we are amazingly good at recognizing faces, and pictures of faces. In many cases even a brief glimpse, an obscured or blurred photo, or a line drawing suffices. Yet our capacity is quirky: show someone an upside-down photo of someone they know well and they are unlikely to recognize it; similarly, gross distortions on the photo can easily be missed. So we probably have a special mechanism: the system we use in recognizing our best friend is unlikely to be a particular application of a more general device that works equally well distinguishing cars or horses.

There are many ways a system of face recognition might work. Lycan discusses one of them to illustrate the recursive strand in homuncular functionalism, and his particular theme of the shading of psychological questions into physiological ones (Lycan, 1981b, pp. 33–34). Here is one way it might go. A memory bank might store only front, right profile, and left profile views. So an executive must require a viewpoint locator to survey a perceptual display, and sort the input into one of the three permitted orientations. That display is then input to an analysis mechanism that produces as output a coding of the display's content. This encoding must then go to a library function, to check against a store. A match will identify the face; that identification goes to the system's output device which issues the identification.

Notice that we can ask questions of varying levels of abstraction. If we had asked about the necessary conditions on a face recognizer, Lycan's answer is too detailed; that's one way to do it but surely not the only way. Lycan's is a candidate answer to the question: how do *we* do it? Someone might have a more specific question yet, not about the system as a whole but about a part. They might want to know the kind of code the analyser produces. Perhaps something like Kosslyn's literal memories: data points from which a diagram can be reconstructed. Alternately, maybe it's a 'feature analysis' that describes the face: 'long nose, thin lips, blue eyes. . .'. How does the analyser work? Perhaps it's a projector which imposes a grid on the perceptual display and assigns a number between 1 (white) and 0 (black) to each square on the grid. If so, the analyser is a light meter and we might want to know how it works, and so on. Let me summarize.

1 Minds can be decomposed into interacting systems of homunculi. Each of these, equally, can be decomposed into still simpler homunculi, until we reach ones whose job is so simple that a straightforwardly mechanical device can carry it out.

2 A successful homuncular decomposition of the mind is an explanation of a sentient being in mechanical terms. That's Dennett's main message about homuncular functionalism.

3 Psychological states are homuncular states. Psychological processes are processes in homunculi. Psychological processors are homunculi.

4 Psychological states, processes and processors differ in *grain*.

Some, while of the same layer, differ in the amount of detail in their identity conditions. Others differ in layer. Lycan's characterization of homuncular functionalism emphasizes these last two points.

In section 1.2 I gave an account of the nature of functional systems; this section has been devoted to the functional organization of sophisticated creatures and devices. In chapter 2, I shall try to identify the distinctive functions mental organs perform, and shall begin to speculate on the way those organs work.

Suggested Reading

Section 1.1

Two excellent introductions to philosophy of mind are Campbell's *Body and Mind* (1970) and P. M. Churchland's *Matter and Consciousness* (1988a). Campbell concentrates on the traditional dualist–antidualist ontological dispute, and defends a very moderate dualism. Recent restatements of dualism are Jackson's 'Epiphenomenal Qualia' (1982), and Nagel's deeply obscure but much reprinted 'What is it Like to be a Bat?' (1979). Churchland focuses more on the debates between different brands of physicalism, and briefly introduces some of the relevant empirical disciplines. Two good collections that cover the issues raised in this chapter are Block's *Readings in the Philosophy of Psychology* vols I and II (1980, 1981), and Lycan's *Mind and Cognition* (1990). Classic early statements of functionalism are Armstrong's *A Materialist Theory of the Mind* (1968) and Fodor's *Psychological Explanation* (1968). Equally early, and equally well known, are a series of papers of Putnam (1975a, papers 16–21). These are the source of the mind – Turing machine analogy discussed in section 1.2.

Section 1.2

The problem of vacuous functional theorizing is pressed in Block's 'Troubles With Functionalism' (1978) and, in a different form, P. M. Churchland's 'Eliminative Materialism and the Propositional Attitudes' (1981). Block calls it the liberalism problem; the functionalist theory of the mind is too liberal, for it attributes mentality to entities which clearly are mindless. The teleological response I endorse here first emerges in Lycan's 'Form, Function and Feel' (1981a) and even more vehemently in Millikan's *Language, Thought and Other Biological Categories* (1984). Millikan's book is unfortunately dense, but a readable synopsis is her 'Thoughts Without Laws; Cognitive Science With Content' (1986). The view that abstract mathematical devices are the subjects of realization, and an associated view that realization is appropriate correlation, is still quite prevalent; see for examples, Haugeland's otherwise superb *Artificial Intelligence: The Very Idea* (1985, chs 2, 3), and Newell's 'Physical Symbol Systems' (1980). Maudlin's 'Computation and Consciousness' (1989) is another recent example which treats realization as an appropriate correlation between a machine table and states of a physical system. I assume an account of biological function in evolutionary terms throughout. That account is defended in Millikan's 'In Defense of Proper Functions' (1989b) and Neander's 'Functions as Selected Effects (forthcoming); a different type of evolutionary account is given in Bigelow and Pargetter's 'Functions' (1987).

Section 1.3

Homuncular functionalism is defended most lucidly by Lycan and Dennett. Lycan's most important writings are two 1981 papers, 'Form, Function and Feel' (1981a) and 'Towards a Homuncular Theory of Believing' (1981b), and a book, *Consciousness* (1987). Dennett's most important papers on this topic are collected in Part III of *Brainstorms* (1978). Simon's *The Sciences of the Artificial* (1981), especially chapter 7, is clear and lucid on the design advantages of the decomposition of the complex into the simple; I return to this point in section 4.5. The criticisms of cruder forms of functionalism are collected and extended in Block's 'Troubles with Functionalism' (1978). Dennett is one of many who has argued that intentional agents are necessarily rational; see especially 'Intentional Systems' (1978) and 'True Believers' (1987). Those views are critically scrutinized in *Language and Reality* (Devitt and Sterelny, 1987, ch. 15). For the idea that perceptual contact with the world is necessary, see Putnam's 'Brains in Vats' in his *Reason, Truth and History* (1981a).

2

Representation and Computation

2.1 The Representational Theory of the Mind

What is the function of our mental states? According to the representational theory of the mind, while mental states differ, one from another, mental states are representational states, and mental activity is the acquisition, transformation and use of information and misinformation. (Hereafter just 'information'.) The perceptual system's causal role is not memory's causal role, but both make available information to other psychological systems.

The scientific and the folk picture converge on the idea that representation is central to human minds. Consider first the scientific picture. There are fundamental contrasts between our mental life and the mental life of some other creatures.

1 We are *flexible* in our behavioural capacities. Many unsophisticated animals behave in complex ways excellently adapted to their life ends. Many insects, for instance, do so. An example much used by Dennett is the Sphex wasp. When it comes to lay its eggs, the Sphex builds a burrow, finds and paralyses a cricket, then drags it to the burrow. She then goes inside, inspects, comes out, drags the cricket in, seals the burrow and departs. In time, the eggs wake in their larder and

the grubs consume the cricket. A gruesome, but certainly a complex and effective, routine. But also a very rigid one. For instance, if an experimenter moves the cricket away from the threshold a few inches, the wasp on emerging from its tour of inspection always replaces it in its original place, and inspects again. And again. And again, if the experimenter repeats the trick. Sphex never learns to take the cricket directly into the burrow. Sphex has a single, invariable behaviour pattern. It is insensitive to new contingencies and requirements; it is unmodifiable by learning. Wasps aren't very thoughtful.

2   We are sensitive to the information in a perceptual stimulus rather than to the physical format of the stimulus. This point is best made by example. Robins, unsurprisingly, feed their young. Rather more surprisingly, they sometimes feed young cuckoos. With somewhat unpleasant consequences for the robins' own chicks, for the cuckoo heaves the robin chicks out of the nest. While cuckoo eggs sometimes mimic the eggs of the species they parasitize, cuckoo young look nothing like robin young. Indeed, they grow to be bigger than the adult robins that feed them. This shows that robin feeding behaviour is not tuned to the information available to the robin. They are unable to learn to use information that shows that they are feeding not their chicks but the killer of their chicks. Instead, their feeding is reflexlike, under the control of a particular physical stimulus that can be mimicked. This type of control by a particular stimulus is quite common, even in animals that are otherwise flexible. Some species of bird are quite territorial, and defend their territories against species mates aggressively. One such is the black-headed gull. This gull not only attacks other gulls; it will attack the bodiless head of a stuffed gull mounted on a stick (Dawkins and Krebs, 1984, p. 384). Attack behaviour is under control of a specific and fixed stimulus.

Many animals are, at least in important ways, unwaspish. Animals can learn both to avoid new dangers, and to exploit new opportunities. Japanese macaque monkeys have, for instance, recently learnt to use running water to wash sand off their food, and to unwrap human food stuffs given to them. Chimps have proved quite adept at learning ways of manipulating their environment to get food. We have this capacity to a very high degree. Our behavioural repertoire is, within unclear limits, plastic. That is, it's modifiable by experience. Sometimes those modifications are appropriate. This plasticity is a consequence of our sentience: intelligent creatures can learn new tricks, can change their ways. Our behavioural repertoire, and that of some animals, is open-ended. Adaptive flexibility, especially learning, requires an ability to represent the world. For it is the information in the stimulus, not its physical form, that our behaviour, but not the gulls', is sensitive to. Thus rigidity and stimulus control are closely linked. Since adaptability is a central part of intelligence, intelligence essentially involves representation.

Intelligent behaviour is stimulus independent. We will attempt to escape from a building on receipt of any signal that reliably indicates fire. We flee because of the semantic content of the symbols, not, within some limits, the physical format of signal. You would leave your house on hearing a certain kind of alarm bell; on being told, in a myriad of different ways, that it's on fire; on detecting certain smells; on seeing smoke; on hearing many different sorts of noises. Contrast our sexual behaviour and mating rituals with invertebrate sexual behaviour. Intelligence involves response to perceptual input in virtue of its representational content (content, for short). Intelligent behaviour is informationally sensitive.

Primate behaviour is informationally sensitive. Frans de Waal (1982), for example, gives a marvellous description of the complexity of chimp social relations. The chimp society he studied was characterized by struggles for power. The rewards for power were sexual privileges; the mechanism of power was not, mainly, brute strength but alliance and bluff. Of course, the contrast between informational sensitivity with stimulus control is one of degree. No organism exhibits perfect informational sensitivity. Some of the data that reaches us we are not equipped to detect. We miss the significance of some we do detect; time and cognitive resources are limited. Furthermore, our reactions, no doubt, have not entirely escaped stimulus control. Gould has written an entertaining essay linking our cuteness judgements to the features of human babies (Gould, 1980). Still, to the considerable extent that our behaviour is adaptively flexible and informationally sensitive, to that extent it must be directed by representations. There can be no informational sensitivity without representation. There can be no flexible and adaptive response to the world without representation. To learn about the world, and to use what we learn to act in new ways, we must be able to represent the world, our goals and options. Furthermore we must make appropriate inferences from those representations.

The physicalist has good reason to see the mind as a builder and user of representations. So does the defender of folk psychology. Section 1.1 began with two examples of folk psychological explanation (otherwise known as *intentional, propositional attitude*, or belief-desire explanation). We accounted for the voting behaviour of Skidnose, and the dietary habits of Zoltan in terms of their beliefs and desires. Here's another. Suppose we wanted to know why Reagan ordered an F111 strike against Libya. A candidate explanation runs this way. (a) Reagan believed that ordering an F111 strike would (in the fullness of consequent causal processes) result in a Gaddaffi-less world, (b) Reagan wanted the world to be Gaddaffi-less, and (c) Reagan had no other (more important) wants that he believed an F111 strike would frustrate.

The representational content of the intentional states seems to play a central role in these explanations. (Though this idea will get much critical scrutiny in chapter 5.) For what the beliefs and desires are about, their *content*, is crucial to the explanation. If Reagan desired not to be rid of Gaddaffi but that he, Gaddaffi, live a long and happy life, then our candidate explanation of the ordering of the strike collapses. If Reagan believed that a strike against *Sarajevo* would do the trick, we no longer have an account of why he ordered a strike against *Libya*. In general, if we take a plausible intentional explanation and transform it by varying the content of the belief or desire clause, the explanation collapses utterly.

If we want then to integrate our two self-pictures: the folk picture and the scientific picture, we need to answer three questions.

1 What are beliefs, desires and other propositional attitudes?
2 What is representational or semantic content; in virtue of what do psychological states have it?
3 In virtue of which of their properties do the attitudes play the role they do in the causation of behaviour?

Furthermore, there are important constraints on the answers I can give to these questions. For I am trying to defend a compatibilist view of the relationship between folk psychology and natural science. That in turn means that folk psychological kinds must be explained by appeal to those of natural science. Functionalists can and do defend the relative independence of the psychological from the theory of the physical processes of the brain. There is a difference between explaining functions and explaining the nature of the occupier of that functional role. But the independence is only relative, for each functional role must have a physical occupier. Functions must be performed; the entities carrying through the performance are physical entities with physical properties. So a theory of the functional role of intentional states must avoid attributing magical powers to mental states. The functions allegedly essential to mental states must be functions actually performable by physical stuff. This sounds like an obvious, almost a trivial, requirement. Not so: it's a constraint enormously difficult to meet, and one that in the history of thought about the mind has been repeatedly violated (see Cherniak, 1986).

How can a bundle of cells in Reagan represent Gaddaffi? Yet more problematically, they must represent nonactual states of affairs. How might Reagan's tissues represent a Gaddaffi-free world, granted that the world is in fact Gaddaffi infested? It's reasonable to wonder whether the representational theory of the mind is in the miracle business. To show it's not, we need to show how physical systems like ourselves could have mental states that (a) represent and misrepresent the world, and (b) participate in the causation of behaviour. There is an account of how this is possible: an account developed in its most explicit form by Jerry Fodor (but see also Harman, 1975; Field, 1978; Lycan, 1981b): the 'The Language of Thought' (1975) hypothesis.

2.2 The 'Language of Thought' Hypothesis

In a series of publications starting in 1975, Jerry Fodor has argued that human (and nonhuman) mental processes involve a medium of mental representation; a medium that has all the central features of a language. Thoughts are sentence-like. There are three important arguments for this view. But the most important argument is tacit, rather than explicit. It is that buying the language of thought hypothesis enables us to naturalize folk psychology. If we grant that hypothesis, we can integrate folk psychology within the scientific picture, as we shall see in section 2.3.

2.2.1 Semantic Parallels between Thoughts and Sentences

There are striking semantic parallels between thoughts and sentences. Consider first the analogies between beliefs and indicative sentences. Both the belief that Gorbachov is a winner, and the sentence 'Gorbachov is a winner' have truth values: indeed, the same truth value. Both the belief and the sentence contain referring elements: both are about Gorbachov, and winning. Both are meaningful: indeed, they have the same meaning. Someone who says that Gorbachov is a winner says what someone who thinks Gorbachov is a winner thinks. Not all sentences have a truth value. In addition to statements, suppositions and assumptions there are orders, requests, and questions. But not all thoughts have a truth value: in addition to believing and supposing, there are desiring and fearing as well. The parallels between thinking and saying are very striking, and one explanation of that parallel is to argue that thought has a language-like character. In a striking metaphor of Schiffer's, we might imagine that in the mind of an intentional agent there are two boxes: a belief box and a desire box. Your beliefs are stored in the belief box; your desires in the desire box. The 'language of thought' hypothesis is a speculation on the form that storage takes. Your beliefs (and desires) are encoded as sentences. According to Fodor, though not other defenders of the language of thought, you do not literally think in English. Your thought sentences do not stand to English sentences as sentences written in morse or other code, or the Cyrillic alphabet, stand to normally transcribed English sentences. You think in a special inner language, *mentalese*. Mentalese is organized into words and sentences. Mentalese words are concepts; mentalese sentences are thoughts.

The existence of codes and variant alphabets illustrates an important facet of languages. It's very crucial for the tenability of Fodor's line that language is *medium independent*. We have two standard media for our natural language: sounds and inscriptions. But we occasionally use others: for example, magnetic patterns on tapes when we record someone's conversation. More exotic media are occasionally described in thrillers and science fiction novels. In principle, the possibilities are unbounded: a suitably powerful species could send morse code messages in English across the universe by sending stars, nova (dot) or supernova (dash). So Fodor's hypothesis isn't crazy: it doesn't require that opening someone's head would reveal a tiny white-board with sentences written recognizably on it. Patterns of neural activity could well be sentential representations. Words can be configurations of neurons as easily as configurations of chalk marks on a blackboard.

So, the belief box contains sentences of mentalese stored in a neural medium. Like English sentences, these sentences are true or false; like English sentences, elements of them refer. That is one reason why there are striking parallels between thoughts and sentences.

2.2.2 The Syntactic Parallels

Thought is *productive*. We are capable of thinking indefinitely many, and indefinitely complex, thoughts. You can think that Ethiopia is hot and arid; that Ethiopia and Chad are hot and arid; that Ethiopia and Chad and Sudan are hot and arid. And so on; there is no nonarbitrary upper bound on the complexity of thought. Thought is also *systematic*. If you can think that goatherds frolic with shepherds, you can think shepherds frolic with goatherds. If you think that sheep are exciting, and if you have the concept of a goat, you have the capacity to think that goats are exciting.

Language, likewise, is systematic and productive. There is no principled upper limit to the length of a sentence. We cannot produce a string of English words, and say that this string is a sentence of the language in good standing, but if you add one word (say, an extra adjective before a noun) the sequence of words is no longer a sentence of English. Obviously, there are pragmatic constraints on sentence length. As sentences become longer, all other things being equal, they become harder to remember and understand. But the degradation of usefulness is gradual; there is a gradual slide from total intelligibility to total opacity. No doubt some similar phenomenon applies to thought as well. Language like thought is systematic. Any language with the resources to express 'Camels smell worse than kangaroos' will have the resources to express 'Kangaroos smell worse than camels'.

There is a standard explanation of the productivity and systematicity of language. Languages consist of a finite lexicon organized by a syntax, into indefinitely many possible sentences. Syntax is a set of rules governing allowable combinations of lexical items. It's a language's instruction manual. It tells how to combine words into larger units, phrases, and how these larger units are combined into sentences. So a language's syntax shows how its sentences are organized into phrases, and how phrases are organized into smaller phrases and words. So the syntax of English tells us, amongst much else about it, that the sentence 'Every dog has its day' is composed of two major units, 'Every dog' and 'has its day' and that the latter is built from 'has' and 'its day' rather than 'has its' and 'day'.

Thought like language is productive and systematic. An 'argument from the best explanation' suggests that it too must consist of a finite bunch of elements (concepts) organized into the cognitive equivalent of sentences.

2.2.3 The Processing Argument

Fodor's principle argument (1975) for the language of thought turned on the nature of mental processing. He argued that processing has characteristics that make commitment to a language of thought inescapable. In trying to show this he worked through three examples of process: rational choice, perception and concept learning. Consider rational choice: say, a highly skilled chess player deciding on her next move. An admittedly idealized account of this decision process requires at least the following:

1   An assignment to the player of a preference ranking. Perhaps a draw is all she wants – say to ensure first place in a tourney. But perhaps she really needs to win or even win spectacularly; she may be playing for a 'best game' prize. To understand her move we must rank her preferences.

2   We must specify the set of options that she recognizes. A brilliant forced mate isn't an option if she misses it.

3   An assignment to the player of a set of beliefs or expectations about the outcomes of various possible moves.

We expect the player, on the basis of her preferences, options and expectations, to *maximize her expected utility*: to make a compromise between most desired outcome and most likely outcome. Obviously, this picture is much too simple, but adding complications to increase realism would not alter the basic moral Fodor wants to draw. For this model, and any based on it, requires an agent to represent the world as it is and as it might be, and to draw appropriate inferences from that representation. Fodor argues that the agent must have a language-like symbol system, for she can represent indefinitely many and indefinitely complex actual and possible states of her environment. She could not have this capacity without an appropriate means of representation, a language of thought. (We will consider a challenge to this claim in chapter 8.)

Fodor draws the same moral from experiments on concept acquisition. The experimental subject is to acquire a certain concept; let's say the concept of a blangle. He is shown a few cards with shapes on them. He is told of some that they are blangular; of others, that they are not blangular. (A card is blangular if it is blue or triangular.) He then gets shown new cards, one at a time, and has to nominate which pile the new card goes into. He is told if he is right; eventually he starts to get it uniformly right. He has acquired the concept. This process, and variants on it, is supposed to tell us something about the cognitive accessibility of various kinds of concepts. It's easier to achieve uniform success if cards are fangular if and only if they are square, rather than if and only if they are square and presented by a female experimenter, otherwise round.

Now what is going on here? Fodor argued, in *The Language of Thought* (1975) and again in the final chapter of *Representations* (1981), that only one theory of this process has ever been seriously considered, though it has had many aliases. It is a hypothesis and test theory. The subject formulates a hypothesis about the identifying conditions of blangularity, and tests that hypothesis against the new presentations.

When the hypothesis is falsified, the hypothesis is modified. But eventually further modification is no longer necessary.

What are the commitments of this model?

1 The subject needs a representational system for stating hypotheses.
2 The subject needs a way of ordering candidate hypotheses for testing: no subject will start with the hypothesis that a card is blangular if and only if either there is a triangle printed on it or it is presented by an experimenter wearing a chef's hat.
3 The subject needs a system for the representation of data.
4 The subject needs a way of matching data with hypotheses.

The model requires something like a language of thought. For the representations must be fit subjects for logical operations and evaluations: for instance, detecting inconsistency between hypothesis and data. Experience can rationally modify hypotheses only if both data and hypotheses are represented in a suitable format.

Fodor, therefore, concluded that cognition involves an inner sentential code. But that inner system is not the public language of the thinker. In part, that's because Fodor believes there to be thinkers that are not speakers. Prelinguistic children and (some) nonlinguistic animals think, and thus in his view house a language of thought. But Fodor's central reason for denying that we talk and think the same language is that learning a language is a special case of concept acquisition. A consequence, he thinks, is that no language can be acquired unless the learning mind already has a representational system at least as expressively powerful as the system being learnt. You cannot learn to say anything you cannot already think.

Consider, for example, someone acquiring the term 'nerd'. What happens? The learner is told of the characteristics of nerds; perhaps some she knows are pointed out. She forms a hypothesis about the defining conditions of nerdhood, which she tests, perhaps by asking questions. 'Is Jerry Fodor a nerd?' She is corrected, but eventually requires no more assistance. Now surely, if this is how concepts are learnt, then there is no acquisition without definition. Our subject must have the capacity to specify the defining conditions of nerdness in advance of learning the term. **Nerd** (I use bold type throughout when a concept is being named) might not be a primitive concept in the subject's language of thought, but it is definable in her language of thought. The introduction of new concepts via definitions may well improve the coding efficiency of mentalese, but not its expressive power. At first glance, Fodor's conclusion is an outrage against sense. If he is right, we can never learn to think thoughts previously unthinkable. Yet surely conceptual growth is frequent in the life of an individual, and the species. One of the differences between us and the ancient Greeks is that we can have thoughts – about protons, computers, violins and the like – that they simply couldn't have.

Fodor is not quite committed to the view that Plato could have had thoughts about neutron stars; experience has an impact on the development of our conceptual repertoire. Still, what he commits himself to is implausible enough, for experience only stimulates the expression of a pre-existent potential. Experience plays roughly the same role in our conceptual development as adequate nutrition plays in the changes of puberty. It is causally necessary, but the process is fundamentally under the control of an internal program. In section 7.4, I discuss Patricia Churchland's claim that Fodor has produced an unintentional *reductio ad absurdum* of the language of thought hypothesis, and shall argue that the *reductio* can be avoided. In chapter 8, I will consider entirely new accounts of concept acquisition that apparently avoid commitment to anything like a language of thought.

Michael Devitt and I (Devitt and Sterelny, 1987) have argued against the thesis that our language of thought is both innate and expressively powerful. Our alternative was to suppose that people start with a rudimentary innate system and on the basis of that system they learn their natural language, which then becomes their system of inner representation as well as their system of communication. But this is a detail that need not concern us. The language of thought hypothesis does not depend on whether we think in mentalese or our public language. Once we see that important parts of mentalese can be learnt, the representational theory of the mind is affected by this distinction in only minor ways.

2.3 Intentional Psychology

Let us suppose Fodor is right; there is a language of thought. If so, we can 'naturalize' the representational theory of mind. That is, we can show that taking the mind to be a representation user does not attribute to the mind functions that no physical stuff could execute. In particular, the language of thought hypothesis supports belief-desire, or intentional psychology. For it enables us to tell a very natural story about thoughts, about thinking, and about the way thought helps explain behaviour. For it enables us to formulate three theses about the occupants of intentional roles.

Thesis 1: Propositional attitudes are realized by relations to sentences in the agent's language of thought.

The exact relationship between intentional psychology and the language of thought hypothesis is a matter of some controversy. Those who think that intentional psychology provides a good account of important aspects of human psychology are intentional realists. Intentional realism, then, is the theory that humans' behaviour and mental states are often the product of their beliefs and desires. It is a theory distinct from the mentalese hypothesis. Intentional realism may be true and the mentalese hypothesis false. Dennett has described mentalese as an 'engineering hypothesis' (see 1978, Preface); he would not accept thesis 1. A language of thought is only *one* possible realization of intentional states, just as a muscled four-valved chamber is one, but not the only, realization of a blood pump.

This view of the relationship seems to me to understate the importance of the language of thought hypothesis to intentional realism. Suppose the ability to think about the world as it is and as it might be, to think indefinitely many and indefinitely complex thoughts, is a necessary condition on having intentional states at all. Intentional agents necessarily have *rich* capacities for mental representation; that is one of the differences between intentional agents and thermostats (section 1.3). Then the best, and perhaps the only, explanation of the truth of intentional realism would be a language of thought; it would not be one potential realizer amongst many. Of course, not all intentional agents need have the same language of thought, but all would have some language-like system of mental representation.

So for Igor to believe that *détente* is dangerous he must house within his mind a sentence token of mentalese, a token that means that *détente* is dangerous. But this is not sufficient, for Igor's so believing is different from his suspecting that *détente* is dangerous, or misanthropically hoping that *détente* is dangerous. For it to be a belief, the token must function within Igor in a way peculiar to beliefs. That is, he must stand in a particular *functional* relationship to the mentalese token. Beliefs mediate perception, action and cognition in their own particular way. Many advocates of this position go further, and suppose that the functional role special to belief is a *computational* role. Beliefs, the idea runs, play a distinctive inferential role. This inferential role, in turn, is implemented by computational processes. Very roughly, a computational process is a sequence of symbol manipulations that are governed by rules that are sensitive to the internal structure of the symbols manipulated. (Much more on this in sections 2.4, 3.3 and 3.5).

Whether or not the functional role special to beliefs can be identified with a computational role is a very moot point. To a first approximation, the play of one belief of Igor's on his others seems to be inferential, and hence carried out by computational procedures. But (a) the distinctive role of belief is not exhausted by its relations to other intentional states; there are links to perceptual inputs and behaviour to be considered as well. Igor's beliefs about his immediate environment are intimately influenced by his perceptions, and it is by no means clear that this causal chain is a species of inference. Furthermore, Igor's beliefs play a causal role in his behaviour. Part of the explanation of his reaching-and-grasping is his belief that the grasped object is a snooker cue. Had he believed the long dark object was a snake, his behaviour would have been quite different. It is not obvious that the causal track from belief to action is any kind of inference. (b) Other propositional attitudes have distinctive consequences for one's inner representations. It is notorious that both hope and suspicion affect our view of the world. But it is by no means obvious that, say, the characteristic tendency of hopes to rearrange one's belief set is an inference.

We should not be too quick to suppose that the functional profile of a propositional attitude is a computational profile alone; that is, an aptness to be transformed in certain ways according to the structural properties of the sentence of mentalese that realizes the attitude.

Thesis 2: The psychologically relevant causal properties of propositional attitudes are inherited from the syntactic properties of the sentence tokens that realize the attitudes.

How do intentional states play their causal role? Stich (1978a) and Fodor (1980), argued for an autonomy thesis. Tokens of mentalese produce behaviour and other mental states in virtue of their intrinsic rather than their relational properties (see also section 2.4 and chapter 5). The rather unclear notion of an intrinsic property is explained by contrast. The representational properties of inner sentences are, it is alleged, not intrinsic. A particular sentence has the content it does in part in virtue of its relations to the outside world. Two inner tokens could have exactly the same intrinsic properties yet be distinct representations because caused by distinct distal events. One might be a visual representation of a horse, the other, of a muddy zebra. The pattern of light striking the retina might be identically processed, leading to intrinsically identical but semantically distinct inner states. Semantic properties are not intrinsic properties. So, very roughly, the intrinsic properties of mental states are organism internal properties.

It is often held that the psychologically relevant intrinsic properties of a mentalese sentence are the syntactic properties of the sentence. But what are those? Consider sentence Z

(Z) Zebras run faster than lions, because many lions have reproduced after failing to catch a zebra, but not a single zebra has reproduced after being caught by a lion.

The syntactic features of Z include its structural properties; i.e. the way in which its atomic elements are combined into progressively more complex ones. So the syntactic properties of Z include having a main clause 'zebras run faster than lions' and including quantificational elements like 'many lions'. The fact that the scope of 'not' does not include 'a lion' is a syntactic fact about Z. Let's suppose that Phillipa believes the mentalese equivalent of Z. So there is a token of Z, near enough, in her belief box. The syntactic properties of that token are clearly psychologically important, for they are important to its inferential potential. In virtue of its structure, 'zebras run faster than lions' does follow from Z, but 'a single zebra has reproduced after being caught by a lion' does not. Syntax is therefore clearly relevant to the causal role of Z, but is it all that is relevant? This question is a main focus of chapter 5. Our answer will depend on the nature of psychological explanation, and the inventory of properties we count as syntactic. For example, the words in it are amongst the determinants of Z's causal role. Consider R.

(R) Rabbits run faster than foxes, because many foxes have reproduced after failing to catch a rabbit, but not a single rabbit has reproduced after being caught by a fox.

Phillipa believes both Z and R, but they have different functional roles in her. Thus, she tends to express her belief in R in conversations about rabbits; in Z, in conversations about zebras. But as Devitt (1989) has emphasized, there is an obvious sense in which R and Z have the same syntactic properties. Thus those who hold that syntax alone is important to causal role need a rich sense of syntax that includes much about individual words. They also need a notion of syntax that is not traditional in some other ways. For some syntactic properties seem to be consequent on the overall nature of the symbol system of which a symbol is part. The fact that 'rabbit' is a noun does not seem to be a configurational property of R. So perhaps some syntactic properties are not major determinants of causal role.

Thesis 3: The semantic content of propositional attitudes are explained by the semantic properties of mentalese. The semantic properties of a token of mentalese are explained by its syntactic structure, and the semantic properties of the concepts that compose it.

The language of thought hypothesis is an attempt to show that the representational theory of mind is compatible with our being evolved animals. But it is wise to wonder whether invoking an inner code is progress, for a multitude of difficult questions obtrude. In virtue of what do those inner structures – whatever they may be – have syntactic and semantic properties? Do we slip into regress in positing an inner code? Fodor avoids a regress of learning: a public language cannot be learnt without mentalese, but mentalese requires no further system in its background because it is not learnt at all. But how are inner sentences used and understood? Ordinary sentences – public language sentences – are understood via much special purpose equipment. We have special purpose perceptual mechanisms for speech comprehension; on Fodor's own theory, special purpose cognitive mechanisms as well. What plays their role in understanding inner sentences? And who or what does the understanding? Trying to solve these problems links the language of thought hypothesis to a computational view of cognition: that is the focus of section 2.4 and chapter 3. Chapters 5 and 6 deal with thesis 3, and, more generally, the problem of representational relations between mind and world.

2.4 Avoiding Magical Theories of Mind

One reason for interest in the mind–computer parallel is that it helps avoid a central problem in explaining cognition. It is very easy, in thinking about mental processes, to slip into circular or question begging ideas about how we think. It's very easy to find yourself giving theories of mental processes that presuppose the very capacities they are meant to explain. Representational theories of the mind – theories that make mental representation central to cognition – risk regress. They risk turning into magical or circular theories of the mental.

How does this happen? How does this temptation arise? Here is an elementary case. Consider vision. Our introspective experience suggests the following story. Vision works by forming a mental picture of the outside world. Introspection has support from other sources. If you ask many people how they perform various memory-related tasks, they often appeal to images. How do they remember how many windows their house has? They say they form an image and count them. A little reflection shows that the appeal to images in the explanation of vision and memory cannot, at least in this naive form, be right. For who looks at the mental image, and with what do they look? If an inner eye produces a further mental image we are at the beginning of an infinite regress. But if the inner eye can extract information from a mental image without needing to make a second, presumably the first is not needed either. Explaining vision in terms of an inner image being scanned by an eye within presupposes the very capacities we are attempting to explain.

This example is a simple instance of a more general problem. In sections 2.1 and 2.2, I argued that thought involves inner representation, indeed, a language of thought. But, prima facie, a language of thought seems to involve the same regress as inner images. Psychologists of language emphasize that we are equipped with a suite of cognitive mechanisms dedicated to language perception. Who hears or sees the inner sentences? Who understands them? Just as positing images seems to entangle us in an inner eye, a language of thought threatens to require an inner ear.

It's a vital constraint on any theory of cognition that it avoids positing an *undischarged homunculus*. That is, we must not explain a cognitive capacity by tacitly positing an inner person with that very capacity. Those who have seen Woody Allen's movie *Everything You Always Wanted to Know about Sex but Were Afraid to Ask* will have seen a perfect example of an undischarged homunculus in the portrayal of the control centre of a protagonist attempting a one-night stand. He had an impotence problem that the control tower traced to a guilt centre, instantiated by a minute, inner but fully functional and guilt-ridden clergyman. Explaining guilt by appeal to a guilty-feeling inner agent is no explanation.

The homuncular problem can easily arise in psychology. Computational models of cognitive processes help psychological theories avoid regress in three different ways.

2.4.1 Individualism

When you think, you use and transform representations of your environment. Thoughts are internal states with semantic properties: reference, truth and meaning. Thinking typically depends on those semantic properties. Free association isn't the normal form of thinking. Reasoning is ordinarily truth preserving; it wouldn't be much use otherwise. Similarly, we almost invariably trust our senses; we believe the world is as it seems. Perception wouldn't be much use unless it was usually veridical, and known to be so. So there is a sense in which the semantic properties of thought are its most important properties; they are the properties that matter to us.

But there is another sense in which thinking is a nonsemantic process. Let me explain. Cognition consists of operations on states of our central nervous system, states which have meaning or content. Now: (a) at least in part these states are meaningful in virtue of their relational properties; in virtue of some causal connection between them and the environment. I see Little Caesar only if some state of my visual cortex is appropriately caused by Little Caesar himself. (Much more of this in Chapter 6.) (b) The processes that access and transform that state are keyed not to those relational properties of internal states but to properties internal to the mind. In now current terminology, the processes that operate on mental representations are sensitive to the *individualist* or *narrow* properties of those representations. For instance, we probably have brain functions specialized for face recognition. That must include some device that reads information off my visual cortex. That reader has no direct access to the distal causes of the stimulated states of my visual system. It must be honed to the relevant intrinsic features of my visual apparatus. For that's its only input. The sketch in figure 3 might make the point.

I see Little Caesar. That is, Little Caesar is causally responsible for

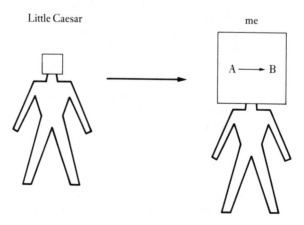

Little Caesar   me

A ⟶ B

Figure 3

A, a state, let's suppose, of my visual cortex. I then think 'Lo! Little Caesar!', a state distinct from seeing him. For we can see someone without having any idea who they are. So *A* causally interacts with memory to produce my thought. Now *A* is about Little Caesar, since it is produced by him in the right way. But that seems to be causally irrelevant to the production of *B*. *B* would be the causal response to *A* irrespective of *A*'s causal ancestry. *A* would have produced *B* (holding the rest of what's going on in my head constant) whether *A* itself had been produced by Little Caesar, his twin, a hologram, a convincing Caesarish robot, or whatever. *B* is a result of features of *A* that are internal to the mind. So a theory of our recognition or categorization of what we see must be, in this sense, an individualistic theory. The features of *A* it appeals to must be the mind internal properties of *A*, not features of its causal ancestry to which our cognitive mechanisms have no direct access. The causal origins of *A* play a direct causal role in mental processes only to the extent that they leave traces in *A* itself.

A good, nonpsychological, example of Fodor's makes this point well. Consider a US dime. Being a dime is a relational property of the coin. Only dimes made in a certain place are genuine; the rest are fakes. No machine, no mechanical device, can discriminate genuine from fake dimes, unless there is an intrinsic difference between the two. If the different manufacturing histories result in coins with identical intrinsic properties, only a magical device could sort them.

So, cognition is the processing of mental representations. But the cognitive mechanisms must be tuned to the structural features that code meaning, for they have no direct access to the extracranial causes of those features. It's in this sense that thinking is an individualist process. Here the parallel between cognition and computation helps. For computation is individualist. Computational operations are specified independently of the meanings of the formulae on which they operate. Cognitive psychologists think that many cognitive processes are inference-like. Perception, for example, is often seen as a process in which hypotheses about the three-dimensional world are confirmed or disconfirmed on the basis of data presented by the sense organs. In constructing computational models of cognition, both the formulae that are the subjects of inferential processes and the allowed inferences themselves are specified independently of their semantics. Elementary formal logic, the 'propositional calculus', provides a simple and straightforward example of how this can be done. The rule of disjunctive syllogism, for example, specifies a transition we may make from any formulae with a particular internal organization; any formulae with an appropriate configuration. We may go from any formulae shaped like not *P* and (*P* or *Q*)

to

Q

This transformation is specified independently of the meaning of the symbols that *P* and *Q* stand in place of; a device could apply a rule like this in complete ignorance of those meanings. We require no miracles, we beg no questions in constructing theories that claim cognitive operations are dependent on configurational properties like these.

2.4.2 Mechanizing Reason

There is a second important way the computational theory of the mind can help psychology avoid regress. It makes precise and manageable a central idea of section 1.3: the idea of decomposing an ability into subabilities. If we could exhibit a complex and sophisticated cognitive ability as an assembly of much more primitive abilities, we would be on the way to understanding that more complex ability. Admittedly, our explanation would not be complete. We would need a story about how the simple capacities are coordinated (and a homunculus can sneak back in here). Furthermore, we still need an explanation of how the simple capacities are realized in brainware. But if those capacities are really simple – say, discriminating light from dark – we are entitled to be optimistic, and in any case we have certainly made progress.

This idea of explaining sophisticated capacities in terms of the coordination of simpler ones is very important in contemporary theories of the mind. I want here to illuminate one strand of it, through the computational notion of a Turing machine, mentioned briefly in section 1.2. A Turing machine is an amazingly simple device, yet one which is, in principle, extraordinarily powerful. It consists of a long tape divided into regions passing through a reader. On the tape are printed symbols from some specified and finite alphabet. The reader views one region at a time, and may carry out the following operations: (a) it may erase the symbol on the region it is viewing and replace it with another from the list, and (b) it may move the tape one region left or right.

No one thinks that the mind is a Turing machine. Turing machines are only in one state at a time, and they carry out only one operation at a time. A Turing machine's set of instructions does not change over time. Human beings are in many psychological states at any one moment. You can be simultaneously: dreading the visit to the dentist, hoping the pain will go away, believing that all things considered you must go, feeling the toothache, seeing the dentist's sign. Many cognitive processes go on in us simultaneously: a whole ensemble of perceptual and cognitive processes can be going on at once. Moreover, our suite of mental operations does change over time, as a result of an unknown mix of development and learning. In the early days of functional theorizing, Putnam speculated that psychological states might be Turing machine states, but for these and other reasons (summarized in Block and Fodor, 1972) no one takes the basic Turing machine architecture of tape, reader/printer/mover to provide a realistic model of the human psychology.

Astonishingly, Turing was able to show that any procedure that can be computed at all can be computed by a Turing machine. That is, any problem for which there is a mechanical procedure guaranteed to solve it in a finite time – for which there is an *algorithm* – can be computed by a Turing machine. In principle, its slender resources are adequate. No one ever uses Turing machines, they are impractical because very very slow. The moral they allow us to draw is theoretical, not practical. Their importance in this context is that they illustrate the way a complex ability can be reduced to simple capacities. Consider a very simple-minded example: a Turing machine that adds. (I here steal an example of John Haugeland's.) A laborious but simple device will work with an alphabet of three symbols '1', '0', 'X'. For any number n can be represented as a string of n '1's. So our Turing machine will add by turning tapes (or sections of tapes) that look like

000X111X1111X00

into tapes that look like

000XX1111111X00

In effect, the punctuation mark 'X' separating 3 and 4 has been erased, turned into a '1', and an initial '1' turned into an 'X'. The ability to add has been decomposed into simple abilities, namely

the ability to recognize '1', '0', 'X',
the ability to erase '1', '0', 'X',
the ability to move the tape right,
the ability to move the tape left.

These abilities are coordinated by the Turing machine's program, which determines the machine's next step as a function of its current input and its current state.

Turing machines aren't realistic models either of minds or of real machinery. But they illustrate an idea central to real machines, and perhaps to real minds as well. Namely, explaining complex capacities as an ensemble of very simple mechanically and physically realizable capacities, sequenced or organized by a controlling program. A theory of cognitive process of this kind avoids one of the ways psychology can fall into the trap of positing an unexplained homunculus.

2.4.3 'Hard-wired' Reasoning Processes

There is a third way representational theories of the mind slip into circularity. How does the mind understand its own rules of operation? The structural or configurational features of symbols explain their role in inference and other cognitive activities. *But how does the mind recognize these structural features?* Recall the example of the disjunctive syllogism. The reasoning device, whether made of silicon or meat, must be able to understand the rule 'From "*P* or *Q*" and "not *P*" go to "*Q*"'. How does it manage this? By understanding further rules about what counts as a '*P* or *Q*' and a 'not *P*'? Again, regress seems to be looming.

The solution to this problem has two parts, the first of which we have just seen. Turing machines, and their more realistic relatives, decompose complex capacities into simple ones. In my toy example, the capacity to add into the capacities to recognize symbols, erase and print. Those capacities are not explained by the machine storing instructions which it follows. The machine will not, for instance, have a description of a zero ('an ellipse') which it must then understand and apply. Rather the machine is *hard-wired* to follow certain procedures. It follows these procedures as the result of its permanent physical configuration. The simplest example of such hard-wirings are the so-called logic gates of a computer: for example, a given connection realizes logical conjunction because its output is 'on' only if it has two inputs and they are both on. Fodor, in discussing this very problem, puts the basic move well

What avoids an infinite regress ... is that the machine is built to use the machine language. Roughly, the machine language differs from the input/output language in that its formulae correspond directly to computationally relevant physical states and operations of the machine: the physics of the machine thus guarantees that the sequence and operations it runs through in the course of its computations respect the semantic constraints on formulae in the internal language. (Fodor, 1975, p. 66)

If the computational theory of the mind is right, what's true of computers must be true of minds as well. There must be a set of basic operations the brain carries out, not in virtue of representing to itself how to carry them out, but in virtue of its physical constitution.

It is time to draw a preliminary moral. I proposed that our intentional states are realized by sentences in the language of thought. The interactions of intentional states in the production both of further mental states and behaviour are realized by the interactions of these sentence tokens, an interaction mediated by cognitive mechanisms of some kind. The upshot of this section is (a) that the properties of most immediate causal relevance to these mechanisms are mind internal properties of some kind, and (b) important cognitive processes are computational processes.

This move was anticipated in section 2.3. Thesis 2 asserted that the interactive role of intentional states descends from the syntactic properties of mentalese sentences. For it is often thought that syntactic properties are the structural properties of sentence tokens. An example is the syntactic marking of semantic scope by bracketing. Contrast: 'not (P or Q)' with '(not P) or Q'. The semantic difference between these two sentence schemas is coded by structural features of the kind a mechanical processor can recognize and act on.

I have now introduced the mainline contemporary position in current thought on the mind, the representational theory of the mind. Thoughts are inner representations; thinking is the processing of inner, mental representations. These representations have a double aspect. They are representations in virtue of relations with the world. Mental states represent in virtue of causal relations of some kind with what they represent. But their role within the mind depends on their individualist, perhaps their syntactic, properties. The syntactic properties of representations – their overall organization and the interconnections between their primitive elements – are properties that can play a direct role in cognitive processing.

As a consequence, the representational theory of the mind is linked to the computational theory of the mind. A computational theory of the mind has the promise, we might reasonably hope, of explaining one aspect of natural minds; of explaining how an entirely natural, physical system can use and manipulate representations. A computational theory of the mind will help explain its internal workings. For computational theories traffic in operations specified individualistically. Moreover, computational theories avoid magic by two ideas prominent in this section: (a) the decomposition of complex operations into ensembles of simpler operations, (b) 'hard-wiring' simple operations so that the system carries them out in virtue of its physical constitution, rather than by understanding explicit instructions about the operations.

In brief. A computational theory of cognition plus an account of the causal relations between mind and world explain how we can have representing minds. The decomposition of the complex capacities into simple ones, plus an account of how simple operations can be built into the physical organization of the mind, explain how we can have computing minds.

This is a nice story. It may even be true. Its elaboration and evaluation will be the organizing principle of this book. In the next chapter, I will discuss in more detail the relations between the various chunks that together make up a theory of the mind.

Suggested Reading

Sections 2.2–2.3

Especially central texts are Fodor's *Language of Thought* (1975), a survey paper 'Fodor's Guide to Mental Representation' (Fodor, 1985b), 'Why There Still Has to be a Language of Thought', the appendix to his *Psychosemantics* (1988a), and his joint paper with Pylyshyn, 'Connectionism and Cognitive Architecture' (Fodor and Pylyshyn, 1988). Other powerful expositions of this line of thought are Lycan's 'Towards a Homuncular Theory of Believing' (Lycan, 1981b), and Field's 'Mental Representations' (Field, 1978). Harman, in *Thought* (1975), accepts a version of the representational theory of mind in which mentalese is English. Maloney argues that even perception involves a mentalese in 'The Mundane Mental Language: How to do Words with Things' (1984). There are plenty of critics of mentalese: A sample is P.S. Churchland's 'Language, Thought and Information Processing' (1981). I will discuss some of them in Chapters 7 and 8, and will give further reading there.

Stalnaker's *Inquiry* (1984) is one important example of intentional realism without a language of thought; see especially the first two chapters. Dretske's 'Explaining Behavior' (1988) is a very robust specimen of intentional realism that is neutral on the language of thought issues. Somewhat less than neutral is Dennett; he is certainly a critic of the mentalese, but it is much less clear that he is an intentional realist. His 'A Cure for the Common Code', reprinted in *Brainstorms* (Dennett, 1978) is an impressed but sceptical review of Fodor (1975). He returns to the same themes many times but especially in 'Three Kinds of Intentional Psychology' (1981b), inaccessibly published in 1981 but reprinted in *The Intentional Stance* (Dennett 1987). 'Styles of Mental

Representation', also in Dennett (1987), also bears directly on these issues. Clark's *Microcognition* (1989), especially chapter 3, is a very recent defence of a Dennettish position on the relation between intentional and theoretical psychology. The issues prefigured in section 2.3 are the focus of chapter 5 and 6; I will discuss further reading there.

Section 2.4

Dennett is the clearest on the dangers of tacitly positing an undischarged homunculus. Particularly recommended are two chapters of *Brainstorms* (1978), 'Skinner Skinned' and 'Artificial Intelligence as Philosophy and as Psychology.' There are numerous logic and computer science texts that introduce the idea of Turing machines. But for this purpose Haugeland's *Artificial Intelligence: The Very Idea* (1985) is in a class of its own. The literature on the use of computational procedures to 'mechanize reason' is huge. All the literature linking artificial intelligence to psychology bears on that issue. Two introductions are Boden's *Artificial Intelligence and Natural Man* (1977) and Gardner's *The Mind's New Science* (1985). Part I of Boden's *Minds and Mechanisms* (1981) bears directly on the isues of section 2.4. Less of an introduction, but still a book-length overview is Clark's *Microcognition* (1989); that work focuses especially on the relations between traditional inference-based artificial intelligence and the newer ideas that are the focus of chapter 8. Even more important individual contributions are Pylyshyn's 'Computation and Cognition' (1984) and Part II of Dennett's *Brainstorms* (1978). Newell's paper, 'Physical Symbol Systems' (1980) is an important insider's overview. An excellent collection on these issues is Haugeland's *Mind Design* (1981).

3

Representation, Computation and Implementation

3.1 Theories, Kinds and Levels

Scientific theories are about natural kinds. These figure in the laws, predictions and explanations that it is the business of science to work out. So in chemistry, the kinds include the elements and compounds; in physics, the fundamental forces; in biology, the species and types of species. So there are, for example, laws about predators: it's no accident that big fierce predators are rarer than the creatures they eat. Contrast the natural kind *predator* with a nonnatural kind; say, the class of *objects the same age as the Eiffel Tower*. The latter is not a natural kind. There are no laws that apply to all and only the age cohorts of the Eiffel Tower.

To explain the behaviour of individual things we sort them into kinds. A particular organ stuck on your face enables you to avoid obstacles and other dangers because it is an eye. A particular large cloud of gas radiates heat because it is a star; it is above a certain critical mass at which gravitation compresses the insides enough to induce fusion.

Scientific domains (evolutionary biology, astrophysics, organic chemistry and the like) have an associated taxonomy; the principles that define the kinds that make up that domain. Because the members of these kinds are never exactly alike in all respects, the taxonomy constitutes an estimate of which characteristics in that domain are important. No two stars are identical. That does not matter; so long as the cloud radiates from gravitation induced fusion it can vary in indefinitely many other respects, and still be a star.

Taxonomies are important; we are not likely to be able to understand the world unless we group together entities which genuinely share important features. We are not likely to understand the interactions of animals with their environment if we classified animals by how cute they are, or how tasty they are. It is unlikely that there are laws that apply to all and only those things which taste good when stir fried with basil and onions. But taxonomies are not easily discovered; our judgements about the similarities that matter are just as empirical and fallible as the rest of science.

Individual objects and processes are typically members of many natural kinds. A particular vial of liquid is a member of many chemical kinds; as it happens, it is sulphuric acid, an acid, a chemical compound, a liquid. Minds, subsystems of mind, and mental processes are likewise members of many natural kinds of psychology. A number of different theorists, in diverse terminologies, have argued that there are three theoretical domains in psychology, and that each individual psychological mechanism and process is in each of these domains.

These domains are the subject matter of three *levels* of psychological theory. The top level is the level at which we specify the function a psychological device performs. It is the level at which we say what a system does. One down is the level at which we specify the information processing means by which the system performs its function or functions. At the base level we specify the physical realization of that information processing device.

Why talk of levels? Taxonomies are relatively but not absolutely independent. The domain described by high-level theories *supervene* on the domain described by lower-level theories. (Chapter 9 considers the stronger thesis that high-level domains reduce to lower-level ones.) Informally, one level of nature supervenes on another if the supervening level somehow depends on the more fundamental level. For example, the basic metabolic processes in physiology – respiration, digestion, excretion – supervene on biochemistry. The range of animal food is so great that we cannot identify digestion with some particular chemical process. One animal's turd is another's tucker. Yet these metabolic processes depend on, and are composed out of, physical and chemical processes. The biological function of digestion has a biochemical explanation. A little more formally, one domain supervenes on another, if there can be no change in the first, supervening, domain without change in the second, base, domain. Think of ageing; not chronological increase but the wear and tear that accompanies it. Animals and plants age in many different ways. It is quite likely that there is no particular biochemical process that is the ageing process in all plants and animals. Yet ageing supervenes on the biochemical, for no organism can age without biochemical change.

Marr, Dennett, Newell, Millikan and Pylyshyn have all defended the idea that there are levels of psychological theory. I will begin with an intuitive sketch of the levels before considering qualifications, problems and objections.

3.2 The Ecological Level

I will call the top level the 'ecological level'. At this level, we specify the cognitive capacities in question. We specify what the system can do in ways that are noncommittal on how the system does it. There is for example some fascinating work on primate deception. The aim of this work is to figure out whether chimps and other primates have the concept of other minds; whether they realize that creatures have beliefs in virtue of which they can be deceived. In one experiment, a chimp becomes accustomed to one trainer sharing food, and another not doing so. The experimental situation then places the chimp in a situation where she cannot reach a box with food in it, but a trainer can. The idea is that if the chimp has a theory of mind, she will point to the box only if the trainer in question is a food sharer. She does. Let's waive the serious complications of interpreting these experiments, and agree that the chimp has a theory of mind. That's an ecological characterization of the chimp's psychology, for it specifies an aspect of the representational capacity of the chimp mind without claims about how that capacity is engineered.

Here's how Dennett puts the point:

The intentional stance profile or characterization of the animal – or for that matter, an inanimate system – can be viewed as what the engineers would call a set of specs -specifications for device with a certain overall information processing competence. An intentional system profile says, roughly, what information must be receivable, useable, rememberable, transmittable by the system. It alludes to the ways in which things in the surrounding world must be represented – but only in terms of distinctions drawn or drawable, discriminations makeable – and not at all in terms of the actual machinery for doing this work. These intentional specs, then, set a design task for the next sort of theorist, the representational-system designer. This division of labor is already familiar in certain circles within artificial intelligence. (Dennett, 1983, pp. 349–50)

Marr (1982) gives a nice illustration (pp. 32–4) of the ecological level by considering the visual system of the housefly. Not surprisingly, what the housefly eye tells the housefly brain is very different from what our eye tells our brain. The housefly sends two most important kinds of signals to its motor routines. If the fly's visual field expands rapidly, the landing motor routines are activated, and the fly automatically attempts to land on the centre of the patch. If there is a small patch in the visual field moving relative to its background (i.e. a candidate for another fly), the visual system plots a pursuing course and issues appropriate instructions to its motor system. That is most of what the visual system of the fly does; in particular 'it is extremely unlikely that the fly has any explicit representation of the visual world around him' (p. 34).

Marr suggests, very reasonably, that if we are to understand how a perceptual system works, we must first understand what it is doing and why. We must have a precise understanding of the information extraction problem the system solves.

The ecological level is neutral on mechanism. A number of other features of this level are worth emphasizing.

First, it is not individualist. An ecological description of a mental processor does not supervene on its intrinsic properties. For we are characterizing the processor's function by appeal to those aspects of the environment it can detect, represent, or change. The sand scorpion recognizes and locates prey by mechanical waves transmitted through the sand. An intrinsically identical device, if embedded in an animal with different hopes and anxieties, would be a predator rather than a prey detector. The intrinsic features of a mechanism constrain but do not determine its function. (Thanks to Peter Godfrey-Smith for this example.) The ecological level supervenes not on the internal workings of the mind alone, but on its environment and history as well.

Second, ecological descriptions can be given for all the units in a homuncular decomposition of the mind. Some theorists are misleading on this point. Newell, especially, but also Dennett and Pylyshyn mislead by concentrating, in their examples of ecological description, on entire agents.

Third, the ecological level is not tied to intentional psychology. Newell and Dennett mislead here both with their examples and terminology. For ecological descriptions can, as the house fly example shows, apply both to simple creatures, and simple modules of complex creatures. Moreover, it is perfectly possible to reject belief-desire psychology as a bad theory of mind, yet still accept Marr's methodological moral. Namely, that we cannot establish how a mental organ works until we know exactly what it does.

Finally, a remark on terminology. There is a bewildering variety of terms for the ecological level. Newell calls it the 'knowledge level', and Dennett the 'intentional' level. I reject these terminologies for the reasons just given. Marr, very confusingly, calls it the 'computational' level; odd, given his own agreement that the ecological level is neutral on the means by which information is processed. Millikan talks of 'remote functional descriptions' for an idea very like this one. Pylyshyn calls it the 'semantic' level: his name, like mine, highlights the nonindividualist nature of the ecological level. I prefer mine because it does not imply, as his does, that *only* at this level are semantic concepts important. That might be so, but ought not be prejudged by a choice of terminology.

3.3 The Computational Level

Below the ecological level lies the computational level. Computational level theories are theories of mechanism; they do not merely specify the task performed, they are theories of the cognitive mechanism that performs that task. Typically, an ecological description of a perceptual or cognitive capacity underdetermines a computational theory of that capacity. When we have one procedure for solving a certain computational task, we normally have many. For instance, suppose we want to explain the ability of some system to add. There are many candidate algorithms. Perhaps the system uses the one we all learnt in primary school: it stores all single digit plus single digit additions as primitive, and decomposes all additions into these primitives plus the 'carrying operation'. Perhaps it converts all numbers into base-two notations, and thus reduces all addition to the primitives of: $0+0$, $0+1$, $1+0$, $1+1$, and carrying 1. Perhaps it reduces addition to counting: it counts (say) marbles for each number to be added into a bucket, then counts the number in the bucket. We typically use the first of these algorithms, a digital computer the second, a young child the third. All are algorithms: formally specifiable procedures guaranteed to solve the problem.

This example is misleadingly simple in some ways. Typically, our algorithms will only approximately carry out the functions specified at the ecological level. We have, for instance, in our visual system, mechanisms whose function is the preservation of colour constancy in vision. Their point is to ensure that we can continue to discriminate an object's colour even when illumination (and hence the nature of reflected light) changes. These mechanisms work very well: objects don't seem to change colour when you turn the lights up. But they don't work perfectly; your visual system can be fooled, for instance under sodium lighting. Usually the algorithms that carry out a job will do so fairly accurately in normal circumstances. But not perfectly, or in all cases. In some ways then, the example of adding by counting marbles into a bucket is the most realistic, for the method works only in a restricted domain. It's limited by the supply of marbles and the size of the bucket.

The computational level is a level in which we specify the *method* by which the device of interest carries out the informational function specified by an ecological description. Having identified some unit as an adder, a computational description specifies the method of addition. For this reason, it is typically assumed that this level of description is of special interest in psychology. For it is here that distinctive *psychological* explanations of behaviour and behavioural capacities can be given. Invoking a computational level commits us to an empirical hypothesis about cognitive powers: namely that they are executed by physical processors that operate on symbols in virtue of their structure. There is no uncontroversial account of the nature of a symbol. But I take symbols to be entities with semantic content that enter into syntactic combinations with one another. To offer a computational account of a psychological process is to claim that cognition *is* computation. That is a much stronger claim than the idea that cognition can be modelled on a computer. Any process can be modelled on a powerful enough computer; that just consists in feeding the initial conditions and the rules that specify how the system changes into the device so that it takes over the burden of predicting change. One can model the Big Bang: that fortunately does not imply that the conditions at the beginning of the universe are replicated in miniature in your machine. It is also stronger than the uselessly vague claim that cognition is somehow analogous to computation. But the computational level is the most problematic of the three levels of psychological theory. For the *computational hypothesis* poses four problems.

1   When is a physical device using some computational method? A car's odometer displays the distance the car has travelled via its connection with an axle, but in no interesting sense does it compute this

distance. A computational description of the odometer, but not human visual recognition, is at best redundant. What is the critical difference?

2   Suppose we know that *some* computational method is being used. We need to identify the essential features of *particular* computational processes. If there is a level of computational theory, there will be a taxonomy, a grouping of individuals into kinds, distinctive to that theory. So if, for example, educated humans' visual recognition is a computational process based on the comparison of features detected in vision with definitions of objects stored in memory, then there will be in those humans a *distinctive method* of visual recognition. Nonhumans with different physical structures might use that same method; other humans, with the same basic neural mechanisms and with an equivalent capacity, might use a different method.

3   It turns out to be very difficult to say just when two minds, or two devices, are using the same method. For there may be no 'the method' which minds or machines use. A comparison with actual computers suggests that methods have many computational descriptions. Perhaps none deserves to be singled out as 'the method' for solving the problem.

4   This multiplicity of descriptions poses a fourth problem, for, as we shall see, it threatens to undermine the distinction between the computational level and the level of physical implementation. I will return to these difficulties after outlining the most straightforward level, that of physical implementation.

3.4 Physical Implementation

The third level of Marr's trichotomy is the level of physical implementation. Consider, yet again, addition. A computational process must be physically realized: some system of neurons (if we are thinking of computational processes in organisms) must carry out the arithmetic primitives of whatever algorithm the adder is using. Perhaps it reduces 3 to its binary equivalent of 11. Again, at least in principle the computational level underdetermines the level of physical implementation: different physical structures can realize the same process. That point is easily seen in terms of the Turing machine discussed in the sections 1.3 and 2.4. The colour of the machine tape doesn't matter, nor does it matter whether it's made out of paper or linen. How the machine head recognizes, erases and prints the symbols doesn't matter. Nor do different gearings to move the tape backwards or forwards.

None the less, implementation considerations constrain the computational level in important ways. It obviously constrains the amount of information a memory can contain. Moreover, it is often argued that the slowness of neural interaction shows that our computational organization must be 'massively parallel' rather than serial. Commercial machines only do one operation, and that a simple one, at a time. Getting a machine to do anything interesting takes millions of operations, or 'machine cycles'. That's fine if your device can work through millions of cycles a second, but neurons at best work through hundreds, not millions. So, the argument goes, we must do lots of things at once, and that has consequences for the organization of cognition (see section 8.2).

3.5 Is There a Computational Level?

In section 3.3, I sketched the idea that computational mechanisms perform ecological functions. But that idea faces considerable difficulties. In this section, I explain those difficulties and make some tentative proposals about their solution.

3.5.1 When is an Information Processing System Computing?

Not every information processing system is appropriately explained by appeal to operations on syntactically structured symbols. We explain, for instance, an ordinary mechanical clock directly in terms of its physical structure. We do not regard the clock as executing an algorithm that calculates the time, and then try to explain the workings of the devices that implement such executions. Biological examples make the same point. Hordes of *E. Coli* live in our gut, and a good thing too, for they help us digest dairy food. They do so with the aid of a special enzyme which they produce only when milk products are present. *E. Coli* come equipped with a special gene that suppresses enzyme production except when lactose is present. A bacterium thus has a sense organ which plays a central role in the internal processes and behaviour of the organism (Changeux, 1986, p. 181). But a computational description of this organ would be surely otiose. We can and should give a direct physical explanation of *E. Coli's* recognition of, and response to, a milky environment.

The possibility of a direct physical explanation of information processors poses a problem. If we are, for instance, to explain the extraordinary facial physiology, vocal structures and ears of bats we need to know that they find their way around the world by echo location. Indeed we need to know the kinds of echolocation they use. In addition, we need a story of how the creature can do what it does. Why then cannot we rest content with two levels: an ecological level telling us what the mind can do, and a neurological theory, or suite of theories, giving an account of mechanism. What is the point of a *computational* level?

This is a problem to which we will return, especially in sections 9.4 and 9.5. Moreover, I have no entirely convincing solution to offer. But, very roughly, a computational explanation is required when the system to be explained can recognize the same information in a wide variety of physically distinct signals, and/or use that information for a range of purposes. That is, we explain a system computationally if it shows the informational sensitivity alleged in section 2.1 to be symptomatic of sentience. *E. Coli* react to the presence of dairy products appropriately only if lactose is detected; no other signal switches off the repressor gene. A clock's measure of time is equally stimulus bound: it is completely determined by the easing of tension in a spring. If this suggestion is right, we do not need a computational account of the informationally *in*sensitive mechanisms mentioned in section 2.1: the attack response of the male gulls, and the behaviour of cuckoo-feeding robins. So a computational explanation of an ecologically specified function is appropriate when the capacity to be explained is plastic and flexible. Sentient creatures are *open ended* in ways clocks, thermostats and bacteria are not. Informationally insensitive mechanisms represent but do not compute.

3.5.2 When are Two Systems Using the Same Computational Method?

I suggested in section 3.1 that theories are about natural kinds. So to apply a theory, we must be able to sort individuals into kinds. Since no two individual things or processes are alike in all their details, we must take a stand on which features of an individual matter for the theoretical domain in question, namely computational psychology. Which features of particular computational processors matter for their classification into kinds? When are systems, minds or machines using the same method? Marr and Pylyshyn identify *methods* with *algorithms*. Unfortunately, it is very difficult to state when two systems are executing the same algorithm.

Consider just the epistemological problem. Most of our evidence about method is behavioural. Now suppose that Ron and George recognize, equally well, just the same set of faces. They may not recognize faces in the same way. For there are likely to be many algorithms that are I–O (input–output) equivalent; that deliver the same judgement given the same input. So identical behaviour does not imply identical method. Nor, less obviously, does different behaviour imply different method. For a computational method must be physically implemented. Different implementations of the same method can generate different behaviours. Distinct realizations have distinct speed, reliability and storage profiles. So inferences from what a system does to how it works need to be very subtle.

The epistemic problem is difficult but not utterly intractable. (For the contrary view see Anderson (1978).) Even if two people used different but equally adequate methods, their overall behaviour need not be absolutely identical. For the different algorithms might support different relations with *other* subsystems of the mind. Suppose that Ron recognizes faces by very exact representation of nose shape, and George, by eye colour. If both methods work equally well, Ron and George will do equally well in 'Spot that face!' But their other talents need not be identical; George may well be better at answering questions about eye colour than Ron.

We can bring to bear other data as well. For example, not all methods are equally learnable. Transformation grammarians argue that of the enormous number of algorithms that could support human linguistic behaviour, only a tiny proportion are learnable from the data children actually get. So only those are candidates for being the method we use, despite their having numerous I–O equivalent colleagues. We saw in section 3.4 that the implementation constraint also allows us to eliminate otherwise good candidates. Algorithms run by human brains must be implemented by neural assemblies; not all can be.

Even if the epistemic difficulties are solved, problems remain. What makes a method the method it is? For one thing, we can individuate methods very finely. Consider, for example, the establishment of validity in elementary logic. There is an algorithm that tests for validity in the propositional calculus, the truth table method. An argument is valid, if when the premises are true, the conclusion must be true. So we can set up a truth table in which we assign all the possible truth values to the elementary constituents of the premises of the argument. We then examine each line in the truth table to see if there is a line which makes each premise true and the conclusion false. If there is such a line, the argument is invalid.

Now there are an enormous number of trivially different ways of exploiting this idea. We can vary the order of the items in the rows and columns in the matrix. We can check the lines in a different order:

from bottom to top, or right to left. So do we have one algorithm here, or many distinct but similar ones? Logicians regard these as notational variants of a single algorithm, but programmers cannot, for they cannot afford to ignore housekeeping details. Nor, perhaps, can those studying the human mind. A coarse criterion might count all means of testing for validity as in essence the same; a very fine one might count the most trivial differences in notation as different methods. Addition illustrates the same moral. In section 2.4, I outlined a Turing machine method of addition that turned 111X11 into 11111. Is this the same method of addition as counting marbles into a bucket? It is certainly very like it; intuitively it is machine counting. But there is no widely agreed criterion for distinguishing between essential and inessential elements of a method.

This is not surprising, for it is the theory of human cognition itself that ultimately must tell us which differences matter. Unfortunately, it is not yet well developed enough to do so. As in other sciences, both taxonomy and theory grow together. Intelligent taxonomic guesses promote theoretic growth. We construct good theories only if individuals that genuinely have something important in common are grouped together, but intelligent taxonomy is not easily come by. Consider, for example, the phenomenon of consciousness. Are our conscious mental episodes a psychological natural kind, distinguished, perhaps, by some kind of informational access? Without a good theory of consciousness, none can say. But without a good taxonomy of the mental, we will not get a good theory of consciousness.

We do not have a good taxonomy of computational method. That is a serious problem; however, it is not a refutation of computational psychology but rather one symptom of its immaturity.

3.5.3 Is There a Distinguished Computational Level?

A comparison with actual computers suggests a further problem in determining the computational level. Consider a computer running a chess program. Chess programs have a common basic structure. The computer considers each legal move in a situation, each reply to that move, each reply to that reply and so on, to a certain depth of analysis. Thus the computer constructs a set of enormous branching trees, the root of each being a legal move in the position being analysed. The program evaluates the position at the end of each branch; assessing a numerical value for the material balance and various positional features. The computer then backtracks, choosing that move such that, if each player makes her/its best move, the position results that the computer regards as its most favourable. So the computer doesn't gamble; it does not deliberately play a move that results well for it against a weak reply, but badly against a strong one.

That, at least, is the overall structure of the program. Details vary widely. The algorithms that evaluate the positions at the end of search trees vary most, but there are other differences as well. Current programs now continue the search deeper in crucial lines; they extend the tree if, say, either player is in check at its standard search depth. Most also add a few bells and whistles: allowing the player to change the search depth, take back moves, change sides and the like.

Take one of these programs – say Sargon II, available on many home computers. Suppose that a human used the same set of algorithms to generate move options, construct trees of analysis, evaluate positions and choose the best move as Sargon II uses. Should we then say that this person and a Mac running Sargon II play chess in the same way; that the same cognitive processes are taking place in the human and in the Mac. From the way I have told the story you would think so. But we can describe the algorithms the Mac follows in a very different way. For the instructions of the chess program are not directly implemented by the Mac's hardware. In section 2.4, I pointed out that the primitive operations of a Turing machine pose no problem to physicalism. For those primitive operations – recognizing and printing symbols, moving a tape and changing state – are carried out by the device in virtue of its physical structure. It needed no instructions about how to recognize the symbol for zero. The chess-playing instructions of Sargon in the Mac are *not* directly implemented. The Mac does need instructions to tell it whether it is in check. The instructions directly implemented by the Mac are those of its assembly language: instructions that direct it to addresses in memory where data are stored; instructions that carry out same/different checks between distinct addresses; instructions to 'add one' to a number at an address and the like. It is only elementary operations like these that are directly implemented by the Mac. The instructions in the chess program have ultimately to be defined in, or *compiled* into, these elementary instructions, often via several intermediate stages. So there are a number of differing descriptions through which the operations of the Mac can be described. A 'machine language' describes its activities in terms of its directly implemented operations. A high-level language describes its activities in chess talk. So does the *appropriate* computational description of the Sargon-employing chess-playing Mac talk of moves, and trees of moves, and positions. Or does it talk, at considerably greater length, of checking, moving and altering bits of information at divers locations in the machine's memory. If it is the second, given the radical difference in hardware, it is certain that the person is not playing chess in the same way as the machine.

The standard response to this point in computer science is to argue that there is not one level of computational description but many. The Mac is using various linked chess algorithms, and it does so in virtue of running algorithms in assembler and others in between as well. The question of whether a person and a computer are playing chess the same way is ambiguous.

Pylyshyn has argued a contrary position. He argues that there is a *distinguished* level of description. The Sargon-level description and the assembly-level descriptions are not of equal importance. The theoretically salient description of a system or subsystem is a specification of its repetoire of primitive representations and the primitive operations. Furthermore, it is this level of description that is the special province of psychology. The explanation of those primitive operations is the province of the neurosciences, not psychology. So Pylyshyn thinks that there is a clear demarcation between psychology and the sciences of its physical realization, and that is the boundary between symbol processing, and the implementation of symbol processing.

There is one consideration that should push us Pylyshyn's way on this. The cascade of languages that we use to describe Sargon II is an artifact of the tension between what we want languages to say, and how the machine operates. Low-level languages have straightforward implementations, but are hard to 'use', i.e. it is hard for us to see how to express in that language what we want to express about the world, and it is hard for us to express the operations we want to perform on those representations. Hence the invention of 'high-level' programming languages which are easy for *us* to use. So we need, as well, intermediate bridging languages. The multiplicity of computational descriptions of standard computers is the consequence of needing programming languages that will run on two very different machines: computers and brains. Even if cognition is computation, we face no such conflicting demand, so in this respect the comparison with machines may well be misleading.

3.5.4 Is There a Primitive Computational Level?

So let us suppose our task is to specify the primitive operations of the mind. Our choice ought not to obscure genuinely psychological processes, by treating as a unitary step that which is complex. But nor should we treat as assembled a process that is psychologically a primitive single-step operation, even if it is physically complex, or hard to program on standard devices. We need some criteria of primitiveness. Pylyshyn suggests some. We need to ask four questions about his tests. (a) Do they pick out the same operations? (b) Are they clear enough and empirically well defined enough to be usable? (c) Are they theoretically well motivated; that is, do they nonarbitrarily pick out a distinguished level? (d) Granted that the tests define an important level, is it the level at which psychology is demarcated from neuroscience?

Perhaps not surprisingly, the considerations suggested by these considerations tend to tug against one another. So let's look at his suggestions.

No intermediate steps

The operation of transforming symbol structure A into symbol structure B is not primitive if there are representational intermediaries between A and B.

This is at least a necessary condition on primitiveness, for if C is a representation that mediates the transformation of A into B, then there are two steps, A to C, and C to B. Hence the move from A to B is not primitive. But how can we use this test? Let's consider an example.

Chomsky introduced a famous idea into natural language syntax, the distinction between the deep and surface syntactic structure of sentences. The point of deep structure is to capture the fundamental organizational similarity of sentences that differ superficially, in the order of their elements, and the like. The following pairs of sentences illustrate the idea of superficial difference with deep identity.

It is hard to eat soup without a spoon.
To eat soup without a spoon is hard.

Igor threw up his lunch.
Igor threw his lunch up.

Nicole believed that Paul monstered her sister.
Her sister was believed by Nicole to have been monstered by Paul.

Transformational grammars assign to each sentence of the language they are about, two structures. Deep structure specifies the basic grammatical relations between the parts of the sentence. Surface structure specifies the phonology and graphology of the sentence. Many linguists hold that the language processing unit of the mind has one of these grammars built into it (Berwick and Weinberg, 1986). So speaking a sentence involves some kind of transformation of its deep representation into its surface representation: understanding it requires the converse operation. Is the surface-to-deep match (and its inverse) a primitive step? One might think so. Both structures are available to a variety of cognitive functions; it is this variety that requires a symbolic rather than a directly physical explanation. Yet transformational grammars typically do not map deep structures *directly* onto surface structures; the derivations are often complex, and run via intermediate structures.

Consider, for example, 'Her sister was believed by Nicole to have been monstered by Paul'. On some standard versions of transformational grammar, that would be derived from some thing like:

Nicole [believed [that [Paul [monstered her sister]]]]

via:

Nicole [believed [that [her sister [was monstered by Paul]]]]

and

Nicole [believed [her sister [to have been monstered by Paul]]]

to

Her sister [was believed [by Nicole [to have been monstered by Paul]]]

On this view of the matching process, the subordinate clause of the deep structure, 'Paul monstered her sister' first is passivized; that is, 'her sister' becomes the topic of the clause. Then 'her sister' becomes the direct object of the main verb, 'believes', and the subordinate clause becomes some kind of remnant. Finally, 'her sister' becomes the topic of the whole sentence. The alleged existence of these intervening structures suggests the match between deep and surface structure is not primitive. But these are not available to any other cognitive functions: if we take them to be psychologically real, their only role is to mediate between surface and base. They are not *transparent* to other processes. Two intuitive tests, complexity and transparency, pull in opposite directions.

Complexity equivalence

A process is primitive only if its resource use does not vary with input. A primitive process is a *fixed-resource* process.

The intuitive justification of this suggestion is not easy to see. Nevertheless, there is one. For consider an example, visual perception. On the retinal image, there is at best a mess of blobs, lines and squiggles. That has got to be sorted into an array of objects in a field of view. Normally some of these will occlude others, and all will occlude the backdrop. Working out the 3-D array involves first the detection of boundaries; edge detection. That is a moderately complex physical process, involving banks of cells that basically heighten contrast, and thus make discontinuities more overt. Is edge detection a *psychologically* primitive process? We see the intuitive point of Pylyshyn's suggestion when we consider the possibility of the detection of edges on complex figures taking more time or trouble than on simpler figures. For that would strongly suggest that we could decompose the process into the detection of edges on individual segments of the figure. If so, it is that that is primitive.

If we accept this criterion, matching deep and surface structures is primitive only if the computational expense of a match is fixed, not varying with the sentences whose structures are matched. Pylyshyn's two suggestions may not be equivalent, for the first counsels us to take the matching of deep with surface structure to be primitive unless we find good reasons for positing intermediate representations. Even if there are no such reasons, the structures of complex sentences might take longer to match than the structures of simple ones.

Is computational complexity empirically accessible? Pylyshyn himself points out that there is no clear behavioural test for computational complexity. In particular, reaction time, despite its wide use in cognitive psychology, is not such a test. Two complexity-equivalent steps can take different times to carry through. For in the first instance time measures a property of the *physical realization* of the computational process. Pylyshyn is confident that reaction time can be made to bear on the question of the algorithm an agent is using. But he insists that their import is indirect and always via hypotheses that require independent justification.

So far, our situation is this. We have two suggestions. They both enjoy intuitive plausibility, but they are not obviously compatible, and they both require a good deal of a theory of mind to be in place before we can actually use them. They are both very blunt tools at the beginning of theorizing. Pylyshyn has most faith in a third idea.

Cognitive impenetrability

A process cannot be primitive if it is cognitively penetrated; that is, if it changes adaptively in response to changes in the agent's beliefs and goals.

This criterion has a good intuitive motivation: the idea is that a device cannot explain cognitive operations if its own workings are in part cognitively explained. So the basic processes cannot be affected by, or under the control of, the intentional states that they are meant to explain.

None the less, this proposal raises all sorts of difficulties. There is no need to suppose that penetrability marks the distinction between psychology and the neural implementation of psychology. For there may well be all sorts of impenetrable nonprimitive processes. Fodor is fond of pointing out the impenetrability of the standard visual illusions; knowing that these are illusions does not make them go away. Yet both Fodor and Pylyshyn claim that visual perception is complex and inference-like (see Fodor and Pylyshyn, 1981). Fodor argues that there is a whole class of perceptual systems that are cognitively impenetrable. So, at most, impenetrability is a necessary condition of being primitive. But even that is problematic.

Pylyshyn's idea is very difficult to make precise. For putative counter-examples need to be nonarbitrarily excluded. Moods and emotions have an intentional component yet seem to affect the whole range of our activities. Feeling tense includes an intentional element, for worrying involves both beliefs and desires. Yet it can affect your digestion, but surely digestion is not a psychological process. If intentional states can affect anything inside us, they can affect the primitive operations of our mind. If so, primitive operations are cognitively penetrable, and the suggestion is no good at all. Moreover, attention affects all sorts of perceptual processes and certainly helps determine what you perceive. It may affect all psychological processes. Yet what you attend to is most certainly affected by beliefs and goals.

The criterion is hard to apply. Typically we want to know whether a subprocess – say, locating the nose on a face – is primitive, hence impenetrable. But we have access only to the output of the whole system: even if that is penetrated, we must discover the locus of penetration. According to Pylyshyn, penetration is the *rational* sensitivity of a process to beliefs and goals. If an illusion went away when we knew it was an illusion, that would be rational sensitivity of a process to information and hence penetration. Just any old change is not penetration: stomach pain is not a rational response to worrying about where the rent is coming from, and for that reason the causal influence of anxiety on digestion does not demonstrate digestion's psychological nature. Rationality is important to Pylyshyn, because he thinks it is the rationality of a set of procedures that demonstrate the need for a symbolic and semantic theory of them, and the inadequacy of any merely mechanical explanation. But rationality is always an idealization. No physical system is perfectly informationally sensitive and plastic: we are all a bit tropistic, rigid and subject to breakdown. So which sensitivities of outcome to information constitute rational adaptivity, and thus exemplify cognitive penetration? There are other problems of application: consider, for example, biofeedback relaxation. These techniques enable people to learn to lower their heartbeat at will. Does this show that heartbeat is a psychological process? Obviously not. Heartbeat is as mechanical as any process in the body; you hardly need a brain for it at all. So the causal route of penetration matters, and the criterion becomes at best very messy.

There is therefore no clean criterion of a primitive process, but rather a set of messy indicators. Ought we to expect a clean cut? Lycan argues persuasively against there being any sharp demarcation between the psychological and the physiological, on the grounds that the kinds in question are functional 'all the way down'; they just abstract away from fewer physical details as we come down to the neurons and assemblies of them that neurophysiology traffics in. He emphasizes the cascade of languages that I mentioned in discussing Sargon, and points out that even the binary machine code can be redescribed as settings in memory addresses (Lycan, 1987, pp. 81–2).

Lycan is surely right in pointing out that even 'neuron', 'axon', 'dendrite', 'neurotransmitter' and so on – the atoms of neurophysiology – are functional terms. But though it is functions all the way down, it by no means follows that it is symbol processing all the way down. It is surely redundant, at best, to conceive of neurons as following an algorithm when an excitation is passed from one to another across a synaptic connection. While it is reasonable to see this as an informational as well as a bioelectric flow, it is otiose to look for syntactic structures and their transformations here. There is no syntax, and hence no computation at the bottom. Perhaps that does not demonstrate that Pylyshyn is right to look for a distinguished level which is symbolic, but which is explained by nonsymbolic neural devices. Perhaps having a syntactic structure fades away, rather than gives out abruptly. But I doubt it: having syntactic structure is a pregnancy-type property, all or none. So I think Lycan is right in denying that there is a sharp break from functional to structural properties, and hence is right in denying a sharp psychology/ neurophysiology distinction. I think he may be right in arguing that there is more than one true computational description of a cognitive process, though I have reservations about the mind–machine parallel here. But it would be wrong to infer that there is no distinguished computational level, the level of the primitive operations. But at the moment we have no clear and empirically well-defined test of that distinguished level.

3.6 Conclusion

The idea of theoretical levels, in different guises and different forms, is widely accepted in the various sciences of behaviour. It allows disciplines to formulate problems with a considerable degree of autonomy. Ethologists, for example, can study and describe the range of chimpanzee behaviour (and hence describe the shapes of their underlying capacities) without committing themselves to a view of the neural or computational process through which chimps recognize each other. Cognitive psychologists often propose views about the computational or representational structure of the mind that are relatively independent of the neural structures that carry out computational tasks.

For example, it is common within cognitive psychology to represent information in long term memory as a network of 'propositions', representations that are sentencelike in their semantic properties and in being built out of more elementary constituents, but which do not have the linear order distinctive of sentences. This model makes no detailed claims about the neural organization of the mind; it's compatible, for instance, with memory being localized in a given section of the brain, or with its being widely distributed. But the cognitive proposals are, at most, only relatively independent of neural claims: a network model of memory implies that there must be neural connections between whatever structures represent 'the lion was hungry' and 'the lion ate Max' if these are linked in a network. Computational theories have implications for theories of physical implementation; theories of physical implementation constrain computational theorizing.

Suggested Reading

Section 3.1

In arguing that theories are about kinds, I am not entering the debates about the nature of scientific law. I am not, for example, endorsing the view that laws of nature are relations between properties that Armstrong defends in his *What is a Law of Nature?* (1983) All I mean to do is emphasize the importance of taxonomy in the development of good explanation. But I am committed to scientific realism, to the view that the entities and their relations that are the domain of the natural sciences exist independently of their investigators. For it is crucial to much of what I say that the business of science is explanation rather than prediction. For two contrasting contemporary defences of realism see Devitt's *Realism and Truth* (1984a), and Churchland's *Scientific Realism and the Plasticity of Mind* (1979). For contemporary antirealism, see van Fraassen's *The Scientific Image* (1980).

Section 3.2–3.5

Marr's views on theoretical levels are developed in the first chapter of his *Vision* (1982). Newell expounds his version of the idea in two papers, 'Physical Symbol Systems' (1980) and, especially, 'The Knowledge Level' (1982). Dennett discusses the idea of 'stances' throughout his work. Most to the point are 'Intentional Systems' in *Brainstorms* (1978), and two papers from *The Intentional Stance* (1987), 'True Believers' and 'Three Kinds of Intentional Psychology'. Practically the whole of Pylyshyn's *Computation and Cognition* (1984) is relevant to this chapter. But the second and third chapters are most crucial. Millikan's version of the distinction between the ecological and the individualist levels is given in 'Truth Rules, Hoverflies and the Kripke–Wittgenstein Paradox, (forth coming a). Peacocke gives an even more complex version of this set of distinctions in 'Explanation in Computational Psychology: Language, Perception and level 1.5' (1986), arguing for theories intermediate between the ecological and computational levels. Lycan rejects a principled psychological/ neurophysical distinction in the fourth chapter of his *Consciousness* (1987). The distinction is applied to the special case of linguistics by Stabler in his 'How are Grammars Represented?' (1983).

4

Marr on Vision; Fodor on the Mind's Organization: The Theory in Action

4.1 Introduction

I shall illustrate the discussion of section 1.3 and chapter 3 with a famous example. In 1982, David Marr's *Vision* was published and it is already a classic (perhaps *the* classic) exemplar of a computational theory of the mind. I shall recycle this example to illustrate both the decomposition of a complex ability into simpler abilities, and the idea that psychological theories deal with phenomena at a number of distinct levels. In 1983, Fodor proposed a general theory of human cognitive organization partly based on some ideas of Marr. Fodor's theory is both interesting in itself and is of considerable philosophical importance. So I follow my account of Marr with a briefer treatment of Fodor's modularity thesis.

4.2 Vision

What is the function of the visual system? This question has no single answer. The visual systems of invertebrates are often specialized. They don't deliver a general representation of the world, but rather factors of special biological interest: mates, predators, food. J. J. Gibson (see, for example, (1979)) argues that this is true of all animals: we all see the world in biologically meaningful terms, in *affordances* of various kinds. We see parts of the world *as* barriers, shelters, paths, opportunities, dangers, rather than seeing it as a collection of shapes, surfaces and textures. Moreover, we see it as affordances directly, not by first detecting its geometric properties and then inferring their biological import. Gibson's work has not won widespread acceptance. Most are convinced he understates the degree to which the information hitting the eye underdetermines the percept, and the complexity of the operations needed to extract the data that are in the stimulus (see, for example, Ullman, 1980). But his theory shows that specifying the function of vision requires a delicate empirical investigation. For while we need to know the output of a *perceptual* system, our behavioural and introspective evidence is typically the result of both perception and cognition. An account of the function of vision draws a vision/cognition boundary. There is great debate about the place and nature of that boundary.

Marr suggests that vision delivers a 3-D representation of the shape, size, colour and motion of what's in the field of view. Moreover, the format of those representations makes them suitable for immediate use by the cognitive mechanisms that enable us to recognize and categorize what we see. Marr thus supposes that *purely perceptual* processing provides a sophisticated representation of the world. The alternative is to suppose that perception provides only a representation of the stimulus, and leaves it to our central cognitive processes to work out the tale this stimulus tells about the world.

What is the input to the visual systems? Light falls on the retina. We can think of the retina as a two-dimensional grid of about 126 million points (pixels), extremely dense around the centre. For the retina is simply a surface packed with light-sensitive cells. When light falls on the retina, cells respond. If we disregard the complication of colour, the strength of that response represents dark, white, or some shade of grey in between. This response is the input to visual processing.

Each pixel's response represents the intensity of light at that point. But the retina may give more than a representation of light intensity at a single moment in time. The variation in intensity across time at a point may be part of the input to the visual mechanisms. So too may be the difference between intensities at corresponding points in the two images binocular vision gives us. So the input is a representation of intensity values and perhaps their changes; the output is a 3–D representation of the world suitable for thought.

It is worth reflecting for a moment on just how surprising it is that we can see. For the intensity value of the light that strikes the retina has an extremely messy causal history. It is partly caused by the reflectance of the surface from which the light has bounced. Surfaces vary in the proportion of light reflected to that absorbed. A low intensity value might be the result of the light having bounced off charcoal. But intensity depends on many other facts about the environment. Most obviously, the illumination. An energetic light source, all else equal, will result in higher intensity values. Intensity also depends on the geometric relations and the distances between the light source, object surfaces and the eyes. Naturally, the greater these distances, the less the light. But orientation is also important. If the surface is tilted away from the illuminant, less light is reflected. If it is tilted away from the line of sight of the eye, less reaches the retina. These physical facts imply that the light reaching the retina is decidedly equivocal about its source.

It was thus no easy matter for natural selection to engineer a system that can resolve these ambiguities to deliver a field of view. It is hard to construct a representation of how the world looks from the point of view of the perceiver from such messy evidence. She needs a representation of the shapes, sizes, colours and distances of those surfaces, contours and curves of the objects in her line of sight. But even granted success in that far from trivial task, consider how much remains to be done. For the field of view is *not* a suitable input to her general cognitive mechanisms. Consider recognition. The agent's viewpoint of an object is markedly idiosyncratic. It will depend on (a) her perspective: whether she is in front or behind, to the left or right; (b) the orientation of the object: whether it is upside-down, upright, tilted, or on its side. (c) It depends as well on the distance to the object. It is not just that apparent size changes with distance, for it is easy enough to imagine mechanisms that would cope with that. Rather, at distance, details disappear, and, when close to large objects, apparent proportions and distances between parts change. If you are one inch from the front of an elephant, the trunk looks bigger than the rest of the animal. (d) Finally, viewpoint depends on the degree to which the object is occluded by obstacles on the lines of sight between surface and eye.

Surprisingly, our recognitional capacities are relatively constant across such changes, though ecologically unusual orientations, in particular, can fool us. It is surprisingly hard to recognize upside-down photos of faces. It is hard to believe that we store in long-term memory a match for every possible viewpoint of every kind of object we can recognize. On one estimate, that is 3000 kinds, plus subvarieties

(Stillings et al. 1987, p. 491). For there are an enormous number of views of even a single object. So, if Marr is right in thinking that vision provides input in a form suitable for recognition, then we need more from vision than a 3-D representation from the agent's perspective. We need to convert the egocentric perspective into an object-centred one. That is an extra task for the visual system, and a difficult one.

So our visual systems solve hard problems. One of the great virtues of Marr's account of vision is that he offers both a general, and a detailed, picture of the visual mechanisms. (a) He gives an architecture of vision, outlining the intermediate representations between the retinal image and final output, and of some of the subsystems that compute them. Some of these subsystems are only outlined. But, for some, Marr offers a detailed theory, suggesting specific algorithms, and even making proposals about neural implementation. (b) He suggests criteria that the algorithms computing visual representations should satisfy. (c) He tentatively identifies the crucial informational clue in the retinal image. Let me elaborate.

4.3 The Architecture of Vision

Marr believes that the fundamental informational clues in the retinal image are sudden discontinuities in light intensity. In suitable circumstances, these are correlated with physically significant features of surfaces; boundaries between objects, contours of objects, one surface peeping out from behind another, textures and marks on surfaces. So the first task is to represent explicitly represents these discontinuities. The *raw primal sketch* is a 2-D representation of the lines, closed curves (blobs) and termination points of the discontinuities found on the retinal image. From this, the primal sketch is computed, namely a representation of the two-dimensional geometry of the field of view. The primal sketch will differ from the raw sketch in a number of ways. For instance, it explicitly represents larger-scale organization only implicit in the raw sketch. It will group together similar elements to form larger units from smaller ones. An instance is the embedded square and triangle in figure 4 (from Marr, 1982, p. 94).

The next stage in this process is the computation of the $2\frac{1}{2}$-D *sketch*. This represents (a) the distance from each point in the visual field to the perceiver, and (b) the orientation of the surface on which each point rests. The surface may be perpendicular to the line of sight, or sloping towards, or away from, the viewer. The $2\frac{1}{2}$-D sketch will show this for

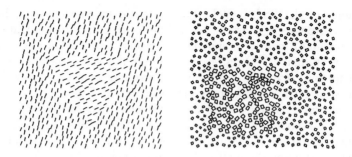

Figure 4

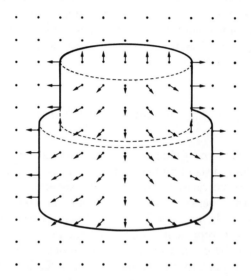

Figure 5

each point in the field of view. Figure 5 (from Marr, 1982, p. 129) is Marr's standard illustration of the central idea.

Finally, the 2½-D sketch is input to processes which construct the 3-D object-centred shape representation that is vision's goal. Thus the *gross* architecture of the human visual system, if Marr is right, is as shown in figure 6.

Marr gives, as well, a less gross account. The construction of the 2½-D sketch, for example, relies on subsystems that are sensitive to

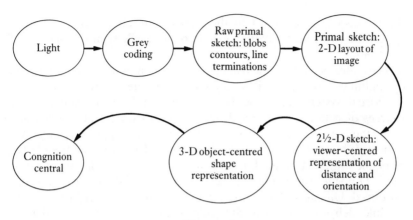

Figure 6

difference in light intensity across time or across images. Such differences are very informative. The apparent motion of an item over successive images is a source of depth information. If, for example, an item grows in the image over time but does not change position, you are on a collision course. If it grows and moves, something is closing on you (or vice versa), but the motion has an oblique component as well. Motion against a background is extraordinarily effective in segmenting superimposed 2-D shapes into 3-D objects. For if adjacent points have different apparent motions over time, they are not on the same surface, likely not the same object.

Another instance of the same general phenomenon is 'structure from motion'. Ullman, in particular, has shown that we have a surprising ability to infer the shape of an object from motion information alone. His most extraordinary demonstration of this ability is the 'two cylinders' experiment. The faces of the two cylinders – one nested inside another with the same axis – are defined by nothing more than 100 points lying on the surfaces of the cylinders. The cylinders are completely invisible except for these freckles on their surfaces. These points are then projected onto a surface; that is, a straight line perpendicular to the axis of the cylinders is drawn from each point to a surface, and a point is drawn at the place of intersection. The result is an apparently random array of dots on a plane. The cylinders are then rotated, in opposite directions, about 10 degrees, and a projection taken again. The result once more appears to be a random collection of dots on a plane. The same procedure is followed a few more times. Each static display appears to be a random set of dots. If, however, the six displays are shown to the subject one after another at movie speed, the two counterrotating cylinders are easily seen (Ullman, 1979, pp. 134–5).

Marr draws four conclusions. (a) Discontinuity over time, like discontinuity over space, is a very important clue for the visual system. (b) Visual systems are modular, for they work even when all other sources of data are suppressed; the counterrotating cylinders are seen even though all other cues but motion are suppressed. (c) It is important to see that the output of the shape-from-motion module is in principle underdetermined, even if we insist on a 3-D interpretation of the 2-D image. An indefinitely large number of 3-D scenes could have produced Ullman's dots; most simply a cloud of blowflies. Yet the module delivers a determinate judgement. Marr concludes that the hypotheses our modules entertain are restricted, and that the shape-from-motion module is typical in this respect. (d) He concludes that the shape from motion problem is very hard. Because the module operates early, the *matching problem* is very difficult. That is, how does the module match an element of the image at time t with an element of the image of $t+$? If systems that recover information from apparent motion took highly processed inputs, this problem would not be too serious. How many albino chickens will be represented in any one image? But Ullman's experiment, and many others, shows that shape-from-motion operates early in the process. It contributes to the recognition of albino chickens, rather than relying on that recognition. It takes an early representation: in Marr's view, the primal sketch. Now on any two images, there will be *lots* of blobs, lines, terminations. So which corresponds with which? This problem is *especially* difficult because objects can merge, split, or disappear. So the projection of an object onto one retinal image might correspond to one, none, or several projections on a later image. The matching problem is hard. Furthermore, even granted a solution to it, the recovery of shape is by no means easy.

This example, and others like it, lead Marr to substantial proposals about the nature of the algorithms that solve these problems.

4.4 *The Nature of Visual Algorithms*

What kind of algorithms are likely to be employed by the visual system? We cannot say yet exactly which algorithms vision uses, but Marr does think we can narrow down the range of candidates.

4.4.1 Modularity

Marr thinks that the algorithms that serve specialized functions are modular. They operate independently of one another, with at most a limited information flow between them. For example, Marr thinks that there are at least four mechanisms that give depth information: (a) stereopsis, i.e. inferring depth from the difference in position of an object's representation in the left and right retinal image; (b) motion on the retinal image due to the movement of objects in space; (c) optical flow, i.e. motion on the image caused by the agent's motion through space; (d) the recovery of 3-D shape from 2-D silhouette. Marr thinks, on experimental and theoretical grounds, that these are all computed independently, by devices that do not exchange information. Experimentally, because these processes can be shown to operate even when all other information is suppressed. So independent operation is *possible*. Further, we ought to *expect* independence. For it would be good design. If everything depends on everything else, natural selection would find vision very difficult to debug. Natural selection works on small random tinkerings, keeping the best. But if All was connected with All, random tinkerings with, say, stereopsis would ramify through everything else. So even if stereopsis were improved, it is likely something else would be worse.

4.4.2 Nativism

Marr, like many other cognitive psychologists, argues for a nativist theory. Nativists think that important chunks of our information about the world are innate. The most famous example is Chomsky; he thinks the language learning problem solved by children is so hard that they must be preequipped with information about the grammar they are to acquire. Marr thinks that the light that strikes our retina is ambigious about the world it comes from, and that the task of extracting the information that is in it is demanding. So he thinks that we come preequipped with information about the causes of the changing patterns on our retinas. At each stage of visual processing, the processor must have access to facts about the world if that world is to be veridically perceived.

The causal history of the light that strikes the eye is complex. Vision must first sort the consequences of surfaces from the consequences of illumination. I have already mentioned that the central clue here is discontinuity. Normally, the illumination on a scene varies gradually from one place to another. Sudden changes are typically the result of some property of the reflecting surface: an object boundary; one surface partially occluding another; a colour or texture change; a curve or bend on the surface. So the first thing to look for are these discontinuities. This is an appropriate procedure, but one that depends on a contingent fact about our viewed environment. After all, illumination boundaries can be sharp; there are knife-edged shadow boundaries. Moreover, colour changes, and changes in the 3-D geometry of a surface can be gradual. Early vision builds in a substantial and fallible physical assumption, namely that sudden changes in light intensity between adjacent points on a retinal image are caused by the surfaces from which the light is reflected and not by the nature of the illumination.

Nor do the assumptions stop here. Grant that discontinuity in light intensity signals a real property of surfaces. Which? Discontinuities may be caused by colour or texture changes; bends on a surface; a joint of a surface with another in a different orientation; or by one object partially eclipsing another on the same line of sight. How is all this to be sorted out? Marr emphasizes the importance of comparing different images in resolving these ambiguities. Our two retinal images are not identical. The closer an object the greater the *displacement* (i.e. the difference in retinal position) of its representation on the retinal image. This is stereopsis. Displacement across images, a 2-D property, carries information about depth, the distance of viewer to object.

Motion also helps resolve ambiguities. If two points have different apparent motions on an image, they are unlikely to be on the same surface in space. But both stereopsis and apparent motion yield usable information only if the *correspondence problem* is solved. That is, we must pair a point, line or blob on one image with *the* right point, line or blob on the next image. The algorithm that solves the matching problem has physical assumptions built into it. The match (a) pairs uniquely, (b) pairs like with like, and (c) assumes that displacements are small and vary smoothly. That is, if two items are close on one image, their matches will also be close. These physical assumptions work well, but not perfectly, but only because of contingent facts about the world. Similarly, Ullman has shown we can recover shape from motion, even with restricted information. But only because the shape-from-motion system has built into it an assumption that the objects in its field of view are rigid and in motion, not flexible but undergoing distortion. For these could have identical 2-D projection. A balloon swelling throws the same retinal image as a sphere travelling towards the eye. Despite that, our perceptual representation is not ambiguous. We determinately see the world in a particular way even when the information the eye receives is equivocal. Even notoriously ambiguous figures cannot be seen both ways at once. You cannot see the Necker cube, or the duck/rabbit both ways at once.

So far, I have discussed examples of physical assumptions built into early visual processes. But Marr wants to draw the same moral quite generally. His research strategy is to find some general feature of the world that can be built into the visual algorithms. The aim is to constrain the set of possibilities the visual modules consider. If one can do so, the information in the light may be sufficient to select just one from the narrowed class of possibilities. His theory of late vision shows this idea too. How can we construct a 3-D object-centred representation prior to the recognition of the object itself? Marr suggests we might represent objects as generalized cones, or connected networks of generalized cones. Roughly, a generalized cone is any object which has an axis of symmetry, straight or curved. More exactly, it is any shape that can be represented by two vectors.

1   A vector that describes the path of the figure's axis of symmetry.
2   A vector that specifies the perpendicular distance from every point on the axis to the shape's surfaces.

Now this is a compact representational system, yet quite rich. Many shapes are generalized cones, or ensembles of them. Marr shows, for example, that the human body can, to a first approximation, be represented as an ensemble of such cones. Importantly, this is the kind of representation that the visual system may be able to construct. When an object is a generalized cone, its 2-D projection encodes that fact. So, for example, we can recognize silhouettes when they are silhouettes of generalized cones. But most importantly, many of the natural objects we do recognize are ensembles of generalized cones. One nice example Marr gives is a set of animal shapes constructed out of pipe cleaners. They are easily recognizable.

The point is that if our natural environment was not crowded with objects so representable, representing shapes as cones would be worthless. If we mostly saw balls of crumpled newspaper or clouds, being set up to represent the world as systems of cones would do us no good whatsoever. For these have no axis of symmetry, nor are they decomposable into parts with such axes. However compact that symbol system, however inferable from 2-D data, it would be valueless in some worlds. The representational system used by vision at its final most cognitively sophisticated stage is up to its neck in commitments about the sort of things we see. It is no neutral and uncommitted symbolic medium, but rather one tailored for a specific domain.

4.4.3 Robustness and Realizability

For some of the components Marr isolates in the visual system, there is no known algorithm. We don't know how the visual system recovers shape from shading, that is, from the variation in light intensity caused by the interaction of contour and light source. But for a number of important elements of vision, Marr and others provide quite precise algorithms. Marr himself provides algorithms for stereopsis, for calculating depth from displacement. He reports Ullman's procedure for computing depth from motion, and Land's work on colour, amongst a good deal else.

But of course it is one thing to have *an* algorithm. Quite another to have *vision's* algorithm. Where we have one procedure that solves a problem, there will be many. So do we have, in any of these cases, the right algorithm? This question is especially pressing, for none of these methods come with an implementation theory, except perhaps for very early visual processing. Marr is sensitive to this issue, and suggests constraints that psychologically plausible algorithms should meet in addition to reasonable agreement with experimental data. In particular, he argues that algorithms should be *robust*; they should degrade gracefully. That is, they should give fairly accurate results from inaccurate data and they should give fair approximations if their normal physical presuppositions are not quite met. So, for instance, a shape-from-motion method ought to give a fair approximation to an object's shape even if it is not quite rigid, if, say, it bends a bit due to wind resistance while moving. This constraint is not idle: Marr doubts that Ullman's shape-from-motion method meets it. Our perceptual systems are strikingly robust, coping admirably with noisy or inaccurate data. We often, for example, understand ungrammatical sentences without even noticing that they are ill-formed.

Perceptual algorithms must be neurally realizable. Now even in the absence of a specific proposal about realization, a method can be a plausible candidate for realization. Neural plausibility requires that the processors that execute an algorithm meet three conditions.

1 *Parallelism*: The processors that compute the elements of a problem must operate simultaneously. The basic units out of which the brain is built are slow compared to electronic components. Yet vision solves computationally complex problems very quickly, so many elements of a problem are worked on at once.
2 *Locality*: Neurons and neural assemblies have very rich connections to neighbours but far fewer connections outside their local area. So, as a first approximation, we should assume that each processor is connected informationally to, but only to, its neighbours.

3   *Simplicity*: The conditions of parallelism and locality imply that there are a large number of processors. So we should not expect these to be individually powerful or sophisticated; rather we should expect them to be simple devices.

Marr shows that his theory of stereopsis meets these conditions and is therefore a plausible candidate for neural realization; Ullman shows that the same is true of his account of shape perception.

4.4.4   Zero-crossings

The ecological, computational and physical perspectives come together best in our theory of early vision, in the detection of intensity on the retinal image. The task is to detect edges and other boundaries. The method is to detect sudden changes in intensity on the retinal image. We can think of the retinal image as an array of intensity values. Let us consider a fragment of such an array, albeit an unrealistically noise-free one.

$$
\begin{array}{ccccc}
x & x & x & y & y \\
x & x & x & y & y \\
x & x & x & y & y \\
x & x & x & y & y
\end{array}
$$

For a noise-free discontinuity, the computational task is trivial. Any algorithm suffices which gives a null output wherever the horizontal pairs are identical. For example, an algorithm which forms a new matrix by subtracting left from right will yield a new array with zeros in all but the fourth column. The fourth column will be positive if the 'y's represent a light bar on a dark background; negative if vice versa. Of course, for real images, constantly varying and with more gradual and more frequent transitions, we need a more subtle measure. One idea is to form a graph of the change in intensity. No change gives a flat line, gradual change a gentle slope. Discontinuities emerge as steep sections on the graph. So our visual system needs to do a little calculus in measuring the slope of the graph. Still, the graph will have peaks and troughs, signalling maxima of light and its absence. At the change of one to another, positive values change to negative values, or vice versa. The curve crosses zero; hence Marr calls detectors of these changes in intensity zero-crossing detectors.

But how could such discontinuities be detected? As it happens, there is solid evidence for pairs of 'reversed-polarity' photoreceptive cells. These are 'on-centred' and 'off-centred' cells. They have circular receptive fields with a small central circle embedded within a larger outer one. So their receptive field looks like a doughnut. On-centred cells fire if the centre of their visual field is stimulated, and are inhibited if the outer doughnut is stimulated. Off-centred cells have the reverse arrangement. Marr has pointed out (1982, p. 66) that zero-crossing detectors can be built out of pairs of off- and on-centred cells and an 'and' gate. Pairs of these cells can be linked so that they both fire only if there is a discontinuity between them. An 'and' gate firing only if both cells fire into it thus signals the discontinuity. Banks of paired cells firing into a single cell will detect a line on the retinal image of the same orientation of the bank of cells.

Marr's theory of vision is rich and in places detailed. It is controversial but continues to fuel an ongoing research program. But independently of its ultimate empirical fate, it is an excellent example of the ideas of sections 1.3 and 3.2; of the decomposition of a complex system into simpler units, and of the availability of differing but complementary theories of those units.

In discussing Marr's theory of vision, I have attempted to make more concrete the idea of a theory of mental processing. I discussed Marr's account of the ecological function of vision: it takes changes in light intensity at points in the retinal image, and makes an object-centred 3-D representation of the field of view. I have shown how he thought this very complex function could be decomposed into simpler ones. I have not specified any particular algorithms to perform these simpler functions, but talked about both the nature and the neural realization of these functions. The sketch of Marr's theory should illustrate how the three levels of a psychological theory are intended to inform each other. The ecological level specifies, in a fine-grained way, the output of our systems of visual perception together with the informational basis from which that output is extracted. Marr outlined algorithms that could perform (some of) these extractions, and attempted to show – especially for early visual processes – that those algorithms are biologically plausible. That is, that the neural organization of early visual processes might well implement those algorithms.

4.5 A Second Example: The Modularity of Mind

In this section I want to make the computational theory of mind more concrete by sketching a contemporary computational theory of the overall organization of the mind. This theory had its roots in the work of Marr and other MIT-based cognitive psychologists (Ullman, Chomsky), but it received its first explicit elaboration and defence in Fodor's *The Modularity of Mind* (1983).

Fodor proposed a tripartite division of cognitive mechanisms. At the skin there are transducers, which record the stimuli the world provides and send on messages in neural code. Next come the modular 'input systems'. The raw data from the transducers are processed in these systems. The results are passed on to the central processor, the site of the higher cognitive processes. Fodor's view contrasts with a slightly older line in cognitive psychology which drew no sharp distinction between perceptual processing and central cognitive processes.

Transducers are the interface between symbolic processing and the world. They are on the mind–world boundary. The input to the transducer is physical energy in some form; its output is a symbol. If Marr and Fodor are right, transducers are shallow: in their view, the output of the photosensitive cells of the retina is symbolic. For the zero-crossing detectors perform simple computations on these outputs. We have already seen that there are delicate issues hereabouts, for the transduction–input system boundary is also the boundary between processing for which a physical description tells all, and processing which requires a computational description. I mentioned in section 3.5 that there is no untroubled account of this boundary; I will return to this question in section 9.4.

Input systems are specialized; for example, there is not a single system for vision, but one for colour, one for shape, one for face recognition and so on. These input systems or modules are 'domain-specific', concerned with a particular kind of stimulus. Fodor thinks, for example, that the mechanisms involved in speech perception are specialized for that task. English speakers recognize that 'bet' and 'pet' have the same vowel; if he is right we recognize the vowel by a perceptual mechanism that is different from the one used in recognizing a possum fight as a possum fight. Fodor's view is plausible. Consider, for instance, the fact that acoustically different noises are heard as instances of the same phoneme, or the fact that the linguistic differences you can hear depend not on your general acuity but the distinctions marked in your native languages. Thus monolingual Cantonese notoriously have difficulties with the English l/r distinction; English speakers notoriously have difficulties with the tonal distinctions of Asian languages. If a computational mechanism is exclusively used for a particular task, it is fair to assume that it is specifically adapted to that task. The algorithms used by a chess playing computer to evaluate chess positions cannot be used to evaluate football players. They are domain specific not just in being use*d* only for chess, but in being us*able* only for chess; we would expect the special purpose mechanisms of the mind to be domain specific in this stronger sense as well. Specialization has implications for learning. If we all have a common suite of special subsystems whose operating procedures are tailored to their particular domains, it would be an advantage to have those procedures built in. For learning is time consuming, and mistakes can be disastrous. So we might expect that input systems are 'innately specified', with structure not for the most part formed by learning, even when the procedures in question could be learned. Fodor thinks that there are even stronger reasons for expecting some input systems, at least, to be innate. For he thinks some are not learnable at all: he follows Chomsky in thinking that the task of learning a human language genuinely from scratch is so difficult as to be impossible. Language learners already have a big chunk of their language processing module installed before they start. Similarly, suppose Marr is right in thinking that vision represents the things we see as networks of generalized cones. It is difficult to see how we could possibly have learnt such a system of representation.

So input systems are specialized and, to a considerable extent, innate. Fodor is also inclined to think that they are supported by dedicated wetware. Input systems are 'associated with specific, localized and elaborately structured neural systems'. Most importantly of all, they are 'autonomous', both in that they get no information from the central processes, and that the central processes have 'only limited. . .access to the mental representations that input systems compute' (1983, p. 57). Marr thought that the mechanisms of early vision that compute the $2\frac{1}{2}$-D sketch were 'informationally encapsulated'; Fodor extends this idea to all the input systems. He enjoys pointing out that visual illusions do not disappear once their victim is convinced of the illusion. Most of us know that a movie is a sequence of discrete snaps shown fast, but that does not stop us seeing it as continuous motion. As we shall see, the independence of modules is crucial to their philosophical significance. It is also the most controversial, and hardest to test, aspect of Fodor's picture. Finally, modules are independent not just from central information but central decision. For they are 'mandatory'; there is no decision to operate, rather they are automatic, rather like a reflex.

Input systems send information to the central processor. The central processor is in two ways a global information processing mechanism. First, its cognitive processing is unencapsulated; its sources of information are not domain specific. Thus the visual module, in presenting to me a visual representation of the early morning state of my ceiling, has access only to a limited range of domain-specific information; essentially only the structure of the ambient light striking my retina, together, perhaps, with some general truths about the world. It does not, for example, have access to information about what is normally on my ceiling. But I, in deciding whether the squashed-blowfly appearance my visual system is presenting to my central processor is really a blowfly squashed on the ceiling, or merely a trick of the early morning light, can access my information on an indefinitely wide range of topics. Is it blowfly weather? Do I remember squashing one on the ceiling? And the like. Fodor calls this the property of being isotropic.

Secondly, central processes are Quinean. That is 'the degree of confirmation assigned to any hypothesis is sensitive to the properties of the entire belief system' (Fodor, 1983, p. 107). Thus I'm entitled to believe that – despite what my ears are telling me – there are no fairies at the bottom of the garden (but only a white cockatoo) because the admission of fairies into my ontology would grossly complicate my entire belief system. Fodor is pessimistic about the prospects for a good theory of central processing, for he does not see any good candidate for a computational theory of rational belief formation. In chapter 10, I will discuss the frame problem, and will find too little reason to disagree with this assessment.

The modularity hypothesis is not just a useful illustration of the themes of the last chapter, it is of direct importance to both epistemology and to the account of intentionality I offer in chapter 6. We can begin to appreciate this importance by considering *why* the mind might be modular. Marr suggests an evolutionary engineering reason. Nonmodular systems are much harder to debug, for a change anywhere in a nonmodular system can have consequences anywhere else. That must make it harder to use natural selection's design technique of making small but random changes, and keeping any improvement thus made. This argument is not very strong, for natural selection does work on nonmodular organization; genomes, the genetic codes of plants and animals, are not modular. A given gene does not have a single special consequence for the developed organism; typically a gene has many effects, and those effects will depend as well on the other genes of the genome. But the nonmodularity of the genome does not prevent its debugging by natural selection. Still, the modularity idea is evolutionarily plausible on other grounds, for modular input systems are useful independently of full general intelligence. Since our minds did not spring into existence all at once, it is important to show how bits of it could be usable before we reached our current exulted level of sentience. Moreover, it is hard to see how a Quinean and isotropic mechanism could arise other than by the gradual generalization of special purpose mechanisms, and by gradual unencapsulation.

In discussing Marr, I stressed the great difficulty of the perceptual task; a fact that makes the modularity hypothesis plausible. For it may be too hard for a general purpose mechanism to take the output of transducers and recover the information we need. We are confronted with eccentric and complex stimulus domains (faces and languages), and need special purpose devices to deliver what we need. Fodor emphasizes a different epistemic consideration. Encapsulated systems ensure that we see the world as it is, not as we want it to be, or expect it to be. If perceptual processing were unencapsulated, it would be much more difficult for us to veridically see surprising situations, a difficulty that could easily be fatal. I have my doubts about this idea. It is clear that background belief had better not *determine* perceptual representation, for it is death not to be able to see an unexpected danger. But encapsulation is the stronger claim that background knowledge does not *influence* perceptual representation. It may well be an advantage to have topdown influence; it might be life to spot an expected danger quickly because it is expected. It might well be good to spot tigers quickly in tiger-infested parts.

Because he thinks perception is encapsulated, Fodor sees his hypothesis as undercutting an important contemporary epistemic doctrine, namely that *perception is theory laden.* It is a truism of much contemporary philosophy of science that there are neither observations nor observation statements that are independent of the theoretical perspective of the observer. This is often thought to have quite radical consequences for the rationality of theory choice. It is claimed that we can rationally choose between competing theories only if there is a neutral language into which we can translate their empirical predictions, and a neutral check of those predictions. It is precisely this neutrality that theory ladenness is supposed to blow away.

In Fodor's view, perception is not theory laden in any epistemically exciting sense. Fodor is a nativist. So he concedes that perception is preadapted to certain very general structural features of the world; to the fact that objects in our field of view are normally rigid, or that illumination causes gradual, not sudden, changes in light intensity. But these are very general features, not at issue in the disputes between rival scientific theories, disputes in which theory ladenness is alleged to play a role. It is not circular, on this picture, to appeal to observation to decide between Newtonian and relativistic theories of gravitation. But it would be circular to appeal to it to decide between a realist and an idealist metaphysics, for the idealist does reject the view of the world built into our perceptual mechanisms.

There are many problems with Fodor's hypothesis, principally concerned with the robustness of the input system–central system boundary. For example, Fodor and Paul Churchland disagree vigorously on whether adopting the kinetic theory of heat could change people's perception of temperature, or only the way they describe those perceptions. It's hard both theoretically and experimentally to establish a robust perception–cognition boundary. It's hard, for instance, to test experimentally Fodor's claim that the systems involved in language understanding have no access to the speaker's background knowledge of social context. But despite such problems, Fodor's proposal is at least coherent, theoretically motivated, and experimentally productive. It is also, as we have seen, of direct philosophic import. It is important not only for the epistemic issue touched on above, but, as we shall see in section 6.9, in constructing a plausible theory of mental representation.

Suggested Reading

Sections 4.2–4.4

Vision (Marr, 1982) is surprisingly readable. There are some very technical passages, but Marr is adept at giving the sense of these. Gardner, in *The Mind's New Science* (1985), gives a nontechnical account of Marr's views, and contrasts them with the noncomputational approach to vision of Gibson. The physical basis of vision is expounded with exemplary clarity by Camhi, in *Neuroethology* (1984). Stillings et al., in *Cognitive Science: An Introduction* (1977), updates Marr's story. The introductory chapter of Pinker's *Visual Cognition* (1985) is a good survey of theories of object recognition. Hubel's *Eye, Brain and Vision* (1988) is an excellent introduction to these issues from a neurobiological, rather than an AI, perspective. Patricia Kitcher (1988) explains the theory and argues for its philosophical significance in 'Marr's Computational Theory of Vision' (1988).

Section 4.5

The basic reference on modularity is, of course, *The Modularity of Mind* (1983). But Fodor summarized the book in 'Precis of "The Modularity of Mind"' (1985a) which appeared together with comments and a reply. Recently, an entire collection on modularity has appeared, Garfield's *Modularity in Knowledge Representation and Natural Language Understanding* (1987). Fodor's views are anticipated to a surprising extent in Stich's 'Beliefs and Subdoxastic States' (1978b). Claims for theory ladenness and its significance are laid out in Feyerabend, *Against Method* (1975), Kuhn, *The Structure of Scientific Revolutions* (1970), and in Paul Churchland's *Scientific Realism and the Plasticity of Mind*

(1979). Churchland, however, resists the relativism and antirealism of the other two. There has been a lively debate in *Philosophy of Science* between Fodor and Churchland on modularity and its epistemic significance. It began with Fodor's 'Observation Reconsidered' (1984a); Churchland wrote a reply 'Perceptual Plasticity and Theoretical Neutrality (1988b)' to which Fodor replied with 'A Reply to Churchland' (1988b).

5

Individualism

5.1 Individualism and Content

Individualism is a doctrine about the natural kinds of psychology, the doctrine that the psychology of an organism depends only on features internal to it. It is a view with two sources. One is an idea about causation and supervenience. Psychological theory had better not posit spooky causal processes, or devices with impossible causal powers. No dime detector can tell legal from counterfeit dimes irrespective of the physical similarity of counterfeit to genuine. Similarly, no face recognizer can tell Ron from his look-alikes irrespective of their similarity to Ron. The causal origin of the stimulus, and hence what the stimulus represents, is not of *immediate* causal import to the face recognizer. So psychological theory must not posit face recognizers that recognize faces except via features of the stimulus that can affect a physical device. This evidently correct line on causation is linked to a claim about supervenience. Psychological properties ought to reduce to, or at least supervene on, the properties that are immediately causally involved in reactions to perceptual stimulation and in the production of behaviour. Otherwise psychological explanation will invoke spooky causation. These base properties are internal to the organism, for they are intrinsic properties of brain states. For reasons discussed in the first two chapters, psychological properties do not reduce to neurophysical properties. But on this view, they should at least supervene on them: no psychological difference without difference in the intrinsic properties of brain states (see sections 2.3–2.4)

The second motivation is vaguer. It is the idea that the mind is a well-defined system. It is not, of course, a physically closed system. But functionalist theories of the mind seem to imply that the mind takes a well-defined set of inputs through the perceptual channels, and that its output consists of commands to the motor system that are translated into action. Computational theories of the mind fit the same picture. They often picture a creature's mind as built from three types of component. Sensors convert energy into symbols, effectors convert symbols into actions and an information processor links the two, taking symbolic input from the sensors, and providing symbolic input to the effectors. If this perspective is right, the mind is connected to the outside world only via a few discrete channels through which it gets symbolic input or through which it acts via symbolic commands to the motor centres. If so, the mind is like a closed system and psychological kinds are identified by their role within this system. No psychological difference without system internal difference.

A point on terminology. Here, as elsewhere, terminology is nonstandard. Individualism is also known as 'methodological solipsism' or 'the autonomy thesis'. Individualist taxonomies of mental states are also called 'narrow' taxonomies; nonindividualist ones, 'broad' or 'wide' taxonomies.

Individualism bears on the representational theory of mind. I claimed in chapter 2 that representational notions play a central role in psychology. Yet representational kinds are not individualistic. There is a standard parable that makes this point. Imagine that, far away in space and time, there is a world just like ours, Twin Earth. Twin Earth really is a twin to Earth; the parallel is so exact that each of us have a doppelganger on Twin Earth, our twinself. A person's twinself is molecule-for-molecule identical to himself or herself. (Obviously, none of this is likely to be true. It is hardly likely that there is a Twin Earth; equally obviously, it is not a scenario contrary to the laws of nature.) Consider now your thoughts, and those of your twin. Note that you and your twin are individualistically identical, for what is going on inside your heads is molecule-for-molecule the same. But the representational properties of your thoughts are not always the same. For consider your thoughts about your mother. These are about *your* mother. But your twinself has never seen, heard, or thought of your mother. That individual's motherish thoughts are about another individual. An individual amazingly similar to your mother, but none the less a different person, separated by eons and light years. So the representational properties of thoughts about particular people don't supervene on brain states; they are not individualist. Variations of the Twin Earth theme have been run by Putnam and Burge to show that thoughts about natural kinds and socio-legal kinds are not individualistic either (see Putnam, 1975b; Burge, 1979).

The conceit of Twin Earth is useful, but not essential. The idea of Twin Earth merely dramatizes the fact that the causal origins of psychological states play a role in their representational content. Hence their failure to supervene on what is inside the head. This fact about representational properties has led some philosophers to urge an *irrelevance thesis* about representation in psychology: semantic kinds have no place in psychology. Dennett, for example, has written that the mind is a 'syntactic engine'; representational notions have in his view real heuristic and predictive value, but they do not have a role in the causal explanation of the mind's inner workings (see, for example, Dennett, 1982, p. 26).

It is widely agreed that an acceptance of individualism is a rejection of the representational theory of mind and of intentional psychology. But it is not universally agreed; an intentional psychology purged of nonindividualist elements might still be recognizably intentional psychology. Stich (1983) floats this as an option. He thinks we could have an entirely nonrepresentational, by still essentially belief-desire, psychology. Others have attempted to construct theories of 'narrow meaning' for psychology. Defenders of that program defend intentional psychology. Furthermore, the intentional states have a content that is essential to their role in psychological explanation, but the notion of content is 'narrow'. Outside-the-head aspects of content are irrelevant, 'bracketed off'. Devitt (1989) defends a theory of this kind, as does Block (1986).

Setting aside this last possibility, the consequences of individualism look to be radical and counterintuitive. I made a case in section 2.1 that representation is the crucial function of cognitive states. If the individualist case is accepted, that must have been a mistake. In this chapter, I consider four responses to individualism. (a) Burge rejects the case for individualism, and argues that contemporary theoretical psychology is not individualist. (b) I discuss at some length a moderate strategy, one that concedes the value of an individualist component in our total theory of mind. But one that claims a nonindividualist psychology can explain phenomena inexplicable to the individualist. Central to the moderate strategy is the idea of 'capturing generalizations'. There are important facts about our and other minds we would miss if we restricted ourselves to individualist psychology.

I consider as well two bolder options. Perhaps individualist psychology is parasitic on nonindividualist psychology. Marr argues for an epistemic version of this idea, in arguing that there is no discovering the algorithms of the brain without first discovering their representational function. There are nonepistemic versions of the same idea. I discuss them in section 5.6. Still more boldly, one can question the significance of the skin as boundary. Underlying individualism is the idea that what goes on inside the skin of an organism is a good approximation of a closed system. So we need to consider only intrasystemic interactions together with the coded sensory input. That is a plausible view, but one open to debate. I will conclude the chapter by airing some scepticism about the importance of the skin as a boundary. These worries are originally due to Dawkins (1982), but have been restated in this context by Millikan (forthcoming c).

5.2 Burge on Individualism

Burge, together with Hilary Putnam, showed that the semantic properties of mental states do not supervene on their intrinsic, nonrelational properties. Folk psychology is not individualistic. In an important recent paper Burge (1986) has two central aims. First, he attempts to discredit the a priori case for an individualist constraint on theoretical psychology. Second, he aims to show that contemporary theoretical psychology is not individualist, and has no individualist reformulation.

Burge considers two formulations of the individualist case. One focuses on causation, and its intuitive force is most easily seen through twin earth fables. Consider Eric and his twin. They behave in the same way, for after all their brains, the controllers of behaviour, are molecule for molecule identical. Surely it is also true that the explanations of their behaviour are also the same. Granted, Eric's thoughts and his twin's thoughts are about different folk and different places. But those differences are irrelevant to the explanation of action, and should be 'bracketed off' in explanations of behaviour.

Moreover, as usual, the recourse to Twin Earth only makes the point more vivid. It is not essential. Consider any two individuals whose internal psychologies are identical in any important and self-contained aspect. Perhaps native English speakers' grasp of the syntax of their own language is such a case. Katie produces and understands sentences containing the name 'Michael', so does Libby. The fact that they are speaking of different Michaels is irrelevant to the explanation of these behavioural capacities. The explanation should be the same because (I am presuming) the internal organization of their grasp of their language is the same.

Burge formulates this argument as follows:

P1   The behaviour of individuals on Earth is identical to that of their functional and psychological duplicates.

P2   Psychology is a science of behaviour.

C1   Since the behaviour of Earthians and their doppelgangers is the same, the explanation of that behaviour, equally, is the same.

C2   So, 'there is no room in the discipline for explaining their behaviour in terms of different mental states' (1986, p. 10).

Even if we grant that psychology is the science of behaviour, the individualist needs to answer two questions. First, not all the activities of a creature are its behaviours, part of the explanatory target of psychology. The wind-buffeted trajectory of a sheep after it has fallen off a cliff is not in psychology's explanatory domain. Another example (from Millikan): a chameleon turns brown in a brown box, as does a mouse in a hot oven. Only the first is behaviour.

Second, we need an explanation of what counts as 'behaving the same way'. For we have many ways of describing behaviour, and some will not count a person and his twin as behaving alike. For consider Eric. Eric thinks about his mother, and sends her a letter. Does twin Eric behave the same way? It depends how we choose to describe twin Eric's behaviour. We could say that because he does not send a letter to *Eric's* mother, his behaviour is not identical to Eric's. Alternatively, we can describe them as both writing to their respective mothers. So described, they behave the same way.

Behaviour is explained relative to a classification. For we explain individual cases by seeing them as instances of natural kinds that are the subject of causal laws (section 3.1). Consider a cat rapidly locomoting after a mouse. That piece of behaviour is, one guesses, appropriately explained by feline psychology. But only as an instance of chasing-a-mouse. Not as an instance of locomoting-at-2.02 pm or heading-towards-Sydney. Even though it was both of these as well. For there are no laws of cat psychology about running at 2.02 pm, or running towards Sydney.

So the individualist owes us (a) an individualist account of the difference between mere bodily changes/motions, and behaviour; and (b) an appropriate and individualist taxonomy of behaviour, an account of which *types* of behaviour stand in lawlike relations to the processes that produce them. It is not easy for an individualist to meet these demands. For example, it is not open to the individualist to distinguish behaviour from mere motion by appeal to purpose, or any representational notions. She cannot say that the change of the chameleon is under the control of its representation of the colour of its environment.

I want to make two main points about these problems. First, and most importantly, it is hard to find a good taxonomy of behaviour; it is hard to say what a creature is doing and when two creatures are behaving alike. Choosing the appropriate language to describe behaviour is a hard empirical problem; it is not settled by a few thought experiments. Second, and more tentatively, I want to put a positive case for the idea that human ethology, the science of human behaviour, relies on a psychological and semantic taxonomy. Two acts are acts of the same kind when they are caused by thoughts of the same kind. Thoughts are the same only if they represent the world in the same way, if they have the same content. If that can be shown, Eric and twin Eric do not behave the same way, because their behaviours are produced by different thoughts. So the argument above would fail.

Let me take these points in turn. The first is easy. For just consider the homely sight of a cat scratching new furniture. Is the cat (a) sharpening its claws, (b) marking its territory, (c) exercising its tendons, or (d) extorting dinner. Answering is a hard empirical problem, yet human behaviour is far more complex.

How can the individualist define categories of behaviour? An obvious suggestion is to define behavioural types by similarities of physical actions. The individualist's rule might be: same motion, same behaviour. But that rule fails to carve animal behaviours into natural kinds. For behaviours can be physically very similar yet be behaviours of a very different kind. Behavioural mimicry is a case in point. Some species of fireflies attract mates by displays of light and movement. Other species mimic those displays to attract the first species as prey. Identical motions; very different behaviours. Another example: the bodily motions of a dog chasing prey may be identical to the motions of that same dog fleeing a danger. But the same motion does not imply same behaviour. Nor does distinct motion imply distinct behaviour. Think of the very different activities that are all acts of hunting.

The ethologist must sort behaviours into natural functional categories. She need not specify that function, for it may not be known. But she certainly never will find out the function of an act if she is fooled by a similarity of motion into lumping together fleeing and chasing. There is no doubt that there are different functional systems engaged when a dog is hungry as opposed to when it is fearful, and the evolutionary and learning history of the dog is central to the explanation of those systems and their work. Obviously, the same physical action is neither necessary nor sufficient for behaviour, in the psychologically relevant sense, to be the same. It is clear that behaviours can be the same only if they have the same psychological causes. But it remains to be shown that the representational properties of psychological states are crucial to our description of behaviour. For equally there are internal differences between a dog in fear and a dog hungry. Perhaps the computational profile of a thought, or more generally, its internal functional role, is what matters to an ethologist. Do we really need to appeal to what the dog is thinking about to capture the difference between fleeing and chasing.

The critical question, then, is whether the appropriate descriptions of acts for subsuming them under psychological laws are intentional; whether they are descriptions like 'Peter was trying to catch Rachael'. For if they are, then the *explanation* of these acts will involve mental representations. For the intentionality of an act is inherited from the intentionality of its mental causes. So if trying-to-catch-someone is a natural kind of human behaviour, then human psychology is representational.

This is a tough empirical question. Folk psychologists describe behaviour intentionally, but we cannot just assume that folk psychology is the right psychology. But, once more, an ethological perspective is illuminating. One currently hot topic in primate ethology is the 'machiavellian intelligence' hypothesis, a speculation about the evolutionary origins of intelligence. The idea is that the original biological function of intelligence is social, mediating cooperative and exploitative relations with one's species- mates. (Though, as the name suggests, exploitative relations are rather more to the fore.)

One important chunk of evidence for the hypothesis is 'tactical deception' among the social primates. Tactical deception is, of its very nature, rare. It is an example of behavioural mimicry, in which an animal mimics a standard behaviour to fool a species mate to its own advantage. Byrne and Whitten (1988, p. 207) give the following example of baboon behaviour.

Juvenile baboons are typically protected from their species mates by their mothers. If threatened, they give an alarm call. Mother will appear and chase off the threat. Byrne and Whitten describe an instance of a juvenile watching a nonthreatening adult laboriously digging up some succulent morsel. The juvenile emitted its alarm; mother appeared and chased off the adult, whereupon junior scoffed the goodies. They noticed that this young individual pulled this trick more than once.

Now, field observations, especially anecdotal observations, are hard to interpret. Maybe the young baboon smelt something the observers did not; getting the food was a happy accident. But there is a moderately large, though scattered, body of similar observations. This suggests, at least, that there is a category of *deceptive behaviour* – behaviour whose *defining characteristic* is the *intent to deceive* a conspecific, and thereby gain some advantage. Note that this behavioural set is very heterogeneous; its particular form will vary widely both within and across species. All that is common and peculiar to all these particular acts is their intentional characterization. The intentional properties of the acts, in turn, derive from the semantic properties of the mental states that cause them.

In conclusion, I have not demonstrated that the natural kinds of human behaviour are identified by their having a common mental cause, where the commonality in question is a commonality of content. But some evidence points in that direction. My main message is that the appropriate description of behaviour is an unresolved empirical issue, not to be settled by a few thought experiments. P1 above is at best question begging.

So despite its intuitive plausibility the causal argument fails. Burge reformulates it to make explicit worries not about causation but supervenience.

P1   The determinants of behaviour supervene on states of the brain.

So

C1   If propositional attitudes are among the determinants of behaviour, they supervene on brain states.

So

C2   Either semantic properties of propositional attitudes supervene on brain states, or the propositional attitudes are irrelevant to behaviour.

This version of the argument recommends an individualist reformulation of intentional psychology, or its exclusion from our theory of the mind. Burge's main message is that this recommendation cannot be sustained on relatively uncontroversial metaphysical claims alone

(1986, pp. 15–16). To reach it, the individualist needs more than physicalism, and more than the claim that causation is local. In particular, the rejection of individualism does not require action-at-a-distance, or any other spooky causal stories.

Let me try to explain the individualist intuition. Suppose our psychological theory of Peter essentially involves his beliefs and desires about Rachael. Peter acts the way he does, we say, because of his representations of Rachael; moreover, the fact that these are representations of *Rachael* matters. The representational elements of our theory of mind are essential to our explanation of his behaviour. Does not this involve a weird causal idea, namely that Rachael somehow affects Peter's mental states directly? Rather than by causing inputs to his sensory organs which in the fullness of cognitive processing affect his cognitive states. Burge argues that this suspicion depends on an equivocation. 'Affect' here equivocates on individuation and causation. Outside-the-skin goings on do not cause inside-the-skin goings on except locally, via causally well-behaved sensory channels. Nothing causally spooky is going on; no ESP. But events outside the skin can play a role in the *individuation* of internal events. Burge gives a nice example illustrating his theme that local causation need not entail local individuation. The lungs operate locally. Nothing affects the lungs causally except via local changes in lung sacs. But lungs are individuated by appeal to overall biological role, not local causal structure.

Burge is right. A nonindividualistic psychology is not ruled out by general considerations about the nature of causality or taxonomy. Burge goes on to argue that current psychological theory is not individualist. On this issue I think he is less convincing. He takes as his stalking horse Marr's theory of vision, arguing that it is essentially and entirely nonindividualist. First, Marr's theory is everywhere constrained (as we have seen) by quite contingent facts about the observed world. We have to take these into account in explaining why vision works. Second, the particular symbol structures Marr suggests make no sense at all unless you bear in mind what those symbols represent. Marr's algorithms are arbitrary if you ignore the quite particular features of the world to which they are adaptations. So the symbols and processes that Marr posits in his theory of vision are individuated by appeal to the entities we interact with in our perception of the world.

Let's consider how facts about the perceived world play a role in Marr's theory. Such facts most obviously enter it at the ecological level (section 3.2). For the problem solved by the perceptual systems is the problem of obtaining reliable information about the world from inputs to one or another of our perceptual organs. How does the sand scorpion obtain reliable and usable information about the direction and distance of prey animals from shock waves in the sand? How do noctuid moths detect and turn away from bats, thus minimizing the bats' chance of detecting them? How do we resolve a visual scene into objects on a surface? How do we resolve continuous speech noise (plus some mere noise) into phonemes? These information processing tasks cannot be specified without reference to the way creatures are embedded in, and relate to, their environment. I illustrated in sections 4.2 and 4.4 the underdetermination of the output of the visual systems by their input. Marr resolved that underdetermination by supposing that these systems were specifically adapted to quite particular aspects of our physical environment, for example to the fact that gradual changes in light intensity are usually effects of illumination, not surface. The ecological level is wide. I do not think that this is controversial. But its significance is, for the importance of the ecological level, and of its nonindividualist components, can be downplayed.

Perhaps the ecological level plays a heuristic, rather than an explanatory role in psychology. Our knowledge of the function of perceptual mechanisms and the problems they solve guide us in the search for cognitive mechanisms. But our theory of how these mechanisms work should be individualist. Psychological *explanation* remains individualist. Dennett may see the ecological level in this way. The main burden of sections 5.4 and 5.5 is to consider, and rebut, this deflationary view of the ecological level.

Marr offers a functionalist theory of vision. I argued in section 1.2 that functional concepts are teleological concepts. Devices have their functions in virtue of the environment and the evolutionary history of the organism. So the world as it is and as it was enters into our theory of the overall organization of vision. None the less, the particular symbols these make can be picked out by their system internal features. For example, the 'primary sketch' is composed of blobs, curves, lines, on a field of view. A blob, for example, is an intensity discontinuity on the retinal image that forms a closed curve. We can give an individualist description of the primary sketch. If we can do this for the primary sketch, why not for the rest of the visual system? The individualist can allow that the structural features forming the causal background of mental processing are functional devices. But they are implemented by neurophysiological structures whose workings are explained by their intrinsic physical make-up. The symbols themselves, the individualist can go on to argue, are defined by their internal properties, so our theory of mental processing remains at heart an individualist one.

Moreover, and most importantly, individualists do not claim that the environment is irrelevant to psychological explanation. Burge (1986) claims of Marr:

1 'that the theory makes essential reference to the subject's distal stimuli and makes essential assumptions about contingent facts regarding the subject's physical environment' (p. 29),
2 'the theory is set up to explain the reliability of a great variety of processes and subprocesses for acquiring information, at least to the extent that they are reliable' (p. 29).

The individualist need deny neither claim. In explaining the interaction of mind and world, we must make essential reference to the world. The issue is whether our theory can be parsed into two components: an account of the world together with an individualist theory of psychological processing. Take a simple case, a cat trying to hook a fish out of a pond, and being misled by the light bending as it moves into another medium. An individualist thinks that to explain the cat's failure to land a fish, we need appeal to only two factors, not three. We need to know the internal psychology of the cat; that suffices to explain the trajectory of the cat's paw, given the stimuli reaching its retina. We need to know where the fish is. Jointly, these two factors explain the cat's miss. We cannot ignore the world in explaining feline behaviour, but we do not need to attribute representational properties to the cat's psychology.

I can make the same point with an example from the next chapter. Churchland and Churchland (1983) describe a certain neural specialization in rattlesnakes as a mouse-detector. For (a) this specialization is activated only by simultaneous inputs from infra-red sensitive organs detecting warmth, and visual organs detecting movement, and (b) these joint inputs are typically caused by mice, the rattlesnake's standard prey.

They thus give a wide functional description of a psychological mechanism. An individualist might offer an alternative description of the same phenomenon: namely, a sketch of the neural connections involved together with the observation that a brain so set up is only adaptive, and could only evolve, in an environment where mouselike objects were the typical small warm moving things. The issue then is not one about the importance of the environment. That is not denied. It is whether our total theory can be segregated into two components, one to do with the environment, and the other, an individualist account of the workings of the mind.

So, though it is clear that our theory of the world plays a crucial role in our theory of how we see it, it is much less obvious that it does so in a way that overturns the individualist's picture. Namely, that vision is a self-contained 'syntactic engine' taking symbolic input from the retina and providing quite different symbolic output to cognition central. I do not think Burge's consideration of particular algorithms overturns the idea that we can see vision this way. Though I will discuss only one of his examples, I think my analysis of it applies to the others.

Burge believes that it is essential to our theory of vision that we see a particular mechanism as an 'edge detector'. I mentioned in section 4.4.4 that the primary sketch is constructed from retinal processors, 'zero crossing' detectors, sensitive to discontinuities of light on the retinal image. The primary sketch is nothing but a map of these discontinuities. Burge points out, however, that the only reason why the outputs of these various devices can be combined into a single consistent map is that the discontinuities typically have a standard distal cause, edges or contours on the objects in view. Were it not for that, there would be no point in engineeering our visual system in this way. So Burge thinks that zero-crossing detectors are edge detectors, and concludes:

If a zero-crossing segment is present in a set of independent channels over a continuous range of sizes, and the segment has the same position and orientation in each channel, then the set of such zero-crossing segments indicates the presence of an intensity change in the image that is due to a single physical phenomenon. (1986, p. 31)

I do not see how any of this need daunt the individualist. Nothing essential to Marr's explanation is lost if we say the following. First, a visual system is engineered so that a processed image enhances contrasts on the preprocessed image. That is what the system of zero-crossings do. Second, such a mechanism is worth having only in certain environments, those environments (like ours) in which the lines of enhancement correspond to edges or contours in the creature's environment. Marr's theory is (the beginnings of) a theory of how such a correspondence is possible. The individualist, that is, distinguishes between two claims:

1 there are features of the physical world on which the usefulness of cognitive processing of a particular kind depends,
2 those cognitive processes represent those features of the physical world.

Burge rightly says of Marr's theory that the particular symbols on which the computational processors operate are selected 'by considering specific contingent facts about the physical world that typically hold when we succeed in obtaining visual information about that world' (1986, p. 34). There is no point in having a sophisticated system for constructing representations of generalized cones if nothing around you has an axis of symmetry. But it remains to be shown that those symbols are about those features, or are individuated with respect to them.

Though our picture of the perceived world is of the utmost importance in constructing a theory of vision, for all Burge shows our total theory can be segregated into two components: an internalist account of the workings of vision, and an account of the world in which that mechanism is adaptive.

5.3 Explanation and the Ecological Level

Dennett is one of a number of philosophers who think that individualist psychology misses generalizations. Intentional states are multiply realizable at a computational level, so creatures can be intentionally similar though narrowly distinct.

Dennett has long defended a distinction between 'design-stance' explanations of behaviour and intentional explanations of behaviour. Design-stance explanations involve the functional architecture of a system, as his favourite example of a chess-playing computer shows. We might explain a computer's failure to avoid mate in five by the fact that it's designed to calculate only six ply (six half-moves) ahead of the game position. The mate is beyond its event horizon, and this is a matter of the system's design. An intentional explanation of its failure would be to claim that it did not want to win, or that it did not believe its opponent would see the mate: a story we rarely tell about computers, but sometimes tell about people.

Dennett suggests that intentional characterization is independent of design-stance characterization, in the sense that systems with very little relevant functional similarity can share intentional states. He reminds us of the way very different experiences can lead people to the same belief, even people whose psychologies are antecedently very different. Such people have an explanatorily useful property in common, but one which is invisible from the design-stance or individualist perspective. Similarly, to use another good example (Dennett, 1978, ch. 2), two systems could be face-recognisers, and be ascribed all sorts of common face-recognition-linked beliefs: the belief that they've just been presented with Napoleon, or that they've seen Michael Jackson's latest face more often than Ronald Reagan's. Yet the two systems might not just be physically different, but may also have different designs. There are lots of very different ways of recognizing faces; one can compare them to stored pictures, or look at the fine details of the eyes, or look for distinguishing features, or analyse facial landscape with sonar. Systems as different as these can only be seen to share psychological states from the representational, not the individualist perspective.

This is a good idea, but I do not endorse Dennett's particular version of it.

1 Dennett links his defence of intentionality to the claim that intentional psychology is a different kind of intellectual enterprise to scientific psychology. It's not an empirical theory in the business of giving causal explanations; it is normative, idealizing, and a priori. That is because Dennett accepts a principle of charity, or a principle of rationality. He thinks there is no coherent intentional description of a seriously irrational belief system; there are times in which he has flirted with the even stronger claim that there is no coherent description of a seriously erroneous belief system. No physical system can actually meet the conditions required for an intentional system, for all are limited in various ways and are subject to breakdown. An intentional description is a description of an ideal system; it is a description of the beliefs and desires an optimally rational agent in those circumstances would have. At best, physical systems approximate intentional systems.

I think this view is both implausible in itself, and without convincing argumentative support. Clinical, devotional and anthropological literature is stuffed with apparently coherent descriptions of fundamentally irrational, and certainly erroneous, beliefs. How else would we describe the views of those who claim: to be Napoleon; that a cucumber *just is* a sacrificial ox; that they are eating God? Cases like this don't settle the matter: its always possible, though often neither easy nor plausible, to reinterpret linguistic and other behaviour to remove the appearance of irrationality. But we need a reason to do, and the odd fact is that principles of charity have often been accepted, but rarely argued for.

I find Dennett's arguments quite unpersuasive. He argues that any intentional system built by natural selection will be rational. But that at best provides a prima-facie case for the reliability of our belief forming mechanism (a) in domains of central biological importance, and (b) in the environments in which those mechanisms evolved. Natural selection gives us fair grounds for confidence that chimps are good at telling whether a female is on heat, or that another chimp is likely to attack. But we have many beliefs about matters of no great biological import. Mother Selector doesn't care about our religious or sporting allegiances. And none of us live in the social environment in which our cognitive powers evolved. Dennett's other thought in support of charity is the idea that intentional individuation is *holistic*. That is, a belief is the belief it is – say, the belief that anteaters have long tongues – in virtue of its inferential relations to other beliefs. Holistic individuation requires that the relations between beliefs be systematic. I take up these issues in detail in the next chapter. Let me just say here that systematicity does not imply rationality. If I inferred from every proposition the conclusion 'I am Napoleon', my belief system would be wonderfully systematic but not rational.

2   Dennett's account of belief-desire psychology turns out to be a kind of holistic behaviourism. People with the same dispositions to behaviour *ipso facto* have the same beliefs and desires. For the point of the attribution of beliefs and desires to some organism is nothing other than the prediction of its behaviour. Intentional explanation is not causal explanation, not at least in the way that design stance and physical stance explanations are. So identity of behavioural dispositions implies intentional identity. But this behaviourism is no more plausible than any other. This chapter started with a description of behavioural identity without intentional identity. We can predict twin Peter's behaviour from our intentional profile of Peter. For knowing how Peter acted towards Rachael, we can infer how his twin acts towards her twin. Nonetheless, there were persuasive reasons to deny that they had the same beliefs and desires (though Dennett himself is unpersuaded; see the Suggested Reading for section 5.1). Dennett's positive theory is heir to all the problems of both holism and behaviourism.

3   A final worry about Dennett's defence of this line is that, in so far as he demonstrates, rather than just assumes, the theoretical utility of the intentional stance, he makes the enterprise of intentional explanation much too pragmatic. According to Dennett, we revert to the intentional stance when we are ignorant of the design of a system but have reason to believe that the system is well equipped for its life goals, being a product of natural selection or deliberate design. In such circumstances we infer, cautiously, that the system will do whatever an optimal system ought to do, however that optimality is realized. The upshot is that there is no question of a creature really having beliefs and desires that is independent of the question as to whether we find it convenient and predictive to attribute such states. Intentional

properties, on his view, are not observer-independent properties. This is an aspect of the difference in status between computational and desire-belief psychology. I think we need to found the explanatory point of wide psychology on firmer grounds than our contingent ignorance of the structure of our subjects.

Pylyshyn, like Dennett, argues that intentional explanation enables us to state similarities between agents that are both explanatorily important and unstatable in individualist vocabulary. For intentional states are multiply realized by computational states.

Pylyshyn makes this point through an example (Pylyshyn, 1980, 1984). Consider the case of Mary, leaving a building because she believes it to be on fire. Maybe she heard a fire alarm, inferred the building was on fire, and left by the stairs. There is no adequate account of Mary's actions in purely computational terms, and hence no adequate individualist explanation of Mary's actions. (Remember, a computational theory is an individualist theory.) The computational account fails because there are a lot of different stimuli which can carry the information that the building is on fire, a lot of different inferential chains which lead from some such stimulus to the desire to leave the building, a lot of different plans designed to bring this about, and a lot of different ways of actually leaving. We should consider not just Mary but her co-workers as well. They all left, and we want to say that they behaved the same way for the same reasons in response to the same threat. But we can't say this within an individualist psychology, because the person who sees flames and flees straight out of the front door is computationally different from those who hear the fire alarm, or smell smoke, and run down the fire stairs or jump out of the window. In each case there will be a detailed computational story to be told, but no computational story can tell us what the cases have in common. Schematically, the situation looks like this:

$$
\begin{array}{ccc}
I & S & O \\
19 & 6 & 13 \\
11 & 27 & 7 \\
22 & 71 & 3 \\
\cdot & \cdot & \cdot \\
\cdot & \cdot & \cdot \\
\cdot & \cdot & \cdot \\
\end{array}
$$

Further, although no computational story can tell us what all the inputs, inner states, and outputs have in common, very plausibly a representational story will tell us this. It will tell us what a fire alarm stimulus and a flame stimulus have in common, and what all the syntactically different inferential processes and physically different behaviours share.

As it stands, there are problems with this argument. Do we really have an argument that Mary and her coworkers behave in the same way in any scientifically interesting sense? Of course, it is important to them and their friends that none became a cinder. But commonalities that strike us as humanly interesting need not correspond to a natural kind: human interest does not carve nature at the joints. The category of weeds is not a natural kind of plant, nor the category of the cute a natural kind of animal. Is the kind 'escapee from the blaze' any better? Pylyshyn appeals to the alleged rationality of intentional behaviour in arguing that we do have a genuine explanatory domain here. But I have already argued, against Dennett, that intentional systems need not be rational. So we cannot appeal to rationality to show that the similarities that intentional descriptions enable us to state are natural kinds.

Moreover, Mary and her co-workers may share individualist properties that explain the similarity in their behaviours. In different ways Devitt and Stich take this line. Perhaps Mary and her companions all behave the same because they all token an instance of the same syntactic string, give or take minor orthographic differences. Alternatively, if they don't all actually token it, they're all disposed to infer it rapidly if called on. Systems which don't have this individualist property just won't behave similarly enough for us to want to include them in our explanation. The syntactic string involved will be a formula of the language of thought which is a rough analogue of 'The building's on fire'. This is the line taken in response to the argument by Stich (1983, ch. 4 and expanded in conversation). Devitt (1989) takes a similar line. I think the Stich–Devitt hypothesis is implausible, partly for reasons I discuss in the next section. But also because I suspect that it understates the multiplicity of computational realizations of intentional states. The flexibility of our cognitive capacities implies that a given individual can encode his intention to leave in many ways. Moreover, there is also likely to be considerable variation across individuals.

Pylyshyn's argument is not conclusive. It is some way from showing that individualist theories fail to capture generalizations.

In Sterelny (1990), I tried to strengthen the case for the explanatory importance of the ecological level. Instead of arguing – as Fodor, Dennett and Pylyshyn all do – against individualism by various defences of folk psychology and its categories, I attempted to demonstrate the explanatory importance of the ecological level without tying that level to intentional psychology. I showed the importance of psychological categories that can apply to more than one species. Such categories are nonindividualist. For the internal difference between species can be enormous. Consider just the difference in perceptual structures between bats and owls. Owls have notoriously acute night vision, whereas bats find their way around by echo location. So if we had reason to attribute to bats and owls the same psychological state – say, that they both perceive mice – then that state could hardly be individualistically defined. Perceptual systems vary greatly; their only common feature is that their function is the extraction of information for the adaptive control of behaviour.

If there are psychological generalizations across species then, those generalizations are generalizations of nonindividualist psychology. But why suppose there are such generalizations? I aired a certain scepticism about Pylyshyn's example of Mary and her friends. Why suppose that they behave the same way in any sense of interest to science? Surely the same point can be made here. So what if there are species of owls and bats that make their living of the same creatures and avoid the same dangers? We can give one account of the psychology and behaviour of bats and a distinct one for owls. What explanatory power do we lose?

The ground work for my answer to this question was laid in section 5.2, where I argued that behavioural concepts used in ecology are psychologically, perhaps even representationally, laden. What makes it true that a cat is hunting? The inner causes of its behaviour, not its outer motions (there may be none). When behaviour is deceptive, it is so in virtue of its psychological causes. Since there are behavioural commonalities across species, and behaviours are defined by their psychological causes, there are psychological commonalities across species. It is clear that there are behaviour patterns common to distinct species. The texts of ecology are stuffed with examples; indeed, chapter headings are often names of behaviours which are in part individuated by appeal to their psychological causes and are found in many species. Not all of these are as subtle as deception. Many arise from the problem of trying to understand cooperative behaviour. Consider just two examples. Many group-living species give warning calls if one sights a predator: monkeys, birds, beavers. Some social species (rather fewer) share food. These genuinely are cases of the same behaviour found in different species. For we want to know how and under what circumstances these forms of cooperation arise, and the role they play in the animal's life. The same sort of problems arise again and again. For example, how is cooperative behaviour insulated against cheating? Prima facie, in any system of food sharing it would pay to take but not give. Giving a warning call can be dangerous, it can attract predators. We can be confident that these are not superficial similarities because they are found in the same conditions again and again. We find cooperative behaviour when the same individuals repeatedly interact, with each having many opportunities to give and receive, and with givers being preferentially aided (Trivers, 1985, ch. 15).

I think that nonindividualist psychology plays an important role in a wide range of evolutionary and ecological theories. For these frequently make implementation-neutral assumptions about the mental capacities of animals. The theories require that the animals in question have certain discriminatory, memory or calculative abilities, but don't care how those abilities are computationally realized. Let me give some cases.

One of the standing problems of evolutionary theory is to explain the evolution of altruistic behaviour. Prima facie, we would expect altruistic individuals to be outcompeted; to contribute fewer descendants than their selfish, and hence more frequently surviving, rivals. The gene allowing altruistic behaviour would gradually disappear. In the last decade or two, a couple of theoretical models have shown how to tame this problem. The central notions are kin selection and reciprocal altruism.

One unsurprising form of altruism is child care. Child care is costly to the parent, and may reduce the number of its own offspring, but in some conditions at least, it's easy to see how a gene for child care could survive. Even though a caring parent may die earlier and with fewer children than its rival, the reduced mortality of the few may leave it with as many or more grandchildren – each tending to receive and pass on the child-care gene. Kin selection generalizes this idea to other kin. A gene for helping those with similar genes to yourself can tend to increase the number of individuals with this genetic material – including the kin-altruism gene. The more distant the kin, the more of them must benefit, or the smaller the cost to the altruist must be. Now this model requires organisms to act differentially towards their kin. How do they manage that? Sometimes the mechanisms are not psychological; proximity does the job, for example, for sterile casts of social insects. But in many kin-selection explanations, psychological mechanisms of recognition are clearly implicated: for example, in the cooperative behaviour of lionesses towards relatives, or in socio-biological explanations of the incest taboo. These explanations require that you can tell who your relatives are. They require a sufficiently reliable relative-detector, but these explanations are indifferent to the way the relative-detector works.

The second strand of the explanation of altruism is the much more homely idea of exchanging favours: reciprocal altruism. Not surprisingly, this kind of explanation is hardly to be invoked for the dramatic examples of altruistic or apparently altruistic behaviour: female birds trying to draw predators away from nests, and the like. But it seems to find a home in the explanation, for example, of the development of mutual grooming by primates, food sharing between vampire bats, and the like. That is, cases where the likely costs aren't too great. Again, it is clear that these models have psychological preconditions: mutual altruism can develop only when animals have suitable recognitional and memory capacities.

A third model involving psychological assumptions is Maynard Smith's notion of an evolutionarily stable strategy (ESS). An ESS is a distribution of behaviour patterns in a community that is immune to invasion from within. I illustrate by the standard simple example. Consider a population and a resource: say, nesting sites. Suppose when two members compete for a resource, they adopt a dove strategy. They threaten and posture for a little while, then one gives up. On plausible assumptions about the costs of fighting and the pay-offs of sites, a population of dove strategists isn't evolutionarily stable. A hawk mutation – an animal that actually fights – will win all encounters at no cost, since doves flee. Doves win only half their encounters, so hawk strategists are twice as successful as doves, so the hawk gene would rapidly spread. But unless the costs of actually fighting are low, or the benefits of the resource are very high, a population of hawk strategists isn't stable either. In such a population, a dove gene could invade, for it would not have to bear the high costs of fighting. It turns out that, in most cases, a mixed population is stable, the exact hawk/dove ratios depending on the details of the pay-off assumptions. The population is uninvadable.

The point here is that many of these models make strong psychological assumptions. For stability depends on the range of behaviours within the repertoire of the population. Thus, on standard pay-off assumptions, a hawk/dove population can be invaded by more sophisticated strategists; e.g. acting like a hawk towards doves and like a dove towards hawks. The bully strategy invades. So, strategies are uninvadable only relative to a range of alternative strategies; strategies aren't absolutely uninvadable. The range of relevant alternatives is determined, amongst other things, by the psychological capacities of the animals in the population. The smarter the animal, the wider the range of alternatives.

All these models attempt to explain the evolution of certain specific behaviours when applied to specific organisms, or certain general patterns of behaviour, when couched more abstractly. *Qua* theories of specific behaviour, they make psychological attributions to animals that are implementation neutral. They are wide attributions: capacities to recognize, remember and react to features of their (typically social) environment. *Qua* general models, they specify that any population of animals with certain needs, certain psychological repertoires and certain resources will tend to evolve in specified ways. Again, the way the repertoire is implemented is irrelevant to its role in explanation.

It is time to sum up the main points of this section. Intentional psychology is not individualist, and it enables us to capture generalizations that we otherwise would miss. So perhaps there is room in psychology for a wide intentional psychology, and an individualist psychology of the computational states that realize intentional states. Dennett and Pylyshyn both run versions of this idea, though Dennett rather downplays the status of intentional psychology.

I think this idea is at least plausible; indeed it is probably right. But it has two controversial commitments. Churchland and perhaps Dennett deny that there are robust generalizations, in effect psychological laws, expressible in the vocabulary of intentional psychology. Even if there are such generalizations, are they capturable only in intentional psychology? Stich and Devitt think not. I side-step the many controversies about the status of intentional psychology by concentrating on more modest representational systems. I have tried both to show the importance of these to the ecological level, and to show the explanatory importance of that level.

In the next section, I discuss the prospects for an individualist psychology. So far, I have, first, granted something to individualism: I agree that an important element of psychology is individualist; second, agreed with Burge in rejecting the a priori arguments for a wholly individualist psychology; and, third, canvassed various arguments that point to a positive role for a nonindividualist psychology.

5.4 Individualist Intentional Psychology?

In the last section I extolled the virtues of nonindividualist psychology. In this section, I argue that we cannot opt for theories that abstract away from the facts of physical implementation, yet are 'narrow' functionalist theories. Narrow functionalist theories define psychological properties by appeal to their causal role, but the inputs and outputs determining a causal role are internal to the mind. Narrow functionalist theories are thus individualist theories. Stich, Devitt and Block have all defended narrow functionalist theories as *complete* theories of the mind. In particular, they think we can develop a theory which retains the explanatory advantages of intentional psychology, but which is narrow or individualist. I doubt this. We can join the Churchlands in rejecting folk psychology, but if we wish to retain intentional psychology, the price is a nonindividualist psychology.

It is, I think, agreed that belief-desire taxonomy involves representational properties. It is generally (but not universally) agreed that we have two intentional taxonomies. *Extensional* or *transparent* taxonomies count thoughts as identical if they have the same truth conditions. On this taxonomy, the belief Ed would express as 'Robert Zimmerman is a menace' and the belief Ted would express as 'Bob Dylan is a menace' are instances of the same belief. Even if neither Ed nor Ted realize that Dylan is Zimmerman. For their belief tokens have the same truth conditions. An *opaque* taxonomy counts these as different beliefs, for the way the truth condition is represented is also important in identifying a belief. Even opaque taxonomies require the truth conditions of two tokens of the same thought to be the same; that's a necessary, though notoriously insufficient, condition on identity.

The issue then is not whether our standard taxonomy of thoughts uses semantic notions. The issue is rather: Can we retain the predictive and explanatory advantages of folk psychology in some successor theory whose taxonomic practices are purged of semantic criteria? Stich has argued that we can strip folk psychology of its semantic encumbrances whilst retaining its virtues, whatever they may be. If we think folk psychology does have the theoretical virtues its admirers enumerate, we can construct a syntactic theory of mind in its image. Devitt hopes to show that narrow content suffices for the explanatory purposes of folk theory.

I do not believe either of these kites will fly. Both Stich and Devitt are functionalists. They identify mental types in virtue of their causal role in the mind. They therefore face two *pruning problems*. Not all causal connections between inputs, outputs and inner states are functional connections. Not all functional connections are essential to type identity. Some of the connections will be merely noisy. The smell of brandy and dry still makes me queasy, for I was once very ill after over-indulging in it. That does not seem a connection that is part of the functional role of the smell. Some of the causal properties of a state it will have in virtue of its physical realization, rather than its functional role. Human active short-term memory seems to hold about seven (unrelated) items. But that fact is very likely a consequence of its realization, not its design. Other connections may depend on quirky and idiosyncratic facts about a person's mental life. There are those that cannot think of worms without shivering with horror. Could that causal connection be essential to the identity of the thought type 'that is a worm.'? Some connections seem just plain unimportant. Contrast the connection between the concepts **horse** and **mammal** with the connection between **horse** and **beloved by young adolescent girls**. The second is not idiosyncratic; girls' love of horses is well known. But it seems unlikely to be part of the identity conditions of **horse**. Other connections can be positively dysfunctional; the breakdown of normal mental functioning. We all have periods of temporary dysfunction, where *everything* reminds us of some hideously embarrassing moment. But these connections are not constitutive of that memory, and that memory is not partly constitutive of all of our mental states. So, (a) there are causal connections between a token mental state and other states, inputs and outputs that are not functional connections at all; (b) some functional connections are essential to identity and others are not. A pruning principle is needed to distinguish the functional from the merely causal, and the essential from the inessential. (My thoughts here owe much to Cowie (forthcoming).)

Failure to give a principled criterion of pruning leads to holism, and a useless taxonomy that fails its main duty of distinguishing between the explanation-relevant and the explanation-irrelevant features of individuals. A holist 'taxonomy' is useless, for no mental state would be tokened more than once. So it would never be true that different people, or one person at different times, act the same way for the same reasons. That is, there would be no true intentional generalizations.

Stich and Block make no serious attempt at pruning, and seem untroubled by their holism. This is legitimate in Stich's case, for he is increasingly sceptical about the value of even a contentless version of intentional psychology. Devitt does try to avoid holism, and in the attempt reinforces my view that no plausible pruning principle will be individualist. I see no prospect of distinguishing the essential from the inessential, or the functional from the nonfunctional that does not appeal to the representational function of these states.

Devitt tries to avoid holism by defining individualist categories by subtraction from nonindividualist ones. In a series of publications, most recently Devitt and Sterelny (1987), Devitt has defended various versions of causal theories of reference, culminating in a causal-descriptive theory (Much more on this in chapter 6.) On this view, the reference of most concepts is fixed partly by causal links from object to mind, and partly by causal links within the mind. So Melanie's concept of dogs refers to dogs partly in virtue of causal links to dogs, partly in virtue of dogish perceptual states, partly in virtue of links to a few especially dog-relevant concepts. Devitt suggests that we get the narrow content of **dog** simply by discarding the Melanie-external chunk of this causal chain, thus getting a nonholistic notion of content that is common to Melanie and twin Melanie. He further suggests that that notion of narrow content is all that psychology needs.

I do not agree that the method of subtraction buys Devitt an individualist theory of the mind. For the truncated causal chains are not individualist natural kinds. There is no individualist property common and peculiar to all those truncated chains. Causal theorists have always emphasized the vast array of different experiences and belief sets people can have without prejudice to their having concepts with the same reference. They delight in pointing out that we and Ptolemy have concepts of Mars despite vast changes in beliefs about Mars. Consider the differences in sensory and conceptual processes that can still be the acquisition of the concept **dog**. Dogs can be seen in very different ways; they can be smelt, touched, heard or tasted rather than seen. Someone can acquire the concept even if they think dogs are gods or their ancestors reincarnated. The concept can be acquired in conversation or from pictures and toys rather than from dogs. What is common and peculiar to the head-internal chunk of these chains? In my view, nothing. What these chains have in common is outside the head, the link – direct or indirect – to dogs. So I do not think Devitt's method defines individualist natural kinds at all, so the question of whether we only need Devitt's kinds does not arise.

In sum, an individualist revision of folk psychology needs to avoid holism; I doubt that it can. If we want folk theory, we must pay the price: naturalized semantics, and a nonindividualistic psychology. What's less clear is that we want folk psychology at all; I discuss the option of abandoning it altogether in chapter 7.

5.5 Do You End at Your Skin?

I have already remarked that one intuition behind individualism is the idea that our skin contains a well-defined and integrated system, though not, of course, literally a closed system. But one whose transactions with the rest of the world are orderly enough for us to regard its behaviour as a consequence of system internal properties, including the deliverances of its sensory transducers. This idea may indeed be more important than the requirement of local causation in driving individualism. For individualists are typically prepared to admit that the internal history of a state is relevant to its individuation. That the current state of Melanie's belief box was caused by a dogish retinal image is strictly speaking irrelevant to its future causal impact. A neurally identical state caused by her smoking dope would have the same causal result. But most individualists allow this difference to count in taxonomy.

In this section, I want to at least raise the possibility that this perspective is mistaken. I want to consider an argument from biological theory which denies that the skin is a bag which contains a well-defined entity. Dawkins (1982) argued, in the context of evolutionary theory, against the view that the organism is the entity of special relevance to biology. Millikan takes a somewhat similar line and applies it to the individualism controversy. In the end, I don't endorse the Dawkins–Millikan line, for it stands in some danger of missing the wood for the trees. There is something very obvious about organisms, and it is hard to believe they are not at least part of the subject matter of evolutionary theory and psychology. But I do want to point out that the individualist's presupposition here isn't mandatory. There is a defensible alternative.

The first point to notice is that it certainly is not a priori true that the skin contains a single integrated psychology. If being one of a pair of Siamese twins was the normal form of human existence, it would be obviously false that the skin contained a single mental life. If a favourite science fiction nightmare, the invasive brain parasite, were a real danger, we would be less tempted to the view. For the behaviour of the brain-parasitized body is the result of two mental lifes, not one. There may be a few circumstances in which the human body's behaviour is the result of two inhabitants, not one. 'Multiple personality' disorders might be an instance, as may be 'split brain' cases. There is a surgical procedure (once used to control severe epilepsy) in which the main communication channel between the two hemispheres of the brain is cut. Under special experimental conditions the two hemispheres seem to act independently.

These examples are either fictional or marginal. But Dawkins' first point is that, for some species of animal, the body snatching nightmare is no delicious thrill, but a genuine danger. There are parasitic species that act directly on the nervous systems of their hosts to the parasite's advantage, and the host's ruin. One parasite of fresh water shrimp has a life cycle that involves passing through the muskrat as well. An invaded shrimp's behaviour changes from being mud dwelling to surface dwelling, materially increasing the shrimp's chances of being eaten by a rat. There are other examples of the same general phenomenon. The symptomology of the rabies infection (and, it has been speculated, VD infection) makes it more likely that the virus will be transmitted. When an invader physically inside a system tampers with the nervous system, the behaviour of the organism is not, on anyone's view, the behaviour of a single biological system.

Dawkins' next point is that the physical location of the interfering organism is surely not crucial. The slaving ant queen that invades a nest and uses pheremones to control the behaviour of the host nest, so that its workers work for her and her brood, surely controls behaviour in just the same sense that the brain worm does, when it tampers with the ant's neural system so that the ant is likely to be eaten by the worm's next host. Behavioural manipulation can be at a distance. I noted in section 2.1 that animal behaviours are often under the control of a very particular stimulus; a particular kind of squark-and-gape often controls birds' parenting activities. By mimicking and exaggerating these stimuli, other animals can manipulate an animal as effectively as an invading parasite. Brood parasites – cuckoos and cowbirds – do just that. While cuckoo eggs often resemble the eggs of the victim, cuckoo chicks do not resemble, for example, robin chicks. They do not need to; the robin is manipulated by a particular signal. Consider a particular robin feeding a cuckoo chick. Dawkins question is: whose behaviour is it? Not, in his view, the robin's *behaviour* even though it is the robin's *physical activity*. It is important to see here that this is behaviour, not breakdown. One might be tempted to respond to Dawkins' examples by saying that the robin is not *doing* anything, any more than a mouse going brown in an oven is *doing* anything. Wrong. There is no breakdown or malfunction in the robin; to the contrary, the manipulation depends on the robin being in good working order.

How is all this relevant to us? Surely, manipulation of this kind is possible just because robin behaviour, like much bird behaviour, is information insensitive. Because our behaviour is the result of information sensitive cognitive processes, we are not susceptible to manipulation of this kind. So our decision about whether the robin is in the relevant sense a closed system is not germane to our conception of human psychology.

Speculations about the gonorrhoeic itch aside, I agree that humans are in little danger of being manipulated *by other species*. But it is no part of the idea that manipulation is always between members of different species. There is plenty of room for conflicts of interest within the human species. Between the sexes, on decisions to do with mating and child care. Between parents and children, and between siblings, over the division of parental resources. I would be prepared to bet that the babies' cry turns out to be manipulation, in this biological sense. Dawkins and Krebs (1984) point out that genuinely cooperative interchanges can be expected to be *unobtrusive*, for loud signals have energy and other costs. Many people must have died because of the loud cry of the human baby. Energetic signalling shows sales resistance; sales resistance shows the message may well not be in the interests of its receiver. Nor is it utterly implausible to suppose there are sexual manipulations within our species. Male sexual arousal, at least, is not exactly delicately tuned to incoming information. It is a candidate for manipulation because it is not caused, even to a first approximation, by the knowledge, all things considered, that a desirable woman may be available. For example, arousal is sometimes caused by looking at pictures of nude women, even in men who know perfectly well that a picture is not a woman.

I think the extent to which human behaviour is manipulated is an open empirical question. If manipulated behaviour is not the behaviour of the system the skin contains, and if significant chunks of human behaviour are manipulated, then the skin does not enclose the action-producing system.

Dawkins gives a different argument to the same conclusion, and it is this that Millikan independently takes up. Crucial to this second line is the idea of control. Why might one think that the skin forms the system's boundary? Because the internal environment is under the organism's control, whereas beyond the skin is a world into which the creature must fit as best it can.

The only interesting principled distinction that can be drawn between that portion of the organic system that is the organism proper and that portion of it that is environment is not determined by a spacial boundary. It is a matter of degree – the degree of control that the system as a whole has over the production and maintenance of normal structure and normal states for its various portions. (Millikan (forthcoming c) p. 34).

Dawkins and Millikan use very much the same sort of examples to show that control is a matter of degree, and that no discontinuity occurs at the skin. Most crabs grow their shells. Many moth larvae extrude a substance out of which they spin their shell substitute. But hermit crabs find their shells, and birds build them, though sometimes in part out of their own feathers. Dawkins suggests that the web of a spider is part of the 'extended phenotype' of the genes that built the spider, and, similarly, the mound of the termite is similarly part of the termites 'extended phenotype'. Control does not begin or end at the skin. Nests and shells show it extending beyond the skin; it can fail to extend as far. For example, the environment might get too cold for the mechanisms of thermoregulation to work.

Dawkins' interests in running this line have nothing to do with psychological theory. He was interested in defending a thesis about the nature of natural selection that de-emphasized the importance of individual organisms. Hence he argues that organisms and their boundaries are less important in biology than they at first appear to be. Millikan's interests are ultimately psychological. She links the biological claim to psychology. For she agrees with Lycan that the notion of function appealed to in functionalist theories of the mind is ultimately a biological one. For when we ask what a system is for, we ask a teleological question. Teleological claims – claims about purpose – are cashed by appeal to natural selection. For the function of a device within a biological system is the effect(s) it has that have been favoured by natural selection. It is Millikan's claim that the system in question is not contained within the organism's skin.

What should we make of these considerations? I do not think they refute individualism. The first argument depended on two ideas. First, that there is no important distinction between manipulation that is the result of direct action on the nervous system of its victim, and manipulation that is mediated by signalling. Second, that interesting chunks of the behaviour of advanced animals, including humans, is the result of manipulation. I am inclined to accept the first of these ideas, but the extent of human manipulation is anyone's guess. The second argument depends on the claim that the crucial variable determining the *extent* of a system is control, rather than, say, integration and mutual adaptation. That is certainly open to question. But even granting it, surely there is usually some interesting jump in this variable at the skin.

All in all, I think we may well end at our skin. But it is not obvious that we do, nor is it a claim requiring no defence.

Suggested Reading

Section 5.1

The classic statements of individualism are Fodor's 'Methodological Solipsism Considered as a Research Strategy in Cognitive Psychology' (1980) and Stich's 'Autonomous Psychology and the Belief-Desire Thesis (1978a). A more recent statement is Devitt's 'A Narrow Representational Theory of the Mind' (1989). The two classics pointing out that content is not individualist are Putnam's 'Meaning of "Meaning"' (1975b) and Burge's 'Individualism and the Mental' (1979). Stich (1983, section 4.3) shows how to make their point without relying on twin planets. Dennett is sceptical about these claims; a scepticism he airs in his paper 'Beyond Belief' (1982) in the section on 'notional worlds'. So is Searle; he argues for the view that meanings are in the head in chapters 8 and 9 of *Intentionality* (1983). A recent and vigorous statement of the sceptical position about content is Godfrey-Smith's 'Why Semantic Properties Won't Earn Their Keep (1986). Field is also sceptical, but his statement of his scepticism, 'The Deflationary Conception of Truth' (1986), is much more difficult than Godfrey-Smith's.

Section 5.2

Burge develops his position in 'Individualism and Psychology' (1986); a recent reply is Segal's 'Seeing What Is Not There' (1989). Fodor's most recent statement of a moderate individualism is in chapter 2 of *Psychosemantics* (1988a); *de facto* this is a reply to Burge. Millikan argues against the view that psychology explains behaviour in 'Thoughts Without Laws; Cognitive Science With Content' (1986), and makes her case against an individualist taxonomy of behaviour in *What is Behaviour? Or Why Narrow Ethology Is Impossible* (forthcoming c).

Section 5.3

The three most important papers of Dennett on this topic are 'Intentional Systems', 'Three Kinds of Intentional Psychology' (1981b) and 'True Believers' (1981a). In these papers he introduces a nice metaphor: the brain is essentially a syntactic engine, not a semantic engine. So an essentially semantic theory cannot be of more than heuristic value. A similar perspective is very clearly expressed in Haugeland's introduction to his collection, *Mind Design* (1981). I think that Haugeland, like Dennett, thinks the real explanatory work is done at the level in which we detail the computational processing of a system. My scepticism about Dennett's behaviourism is aired in Sterelny (1981). The principle of charity is criticized in more detail in the final chapter of Devitt and Sterelny *Language and Reality* (1987). Stich also takes Dennett on over charity in his 'Could Man Be An Irrational Animal?' (1985). Cohen defends the principle in 'Can Human Irrationality Be Experimentally Demonstrated?' (1981). Jackson and Pettit defend a Dennettish view in their 'Functionalism and Broad Content' (1988). The two crucial sources for Pylyshyn's views are his 1980 paper, 'Cognition and Computation', and its outgrowth, *Computation and Cognition* (1984, especially ch. 2). But neither is an easy read. Stich (1983) replies in section 8.4. Dretske argues that Pylyshyn's idea, like Dennett's, merely defends the predictive utility of intentional psychology. He puts this case, and defends his own version of the causal importance of semantic properties in chapter 4 of *Explaining Behavior* (1988). My version of the idea is developed in 'Animals and Individualism' (Sterelny, 1990). Dennett airs some similar views in 'Intentional Systems in Cognitive Ethology: The "Panglossian Paradigm" Defended' (1983).

Section 5.4

The crucial documents in this dispute are: chapter 1 of *Psychosemantics* (1988a), for Fodor's latest defence of the folk, and chapter 8 of *From Folk psychology to Cognitive Science* (1983), for Stich's attempt to show we can have it cheap. Devitt and Block think it is nearly as cheap in 'A Narrow Representational Theory of the Mind' (Devitt, 1989) and 'Advertisement for a Semantics for Psychology' (Block, 1986). Devitt grapples with the holism issues further in 'Meaning Localism' (forthcoming b), and with the arguments for individualism in 'Why Fodor Can't Have It Both Ways (forthcoming a). Maloney also argues that individualist taxonomy essentially depends on a nonindividualist one in 'Methodological Solipsism Reconsidered as a Research Strategy in Cognitive Psychology' (1985).

Section 5.5

Dawkins key work is *The Extended Phenotype* (1982). Millikan joins in with her *What is Behaviour?* (forthcomging c) Kitcher and I argue that Dawkins can have what he wants in biology without downplaying the importance of the organism in 'The Return of the Gene' (1988).

6

Explaining Content

6.1 Introduction

In the last chapter we explored a central problem for the representational theory of mind. Does the explanation of human behaviour, or the explanation of human cognitive skills, require us to posit mental representations? If so, some mental kinds are identified in part by relations between the mind and the world. They are not individualist kinds. The representational theory of the mind is in trouble if there is no need to posit such states. But it would also be in trouble if mental representation turned out to be inexplicable, for it is a naturalist theory of the mind. Mental properties are ultimately to be explained by the nonmental; by more fundamental, because more general, features of our world. The representational theory of the mind isn't committed to any vulgar reductivism. But representational properties cannot be unexplained primitives in our total theory of the world: the demand to explain the mental by appeal to the nonmental is motivated by the demand that psychology should not invoke magical mental properties.

A failure to explain content in naturalistic vocabulary would undercut the claim that the representational theory of mind is naturalistic. Quine, famously, has long been sceptical that any naturalistic account of meaning can be had. In arguing against the analytic/synthetic distinction, he claimed that sameness of meaning, hence meaning, can be explained only by other semantic notions (see, for example, Quine, 1970, ch. 1). We cannot break out of the circle of semantic concepts by explaining one in terms of more fundamental ideas. So these notions have no place in real science, however firm our sentimental attachment to them might be.

If we cannot explain our representational powers, we will instead have to explain them away. That, I think, is Dennett's line. For he thinks it is a serious mistake to give a reductive explanation of intentional properties. If the representational theory of mind fails because representational capacities resist such explanation, it will become the line of us all.

The task of constructing a naturalistic semantics is extremely formidable. In the next section, I will catalogue difficulties that have plagued recent attempts. But some of these have a common dynamic. In the remainder of this introduction, I will try to explain that dynamic. Consider first the resources through which a reductive theory of content might be constructed. Before this century, particularly in the empiricist tradition, *resemblance* seemed an obvious key to the explanation of mind–world relationships. My idea of red picked out redness because the idea resembled redness; resembled it indeed by being red. My idea of Granny, unlike my idea of red, is not identical to Granny, but none the less it is like her and hence refers to her. This idea is all but universally abandoned. It has many problems. For one thing, the notion of resemblance itself can be made to seem suspect (c.f. Goodman 1969). For indefinitely many predicates are true of any two objects, and indefinitely many others are false of them. The predicate 'came into existence in the twentieth century' is true of my idea of Granny and Ronald Reagan; Granny, however, was born in the nineteenth century. Even if one thinks a distinction can be drawn between 'real' properties, and mere predications like 'came into existence in the twentieth century', in what way is a two-dimensional painting of Granny really similar to Granny?

Even if we could revive the notion of resemblance as an objective relation, rather than one dependent on our particular capacities and interests, it would not help. Maybe pictures do resemble what they depict. But concepts are not in general pictures. There is evidence that perception involves maplike representations, and some have argued that mental imagery involves pictorial representations. So there may be mental pictures, but much mental representation is not pictorial (c.f. section 2.2). Contemporary theories of mental representation therefore attempt to construct theories of mental representation out of some species of causal relation between mind and world. This in turn results in a central dilemma for naturalist theories of representation.

The idea is that my concept of tigers depends in some way on the causal connections between me and tigers. But the causal relations in question are crucially ambiguous. Consider the relations between my concept **tiger** and that set of tigers I have encountered at zoos, seen on the movies, read about, been told of, and so on. I want to be able to say that my concept applies to these tigers and to all the others. But how could that be so? *Ex hypothesi*, I have not the most exiguous connection with the rest. Somehow my concept's range of application must be generalized beyond the stimulus set, and just the right amount. It must apply to all tigers, but not more: not to all large carnivores, all felines, all tigerish looking things, or to everything that is either a tiger or was born on a Tuesday. It must include all tigers; not all except those born on Tuesday. (Assuming the stimulus set to contain none such.) Even the notion of the stimulus set itself is problematic. For consider the causal chain as it extends outward from my central processor. (For simplicity, consider only those tigers I have seen.) It goes via the retinal images of tigers on my eye; a structure of ambient light tiger produced; various tiger surfaces; tigers; causal history of tigers being zoo-located. So why isn't my concept **tiger** a concept of tigerish retinal projections on the one hand, or a concept of tiger-directed zoo-keeping on the other.

Thus the causal relations between me and tigers is in two critical ways ambiguous. It is ambiguous both in what counts as the stimulus class (a depth ambiguity), and ambiguous in how that class could be extended (a breadth ambiguity). The natural way to resolve these ambiguities is to appeal to the cognizing mind. My concept **tiger** applies to tigers, not their characteristic retinal projections, because in forming that concept I intended to form a concept of a kind of animal, or perhaps of a being existing in three-dimensional space. (I here follow a standard notation: a word in bold type names a concept.)

Though natural, responses along these lines raise major problems. For they threaten naturalistic semantics with circularity. We are attempting to reductively explain what it is to possess a concept. Once we start to appeal, in that explanation, to cognitive capacities, intentions, or the like, we seem to be presupposing what we are meant to explain. My concept **tiger** applies to tigers because of certain beliefs or intentions of mine. But beliefs and intentions are *composed of concepts*. So I have the **tiger** concept because other concepts of mine are concepts of (say) an animal, or of space. How do they manage to be that? I am not here arguing that all appeals, in the naturalistic explanation of representation, to the activity of the representing mind are illegitimate. That would be mad. We all have the concept of a tiger, and no brick does, however many times it is bounced off a tiger's nose. The difference is surely to do with what goes on in us, and fails to go on in a brick. My point rather is that such appeals must be extremely carefully scrutinized, for they are very liable to be circular.

Naturalistic semantics thus face something like a dilemma. Representational relations seem to be a species of causal relations. Yet the causal relations do not seem sufficiently determinate. They leave too many candidates as the content of any given thought. Winnowing these candidates requires us to move back inside the mind. In turn, this threatens the project with circularity.

We thus need a theory of content that meets at least the following conditions. (a) It should not be circular, nor in other ways should it attribute magical powers to the brain; that is, it should be compatible with a physicalist theory of mind. (b) It should explain how the reference of concepts can be determinate. Some concepts in some minds are no doubt vague to some degree. But my **tiger** concept refers to tigers, not all tigers except those born in the New York Zoo. (c) It should allow of the possibility of misrepresentation. I sometimes misidentify a possum as a cat; I token **cat** when it is really a possum. Further, some concepts are empty. There are no angels, yet the concept is not neural static. Thinking someone is an angel is distinct from thinking they are a demon. Our account should explain the difference between an empty concept and neural static, and between distinct empty concepts. (d) Despite Fodor's opinion to the contrary, we need an account of content that is consistent with the fact that most human concepts are not innate, they are learned. It is one thing to explain how it is that my concept of tigers is, indeed, a concept of tigers. It is another to explain how I come to have a concept with that content. Part of the moral of this chapter is the difficulty of satisfying all these demands at the same time; satisfying one tends to violate others.

6.2 Causal Theories of Content

There are in fact in the literature two quite distinct kinds of causal theory: I shall call these Kripkian causal theories and indicator theories, though in fact my 'Kripkian theories' are rather remote descendants of Kripke's original suggestions. Kripkian causal theories were originally developed as a semantic theory of language, but if they work at all they should work for the language of thought. The essential idea is that the content of a concept is determined by causal links between the individual acquiring that concept and its reference. Paradigms, in the initial development of the theory, were names and natural kind terms. Why does my mental expression **Michael Devitt** refer to Michael Devitt? In virtue of my coining that expression as a result of eyeballing the man. There is an appropriate causal chain leading from Devitt to my concept; hence my concept refers to Devitt. The characteristic that I want to emphasize is that these stories are *actualist*. Counterfactuals play no central role. I would have formed a mentalese expression internally identical to the one I did form, had I met twin Devitt on Twin Earth, or a simulacra of Devitt here. But these counterfactual possibilities are irrelevant – on Kripkian accounts – to the reference of my mentalese expression. However, counterfactual possibilities are important to indicator theories. The essential intuition behind these theories is that my concept **cow** refers to cows because it is reliably correlated with cows. Here counterfactuals do play a role. For to count as having a reliable cow detector, I have to do better than mere current *de facto* success. It is not good enough that so far I have only thought **cow!** in the presence of cows. Perhaps I have only encountered cows and possums; my reaction were I to meet a horse or a bull is relevant to my reliability.

Both Kripkian and indicator theories are still alive, though not in these hopelessly crude versions. But both have great difficulties; especially, I think, wrestling with different manifestations of the problem prefigured in the last section. I think we need both theories. It is hard to extend indicator theories from accounts of perceptual representation to mental representation in general, and from concepts for ostensively definable kinds to other concepts. Moreover, it is obviously difficult to explain the difference between 'that's water' and 'that's H_2O'. For both indicate water. Yet they seem to be different beliefs. A similar problem arises for names. Believing that Clerk Kent is a wimp is not believing Superman is a wimp. Yet my concept of Superman equally well indicates Kent.

Kripkian theories are better adapted to these problems, but seem to presuppose at least part of what needs explaining. Consider names. On the Kripkian view, names are introduced into the language in formal or informal naming ceremonies. I acquire a jet black kitten with fierce yellow eyes; I propose to my friends that we call him 'Satan', and thus Satan is named. Those present, in virtue of their interaction with the cat and the name, acquire the semantic ability to designate that cat by that name. This story is plausible; who knows, it might even be true. But it clearly presupposes that quite sophisticated perceptual, intentional and linguistic capacities are already in place. These are representational capacities, and they need explaining. Indicator theories are appropriate to the most fundamental mental representations, and perhaps explain the conceptual backdrop that Kripkian theories assume.

6.3 Kripkian Theories

Kripkian theories are naturally faced with a vast series of problems of detail. They must, for instance, include a specification of the causal connection between Devitt and me that suffices for my having a Devitt-concept. After all, we must explain the possibility of empty or denotationless terms. The conceptual structure that arises in the mind of the acquirer always has some cause. Yet some concepts are empty. My concept of phlogiston does not designate oxygen even though oxygen was the usual salient cause of the experimental results resulting in the introduction of the concept of phlogiston. **Witch** is not an alternative concept of women. Somehow it will need to be shown that the causal connections between oxygen and **phlogiston** aren't those that constitute reference. Nor are those between **witch** and various alleged witches. There are other problems. We acquire most of our words and concepts from others through language rather than by perceptual contact with their referents. So Kripkian theories need to incorporate a theory of 'reference-borrowing' – a theory of how the causal chain linking my concept of nuclear weapons can run from such weapons to me via other minds. Exploiting perceptual interaction with a tiger to coin a concept which determinately refers to tigers is cognitively sophisticated. Perhaps it is so sophisticated that causal theories are threatened with circularity. Surely acquiring a new concept as the result of the perception of symbols is even more sophisticated, even more parasitic on the prior possession of a rich stock of concepts, than acquiring it from the experience of examples.

The central problem for Kripkian theories is, however, the problem of ambiguity. The causal history of the formation of a concept is complex with many different elements. How do we distinguish an element, in a principled way, as the concept's reference? Why is my concept of Mick Jagger a name for Jagger rather than Jagger's voice? or Jagger's lips? Consider Joseph Banks, Cook's naturalist, confronted with his first kangaroo. How come his concept of roos was a concept of kangaroos rather than (say): marsupials, mammals, critters locomoting by hopping, etc. In earlier work, I have called this the *qua*-problem.

To solve this problem we surely must appeal to more than the causal chain between animal and perceptual organ of the observer. We seem to need (as was emphasized in section 6.1) a more cognitive theory: my kangaroo concept is a concept of kangaroos in virtue of its internal connections with other concepts; in virtue of my beliefs (maybe even knowledge) about what I am perceiving.

This appeal to cognitive processes threatens circularity. If appealing to the connections between my concept of kangaroos and the rest of my cognitive apparatus involves other concepts, this account of the semantics of concepts depends on other concepts. If beliefs or other propositional attitudes are involved, it depends on intentional notions in general. Moreover, if to possess, say, the concept **cow** we must already have in place other concepts, it is hard to see how concepts could be acquired serially, as, presumably, they are.

Michael Devitt and I (Devitt and Sterelny, 1987) proposed a strategy: a hierarchy of concepts: pure causal concepts; descriptive-causal concepts; descriptive concepts. We intended to invoke this hierarchy to simultaneously explain both the nature of the referential relation, and to explain how concepts with those referential properties could be acquired. The idea is to find a class of concepts for which a pure causal theory is appropriate; i.e. a class of concepts whose possession does not require the possession of any other concept. A pure causal concept is one that can be acquired atomically: hence no acquisition problem or threat of circularity arises. Basic concepts could play a role in the explanation of the reference and the acquisition of some nonbasic ones, names, perhaps, or natural kind terms. This larger class could then play a role in our story for others, and so on.

There are two problems confronting this proposal. Firstly, we have to find some way of explaining the less basic in terms of the more basic that does not presuppose that nonbasic concepts are defined. We have very good reason to deny that sophisticated concepts are definable. Kripke (1980) pointed out that names cannot be semantically equivalent to descriptions, for we can use names to refer even when ignorant of, or in error about, their referents. The same is true of natural kind terms: I can refer to polyethelene but know no definition of it; no way of uniquely specifying it. So descriptive elements must be built into a causal theory of reference in ways compatible with its original motivation. In general, our capacity to refer to the world's furniture does not depend on identifying knowledge of that to which we refer. It is also very difficult, at least, to find a nonarbitrary and nonintentional criterion that distinguishes semantically relevant from semantically irrelevant descriptive elements.

Still more serious is the problem of actually finding plausible examples of basic concepts. Sensory concepts at first sight seem plausible candidates, but even for them the *qua*-problem arises. Does my **red** concept (when first acquired) name a colour or a shade of that colour, or even an intensity level of light? Fodor once suggested (1981 ch. 10) that concepts for middle size easily recognizable kinds were basic: concepts like **dog, human, chair** (as distinct from **stool** or

furniture). They are all ostensively definable and easily available to the young mind. But the acquisition (and hence presumably the reference) of these concepts looks cognitively – indeed conceptually – mediated.

1   These concepts can be acquired not just from their instances, but as well from appropriate words, diagrams, models, pictures. Dretske (1981) claimed that children exposed to toy robins learn thereby **toy robin**, not **robin**. But surely that is very implausible: it implies that most of our animal concepts are concepts not of animals, but of pictures or words.

2   The same concept can be acquired by very different perceptual routes. Dogs can be heard or seen or even tasted. The fixation of a concept on its reference can be 'multiply realized': a considerable variety of psychological processes can implement that fixation. The possibility of such multiple implementations is symptomatic of a high-level cognitive process.

It follows that Fodor's suggestion won't do for our purposes. Concepts for which the *qua*-problem does not arise look decidedly thin on the ground. So our basis for bootstrapping our way to the rest of our conceptual equipment may simply not be available. This problem is the key unsolved problem for Kripkian causal theories, and it suggests that the Kripkian story may not be the right story of primitive content, but rather plays a role in the explanation of more cognitively sophisticated structures whose content presupposes a conceptual backdrop.

6.4 Indicator Theories

The central idea of indicator theories is that **cow** refers to cows (hence is a concept of cows) just when thinking **cow** is reliably correlated with cows. At its crudest, your cow concept is the concept you entertain only if you are cow confronted. In Dretske's notation, your thought has the content that's a cow only if it carries the information that that's a cow. But carrying that information requires reliable correlation between thoughts of that type and cows. Some defenders of indicator theories have suggested an even stronger correlation. For **cow** to be a cow concept it must be tokened if and only if there are cows present. The world, if this were so, would carry information about your thoughts; we could infer from the presence of a cow in your vicinity to cow thoughts in your mind. But this seems an unnecessary burden to place on indicator theories; it is hard enough to defend the view that the mind carries information about the world (see Godfrey-Smith forthcoming).

The defenders of indicator theories all know that such crude theories will not work. The crude theory stands in need of revision in two central ways. First, the correlation between **cow** and cows is imperfect, for I can falsely believe of some object that it is a cow. I sometimes token **cow** mistakenly; I don't think **cow** only if cow-ed. It is not just cows but some superset – a set including young bulls, distant water-buffalo, twin cows and the like – that make me token **cow**. Given that the correlation between **cow** and this superset is more reliable than the correlation between **cow** and cows, in virtue of what is that concept a cow concept, rather than a concept of rather cowlike things? This is known as the misrepresentation, or disjunction, problem. There are many candidate solutions, but none of them entirely convince.

Second, the indicator theory, even if it can overcome the first problem, is seriously incomplete. For many of my tokenings of concepts are neither correlated with their references nor misrepresent anything. Sometimes I think **beer** because someone is kind enough to thrust one under my nose. But sometimes I think **beer** because I'm thirsty. That involves no misrepresentation; I don't falsely believe something is beer; I just want a beer. The indicator theory, at best, is a theory of perceptual representation; it needs extending into a theory of cognitive representation in general. For the same reason, it is very hard to fit indicator theories into the division of linguistic labour. I have already noted that we acquire most of our concepts through language rather than through perceptual contact with their referents. It is very hard to see what an indicator theory of reference borrowing would be like.

There is an extensive and growing literature on these issues; especially on the misrepresentation problem. I will not here attempt an exhaustive survey, but will rather describe and discuss two characteristic proposals.

6.4.1 Fodor

Psychosemantics is a monograph developing and defending indication semantics. Fodor proposes to deal with misrepresentation through the idea of asymmetrical dependence. Suppose, for simplicity, that you have the concept of cows, but, like us all, the correlation between your tokens of **cow** and cows is not perfect; you token **cow** when presented with thin water-buffalo. None the less, Fodor argues, your tokens of **cow** refer to cows, not to cow-or-water-buffalo. For the misrepresenting tokens depend on the veridical tokens, but not conversely. You wouldn't think 'cow!' on presentation of a water-buffalo unless there existed a correlation between **cow**-thoughts and cows. But the existence of this latter correlation does not depend on any correlation between **cow**-thoughts and buffalo. Hence buffalo-caused **cow** tokens exist only because cow-caused ones do, but not vice versa. So **cow** refers to cows, not cows-or-water-buffalo.

This is an elegant proposal, but not a convincing one. Firstly, its plausibility depends on the range of counterfactuals we take to be relevant to determining the existence of a reliable correlation. Fodor supposes that there are possible worlds in which **cow** tokens are caused only by cows, but no possible worlds in which those things we mistake for cows are taken to be cows, but cows are not taken to be cows. This depends on the counterfactuals we envisage. There are possible worlds – consistently imaginable situations – in which twin cows, robot cows, cow holograms are so convincingly bovine that we infallibly, or, rather, invariably think 'cow' on beholding them. But the cows in those worlds are so uncowlike (they have been fed strange growth hormones) that we never think of them as cows. Asymmetrical dependence solves the disjunction problem only if these counterfactuals can be nonarbitrarily excluded.

I also think that the suggestion applies at best to natural kind concepts. Consider the concept **brick**. It applies to all and only bricks, oblong clay-based chunks of building material. In particular, it does not apply to twin bricks. Twin bricks are physically identical to bricks, but they are not bricks, for they are not designed, made and used for building. Rather, they are used in twin Iran to stone recalcitrant antiphysicalists. Since twin bricks are physically identical to bricks, in any world in which we think **brick** when confronted with bricks, we will also think it when confronted with twin bricks. There are no worlds in which bricks but not twin bricks produce **bricks**, so there is no asymmetry in the causal routes from bricks and twin bricks to **bricks**. Similarly, Fodor's suggestion cannot explain how our concept of a dime applies to all dimes, but not to all dimes plus perfect dime counterfeits, even though all worlds in which you think **dime** when presented with a dime are also worlds in which you think dime when presented with a perfect counterfeit. Note that there are worlds in which the only objects that cause **dimes** are counterfeits, worlds in which dimes were never legal tender but in which counterfeits were nevertheless passed as legal tender.

Asymmetric dependence may not solve the depth problem. In virtue of what is **cow** a concept of cows rather than cow appearances? Surely here the dependence is symmetrical. Let's grant that we wouldn't think

cow as a result of some cow appearance unless there was a unitary distal cause of cow sight, smell and sound. Would we have the **cow** concept we have if there were no cow appearances, or very different ones? There are possible worlds, I suppose, in which cows are invisible and yet are cows. In those worlds we perhaps have *a* concept of cows. But would they be tokens of **cow**? Note that since Fodor is giving an account of semantic content he cannot rely on a semantic definition of what makes **cow** tokens instances of the type **cow**. Fodor (forthcoming) relies, somewhat unconvincingly, on an orthographic account of type-hood; two token concepts are of the same type if they are spelt the same way in the language of thought. I do not want to overpress the point about depth. The counterfactuals in question are hardly transparent, and the concept of cow appearances is messy and disjunctive. But it is certainly not clear that Fodor has a solution to the depth problem.

There is a still more serious objection. Godfrey-Smith has argued (1989) that cows rather than water-buffalo are illicitly supposed to have an independent link with the **cow**-concept. How so? There is an alternative account of the facts of dependence which seems just as good as Fodor's, and which includes no asymmetry. For it is arguable that there is a privileged link between **cow** and a larger unnatural kind **k**. For the correlation between **cow**-tokens and **k** members is reliable. If **k** includes some buffalo, there is no asymmetry: both cows and buffalo elicit **cow** because they are both members of **k**. Admittedly **k** is an unnatural kind but we have many concepts of unnatural kinds; **weed** is one such. Fodor has thought deeply about the disjunction problem, but none the less I think Godfrey-Smith is right, and the suggestion fails.

6.4.2 Dretske

The first sustained attempt to develop an indicator theory is Dretske's (1981). In this fine work Dretske developed an elegant solution to the depth problem. For he pointed out that our perceptual systems are designed to maintain a constancy between percept and the perceived world, even across considerable variation of the proximal stimulus. For example, if you shake your head, the objects in your field of view do not seem to move even though their images on the retina do move. If the sun goes behind a cloud, the things you are looking at don't seem to change colour even though there may be a marked fall in the amount of light that reaches your eye. The stable correlation, Dretske points out, is between concept and object, not between concept and its sensory intermediaries. So concepts are concepts of those objects, not of the sensory intermediaries.

Dretske grapples with the misrepresentation problem less satisfactorily. He attempts to solve it by first distinguishing between type and token concepts and second distinguishing between the period in which a concept is acquired (the 'learning period') and the period in which the concept is in routine use. The idea is that the content of a concept is fixed during the learning period. So long as the learning period correlation is between (say) wallabies and **wallaby**, hence fixing that concept as a wallaby concept, it won't matter if in the period of routine use that correlation is less than exact and, say, young kangaroos occasionally stimulate a **wallaby** token. Those tokens misrepresent, for in the learning period the correlation was exact.

This account has so many problems as to have been abandoned by even its inventor. The central criticism – pressed by Fodor and others – is that the learning period correlation is not between wallaby instances and **wallaby** tokens. Even if, in fact, wallabies and only wallabies resulted in **wallabys** (let us suppose all the roos had big 'Not a wallaby' signs attached to them) counterfactuals are relevant to reliable correlation. If post-learning period roos do cause **wallaby** tokens, pre-learning period roos would have. Hence Dretske's idea fails to solve the disjunction problem.

Despite the fact that there are clearly very real problems here, I have always thought the dismissal of Dretske's idea has been too swift. Firstly, there are control and feedback mechanisms operating in the learning period that cease to function later (some are teachers), so it's not obvious that the counterfactual 'Kangaroos (without labels) seen in the learning period would stimulate a token of **wallaby**' is true. Of course, if we let our imagination wander freely over possibilia, allowing us to present to the learner perfect wallaby simulcra, twin wallabies, genetically engineered wallaby look-alikes, we will secure a few **wallaby** tokens. No discrimination devices, however well ringed with feedback mechanisms, are immune from deceit. But why is Dretske required to count these merely possible contingencies as undermining the claim that, in the learning period, the connection between stimulus and concept is nomic? A correlation does not fail to be reliable just because it is logically possible for it to fail, or even because it is nomically possible for it to fail. If that is necessary for reliability then no physical device is reliable.

In my view then, the abandonment of Dretske's idea has been premature. None the less, it has been abandoned, and Dretske has developed a new, and much more complex, proposal. It supplements causal notions by an appeal to the biological function of mental representation. So let's look at that idea.

6.5 Teleology

One very popular response to these problems is to appeal to the biological function of a representation-forming mechanism. A mechanism has its biological function in virtue of its evolutionary history. So this appeal is uncontroversially naturalistic, and it seems to have the potential to solve the ambiguity problem. Robins feed their chicks when they gape and screech. But robins are vulnerable to brood parasitism; they also feed cuckoos. But their representation, the idea runs, is **my hungry chick** not **(my hungry chick) or cuckoo**. For the biological function of the representation is to direct the robins in feeding their chicks, not to direct them in feeding their chicks or cuckoos. That mechanism evolved because it led to robin ancestors feeding robin chicks, and despite the fact that it sometimes led them to feed cuckoos.

Dretske attempts to combine biological function with indication semantics, though he does not commit himself to any particular view of the nature of biological function. He shows through a well-chosen example how the appeal to biological function can both resolve ambiguity and explain misrepresentation. Some marine bacteria have magnetosomes, tiny magnets inside them which, like a compass needle, point at geomagnetic north. These magnetosomes indicate both geomagnetic north, and the direction away from oxygen-rich surface water fatal to the bacteria. The magnets thus indicate two properties but, Dretske says, they represent only one: the direction to low-oxygen water. That is the biological purpose of the magnetosome. The appeal to teleology thus disambiguates. It also explains misrepresentation. The magnet misrepresents when it points to high-oxygen water, which it will do if a northern hemisphere species finds its way down south. For in those circumstances the magnetosome will be failing to fulfil its biological function (Dretske, 1988, p. 63).

Millikan and Godfrey-Smith convincingly argue that it is a mistake to graft a teleological theory onto an indicator theory in this way. For it can be the biological function of a device to represent f even when it usually misrepresents. That occurs when it is very important to believe that f when the world fs, and when it does not much matter if you believe f when the world is not f. Predator representation is the usual example. A rabbit that thinks 'fox' when there is no fox loses little; the rabbit that fails to think 'fox' when there is one loses all. So it can be the function of a rabbitish state to *represent* foxes even though it does not *indicate* foxes. Its firings might be usually caused by wombats. It would thus indicate wombats, not indicate foxes, yet represent foxes. So the appeal to teleology should really be seen as distinct from indicator semantics, rather than a supplement to it (Godfrey-Smith, forthcoming; Millikan, 1989, forthcoming b). The appeal to teleology can be modest or zealous. The modest appeal, which I shall endorse, is to teleological explanations of fundamental representational capacities.

6.6 A Modest Proposal

The proposal to add teleological elements to the causal story seems very attractive. For an appeal to the biological function of an internal representation is naturalistic, yet does give us what we desperately need: more discriminatory machinery. Alphonse's mental state has the content that's-a-tiger because its biological function is tiger-representation. That state exists and functions in Alphonse because ancestors of Alphonse with that state were more adaptive in their relations with tigers in virtue of having it; their species mates without it were less fit. Note that the evolutionary history explaining the existence of this state in Alphonse will mention tigers: not twin tigers, genetically engineered tiger-look-alikes, or tigers born on Tuesday. None of Alphonse's ancestors met twin tigers or look-alikes, and tigers born on Tuesday played no special role in their history. So the appeal to teleology enables us to specify the circumstances in which a mental state represents rather than misrepresents. It represents when *the token is caused by circumstances of the same kind as those selectively responsible for the existence of the type.* Alphonse has the cognitive capacity to have tokens of the type that's-a-tiger because tiger-here-now circumstances were critical to the evolution of that capacity. So Alphonse represents when he tokens that thought when confronted with a tiger; misrepresents when he tokens it in other circumstances. Notice that we have not just specified the circumstances in which Alphonse's representations are veridical; we do so in a nonintentional, nonarbitrary way.

This proposal is very plausible when made about animals whose representational capacities are fixed and limited. Let me give two well-known examples, and then consider Fodor's critique of even this limited claim on behalf of teleology. Frogs have rather limited visual capacities, but they do have complexes of cells that respond strongly to small, fast, dark objects. More exactly, there are cells in the frog's visual system that respond strongly to retinal projections that would typically be caused by small, fast, dark objects. Moreover, that response had a distinctive behavioural consequence: the frog's hunting and feeding systems are engaged. The natural representational hypothesis, and one underwritten by teleological considerations, is this. The content of the frog's visual system is: that's-a-fly. For both the relevant visual specialization, and the connections to frog behaviour have evolved because they enabled frog ancestors to sight and catch flies. The frog can be easily fooled, and will visually respond to, and even catch and eat, lots of nonflies. An airgun pellet lobbed across its field of view, and suitably close, will result in a frog sight-strike-feed. Teleological considerations enable us to say that the frog misrepresents, and, hence is fooled. The content of its visual system when so stimulated is: that's-a-fly, not that's-a-fly or an airgun pellet, for the biological function of that state is fly-spotting (see Arbib, 1972).

Let me steal my second example from Churchland and Churchland (1983). The rattlesnake has cells that fire (and hence engage hunting routines) only if two conditions are met. The cells must get positive input from the snake's infrared detectors, signifying warmth, and its visual system, signifying (small) moving thing. When those tectal cells fire, the rattlesnake acts as though there is food about. In the rattlesnake's natural habit, in those circumstances there will indeed be food about. For the combined input is typically caused by a field mouse, the snake's normal prey. Of course, the rattlesnake, like the frog, could be easily enough fooled. An artificially warmed imitation mouse would certainly do it; probably simpler lures as well. Just as with the frog though, we can plausibly and nonarbitrarily say that the snake thinks: that's-a-mouse. Not, that's something warm-and- moving. For it is in virtue of its role in mouse detection that this specialization exists in the snake's brain.

For innate and isolated structures of this kind, I am inclined to accept some version of a teleological theory. Further, I think there will be an important teleological element in our total theory of mental representation, though any attempt to extend the teleological story to the human propositional attitudes faces the most appalling difficulties.

Fodor, however, does not think teleology plays a role underwriting even these rudimentary representations (see Fodor, forthcoming). For Fodor thinks the notion of *selection for* suffers from its own *qua*-problem. Function is indeterminate, unless we can independently ground representational claims. He supports this view by pointing to two alternative accounts of the function of the frog's mechanism.

(Though he actually writes of toads, not frogs.) He thinks we can with equal justice call that visual mechanism a small-black-dot detector, or a fleebee detector. Something is a fleebee just in case it is a fly or an airgun pellet ('bee bees'); the point is that frogs notoriously snap at pellets. Now Fodor claims that there is nothing in evolutionary history alone, nor in the facts about natural selection alone, that warrants the claim that the frog has a mechanism whose function is fly representation rather than black-dot representation or fleebee representation. '*Darwin cares how many flies you eat but not what description you eat them under*'. (p. 21).

I think this is just wrong. Fodor treats his two suggestions as more or less equivalent ways of making the same point, but I think they raise different issues and will take them separately.

Does the frog have a black-dot detector rather than a fly detector? In effect, I replied to this objection in the last chapter. For this is the suggestion that we construe the functions of the mechanism individualistically. Black dots are retinal objects. I argued that we should not restrict ourselves to individualist accounts of zero-crossing detectors, the primal sketch or the function of the rattlesnake's tectal cells. For in doing so we rob ourself of the resources to construct a principled individualist taxonomy. We also rob ourself of explanatory power. One ecological function can have distinct individualist realizations, and internally identical structures can have distinct representational functions. The hoverfly and the frog have moving-black-dot detectors, but for the hoverfly the dot means sex, for the frog, food. Noctuid moths, crickets and lacewings all have bat detectors. They all depend on hearing the bat's ultrasound, but their internal wiring is quite different (Alcock, 1989, pp. 112–23). Both the frog and the toad detect flies, but, for all I know, their internal wiring might be quite different. If so, no matter. They still fall under the same selective explanation. We go beyond the skin here, as elsewhere, because (a) in doing so we capture generalizations, and (b) only in doing so can we construct a principled individualist taxonomy. Frogs *do* have black-dot detectors, but that is compatible with those detectors being fly detectors. The individualist story explains how the ecological function is realized.

But what of the suggestion that Darwin wouldn't mind if we say that frogs have a fleebee detector. For frog ancestors snapped at entities that were flies or airgun pellets. For in the ancestral home of frogs that category is coextensive with the category of flies. Fodor thinks that natural selection does not distinguish between coextensive properties.

Not so, I say. I think Fodor is presenting a standard problem in philosophy of science as though it were one that especially infects teleological explanation. There is a general problem with dodgy predicates. The classic example, due to Goodman, is 'grue'. An object is grue if it is first seen before 2100 and is green, or is first seen after 2100 and is blue. 'Green' and 'grue' are not coextensive, but are, like 'is a fly' and 'is a fleebee', locally coextensive. I see a green object and come to believe that it is green. Is that belief causally based in the object's greenness, or in its grueness? Anyone who takes causal claims seriously will say that it is the greenness that is doing the causal work. Saying so relies on intuitions about causation and the naturalness properties that are very hard to make explicit. But this problem has nothing especially to do with biological or psychological contexts. Consider a positron-free chunk of the universe. In that chunk the category of petrons (a petron is a positron or an electron) is coextensive with the category of electrons. Still, the right causal law in that chunk is that electrons are attracted to a positive charge, not that petrons are attracted to a positive charge.

Fleebees are like petrons and grue surfaces. The frog's visual specialization is an evolutionary response to the property of being-a-fly, not being-a-fleebee, even though in that context all flies are fleebees. I do not think causal claims reduce to claims about the truth of counterfactuals; I think they are semantically primitive. But counterfactuals are a useful prod to our intuitions, and here they are unequivocal. Had flies changed so that their retinal projections were not beebeelike, natural selection would tend to construct mechanisms that tracked the changing shape of flies. Frogs would become less apt to snap at beebees. Had the frog's ancestral environment been from the start beebee infested, natural selection would have tended to construct perceptual mechanisms that could discriminate food from pellets. (These claims have to be phrased very cautiously; natural selection is far from being an omnipotent engineer designing perfect machines.) There is a diachronic tracking between flies and fly representors, albeit a very imperfect one. Thus frog ancestors were selected for fly hunting, not fleebee hunting. So when a frog snaps at a pellet, it misrepresents a pellet as food.

Sober (1984) introduced a distinction that enables me to put this point crisply. Sober distinguishes between *selection of* and *selection for* a trait. Consider a filter that will allow balls of 1 cm in diameter or less to pass. Suppose all such balls are green. In the group that passes through, there is selection for size, but selection of both size and colour. Similarly, there has been selection for a fly detector, but selection of both a fly and a fleebee detector. But there is nothing arbitrary in describing a trait by appeal to what it has been selected for.

6.7 Less Modest Proposals

It is one thing to give teleological accounts of innate structures; quite another to give a teleological account of the propositional attitudes. For scarcely any of them can be innate. Still, some have tried. Most persistently, Papineau (1984, 1987) and Millikan. Let's begin with Papineau's simple theory.

After outlining the ambiguity problem for naturalistic theories of content, Papineau proceeds to make the following suggestion:

> I want to consider then, the following general analysis of truth conditions. The disposition to form a given type of belief is explained by the fact that that belief has typically arisen in certain circumstances and in those circumstances the actions that it has directed have been selectively advantageous. The typical circumstances in question are the belief's truth conditions. And talk of 'typicality' here is no longer empty, for it is precisely because of what happened in those 'typical' occasions in the past . . ., and not others . . . that we have our current belief-forming dispositions. (1984, p. 557)

Ambitious teleological theories of representation have a major empirical burden. For they buy heavily into a debatable view of natural selection. Adaptationism is the view that most of the characteristics of organisms, especially the striking ones, have a selective explanation. That view is very controversial. For some characteristics are the consequences of accidental changes in the gene pool. In small populations accidental changes can be very important. Other characteristics are the result of some kind of genetic or developmental linkage with a characteristic that really is selected for. There is selection of polar bears for warm coats; that results in their having heavy coats as well. There is no doubt that some features of our psychology are adaptations, that some are hangers on, and that some are evolutionary accidents. The debate is about relative numbers. Defenders of teleological theories of our propositional attitudes are betting that our central cognitive organization is a complex of adaptations. For if it is not, important features of cognition central have no biological function. Now this bet may win, but it is very far from guaranteed to win. Our general cognitive capacities may well be a by-product of our growing a big brain for a special purpose, perhaps to cheat each other.

Ambitious theories are thus committed to a special view of natural selection. But that is the least of their problems. For a teleological theory of representation to go beyond frogs and snakes it needs extending in two ways.

1 Human beliefs don't have evolutionary histories. Most of my beliefs, no doubt, are had for the very first time in human history by me. This is no tribute to my extraordinary and original genius. Rather it's due to the egocentric preoccupations of human belief. A large chunk of my beliefs are first person beliefs: beliefs that I have been and done such and such. No one else has such an interest in me. Furthermore, the belief that I currently inhabit New Zealand, arguably at least, is distinct from the belief that Sterelny currently inhabits New Zealand. If that's right, all my first person beliefs are unique to me. Even if it's wrong, many will be. Furthermore, many of my other beliefs have only recently been possible: for they are about recent events. Very few human beliefs have been available to the ancestral population long enough to be the subjects of an evolutionary history. For the overwhelming majority of human beliefs, it's just not true that we have them because, in certain historically typical circumstances, the having of them improved our ancestor's fitness.

2 The representational structures exampled in frogs and rattlesnakes don't have internal structure. The representations of mice and flies are not complex: they don't have a syntax; they don't have component representations. I emphasized in section 2.2 that our representations are complex in just these ways. For thought is both systematic and productive; facts that can only be explained by supposing our thoughts to have a syntax and to be composed from more primitive elements, concepts. For creatures whose representational systems are languages of thought, the fundamental relationship is not between a state of affairs in the world and a sentence in the language of thought. It is rather between elements of the world – individuals and kinds – and concepts. For the semantic properties of complex representations are explained by appeal to the semantics of their primitive elements, the syntactic structure of the complex representations, and how the world is.

On this view, the work of teleology is transformed: it's no longer a theory of where truth conditions come from; it's a theory of where reference comes from. Teleological theories are sometimes (as in the case of Papineau) presented as theories of truth conditions, but if they are to help construct a naturalistic theory of our propositional attitudes, I think they need to be reconstructed as theories of reference.

The prospects for a successful reconstruction are grim. In the first place, if we explain teleological notions in terms of natural selection, we restrict ourselves to innate concepts. It is very implausible to suppose that all our primitive concepts – i.e. all our undefinable concepts – are innate. One way of defending the view that our undefined concepts are innate is to suppose we have a relatively small stock of them – most plausibly sensory concepts together with concepts for kinds that are both very salient and are kinds with which we have had a long interaction – and the rest are defined. Unfortunately, the project of finding such definitions has been tried both in linguistics and in philosophy with singularly little success. Fodor has bitten this bullet, and urged that we have vast numbers of primitive and innate concepts. But he has not confronted the problem of how concepts like **gun** or **xylophone** could be innate, for the referents haven't been around long enough to generate a Darwinian story about how those inner innate structures have come to be in us. Many other kinds have been around for ever, but without our being able to detect them without fancy gadgets. It is hard to find out about viruses without electron micros-copes, so it is hard to see how **virus** could be innate. Here again we see the acquisition problem tugging against the circularity problem. Papineau argues that teleological appeals in the theory of representation don't require that the representing structure be innate. But his claim (1984, p. 557; 1988, p. 66) depends on a dubious analogy between learning and natural selection. (I explain why it is dubious in Sterelny, forthcoming). But even were Papineau right, there is a further problem about teleological appeals in explaining representational states: a problem applying equally to the teleology of concepts or the teleology of belief-like states.

Recall Papineau's basic claims:

The belief has typically arisen in certain circumstances, and in those circumstances the actions it has directed have been selectively advantageous. (1984, p. 557)

or, when the focus changes to concepts,

Concepts get selected because the way they combine to give rise to beliefs ensures that those beliefs are typically found in circumstances where the actions they direct will be advantageous. (1984, p. 559)

Papineau thus requires that beliefs (and even concepts) have typical behavioural consequences. That's necessary if a belief, or more exactly a belief-circumstance pair, is to be selected for. For selection on cognitive states will operate via the behaviour those states give rise to. The problem is that it's far from obvious that there are typical behaviours beliefs, or even belief-circumstance pairs, give rise to. The most telling criticism of behaviourism is that it wrongly supposed there to be a signature behavioural type for each mental state: that there was, for instance, a behaviour characteristic of believing that the earth was spherical. There is no such characteristic behaviour, for the behavioural consequences of a belief depend on the other beliefs and desires of the agent. That's true even for the veridical perceptual beliefs that Papineau's basic analysis is designed for. A tree is in front of me; I notice it and come to believe that that's a tree. Why, in general, should we expect the behavioural consequences, if any, of that process to increase my expected number of descendants? Why expect the analogous processes in my predecessors to have increased the expected number of their descendants? The behavioural salience of this new belief will depend complexly and initimately on my other cognitive states, and there is no reason to suppose that these will be, in general, adaptive. It needs a good deal of work to show that false belief is mostly maladaptive. First, because an observationally adequate belief set leads to the same expectations about the world as a set of true beliefs would. Second, because the way and circumstances in which beliefs are false matters. Thinking that's a very big bush when it's a tree doesn't seem maladaptive. More radically, it's been urged that selection might favour false beliefs: it might favour over- caution about whether predators are about, or whether certain novel food items are poisonous. It might favour women underestimating the pain and danger of childbirth. But even setting these doubts aside, assumptions of the adaptivity of belief-circumstance pairings seem seriously undercut by the holistic nature of action causation.

Godfrey-Smith has urged a related point. He points to the distinction between teleological accounts of a cognitive mechanism, and teleological accounts of the products of that mechanism. Teleological accounts of mechanism – for example of the eye and the rest of the visual system – present no more difficulty than the teleology of any other organ. It's as appropriate to ascribe functions to the retina as it is to ascribe functions to the liver. Not so the products of a mechanism. My current retinal image (an image of a chunk of text) has no biological function. For there is no discriminatory pattern of replication. People with that retinal state are not thereby likely to have more descendants who also have it. Being in that state doesn't increase in frequency in the descendant population. Contrast having a mechanism which forms retinal images. Having that property, a properly functioning retina, most certainly did lead to having more offspring with that very property.

Let me turn to Millikan's more complex theory, which avoids some of the problems of Papineau's account. In particular, she is not committed to the view that beliefs and desires have a behavioural signature in virtue of which they are selected. She does not think concepts have a natural selective story to call their own. The biological functions of particular concepts, and of particular intentional states they constitute, derive from the selective history of the brain, the organ that forms these particular states. She is sensitive to Godfrey-Smith's distinction between a mechanism and its states. Yet she claims that particular states, even unique ones, have proper biological functions. She supports this view with many apt examples. The chameleon has a mechanism that changes the colour of its skin; the function of the mechanism, obviously, is camouflage.

> If we look at any particular colour pattern . . . we can say what the proper functions of this pattern are, even though it's possible . . . that no chameleon has ever displayed just this particular pattern before. The proper functions of this pattern are to make this chameleon invisible and to prevent it being eaten – functions it derives from the proper functions of the mechanism that produced it. (Millikan, 1986, pp. 52–3).

The proper function of a *state* of a mechanism is (a) an effect of the mechanism operating Normally, and (b) an essential means of that mechanism's biological function. This is important, for intentional content is the content of states produced by biological mechanisms. (By 'Normally', I mean as it has been selected to operate; this may not be the same as its usual operation. I will follow Millikan's convention of capitalizing to indicate my use of a teleological rather than a statistical notion.)

Millikan then goes on to point out that many mechanisms, and hence states of those mechanisms, can carry out their function only if the world cooperates. The immune system can only carry out its function if microorganisms invade. The immune system is not functionless in a sterile environment, but neither it nor any of its states are performing their biological function. The conditions necessary for the performance of the function, the external conditions natural selection has tuned the mechanism to, are the Normal conditions for the performance of the function. Normal conditions can be very very rare. Millikan's flagship example is human sperm; sperm is adapted to, and has the biological function of, uniting with an ovum. Almost none fulfil their destiny; they suffer a drier fate. Normal conditions are sometimes optimal conditions, and optimal conditions can be hard to find. This fact is crucial to underwriting her account of desire. For the content of a given type of desire is *that state of the world it would produce if conditions were Normal.* It is no rebuttal of this account that most desires do not get fulfilled. If Normal conditions are optimal conditions, optimal conditions for desire fulfilment may be decidedly thin on the ground.

I think, however, that this account faces tough problems. Do most human desires have a proper function? My guess is that the function of the desire-making system is to produce motivational states that contribute to survival and reproduction. I think it is an entirely open question whether most of our desires are Normal states of the desire-making system. For I think many are produced by Abnormal means. Their problem is not that optimal conditions are rare but they are pathological, and hence functionless. Consider a chameleon whose skin has a certain pattern not because of the Normal operations of its system, but because experimenters have put it on a wierd diet, or injected its skin or irradiated it in some way. The chameleon's skin-colouring mechanism still has a biological function, even if the experimental activity is such that it is permanently cactus. But I do not think that that *particular pattern token* does. Now it strikes me that many of our desires may be the result of an Abnormal mechanism because of our Abnormal physical, social, psychological and chemical environment. Pathological systems still have functions; states of them produced bizarrely do not. It may well be that many of our desires have, from the perspective of our evolutionary history, a bizarre history. If so, no condition is Normal for their fulfilment. If so, according to Millikan's theory they have no content.

I have another worry. I suspect the notion of a Normal condition of desire's fulfilment is covertly circular. Let me get at that idea by first considering some extreme cases. For there are plenty of desires that are worse off than sperm: they are nomologically impossible of satisfaction. There are not even optimal conditions in which one can do God's will, live forever, or speak one last time to a friend now dead. (I leave aside logically impossible desires; everyone has trouble with them.) What are the Normal conditions for the satisfaction of these desires? There are no conditions, actual or possible, in which an agent can realize his desire to teach Darwin genetics. So there are no conditions in which the content of that desire can be determined by an action which expresses it. So it is at least unclear whether impossible desires have, on this account, determinate content. This suggests a more general problem. Do we have a naturalistic and noncircular account of Normal conditions for even run of the mill desires. Notice that a desire will often produce satisficing behaviour; I want a good wine but settle for a New Zealand one. How are we to exclude *those conditions*, the conditions in which I satisfice, as Normal and thus attribute to me the desire for any old plonk. That is, how can we do so without appealing to the content of my desire.

I think Millikan understates the terrific contrast between her striking case of rare Normal conditions, the sperm about to encounter an ovum, and the Normal conditions of desire. A little physiology, a bit of experimental manipulation, a dash of evolutionary history, and the conditions under which a sperm scores are noncircularly described. But this is not so for desire. I think precisely the same problem arises for her account of belief.

In other respects, the account of belief is quite different, for belief types are not named after their function, but after a normal condition of that function's operation.

Beliefs are named ... in accordance with certain of their Normal conditions for functioning properly. For example, if both John and Bill believe that Jane languishes in Latvia ... (they) have in common ... something ... that cannot perform ... Normally – that is, in accord with principles relied upon during evolutionary design of the cognitive systems – unless Jane does languish in Latvia. (Millikan, 1986, p. 69)

I do not see how to specify the Normal condition of a belief's participation in the production of behaviour and other cognitive states independently of semantic notions. What is Abnormal about a false belief's inferential involvement in a *reductio* inference? What is Abnormal about the reliance on belief that is merely observationally adequate rather than true? The claim that a belief system is true is much stronger than the claim that it is observationally adequate, but I doubt that this is a distinction that the principles natural selection has crafted worries about. Surely Mother Selector is a pragmatist. The notion of a Normal condition here may be an intentional notion; if so, Millikan is using what she is meant to be explaining.

It's time to pull the threads together. I have only discussed a few examples of teleological approaches. Teleology gives us a real insight into representational structures that are self-contained, and which contribute to behaviour in a distinct and identifiable way. But at the very least there are great problems in extending this recipe to representations that aren't innate; in particular, to representations produced by general purpose mechanisms that then interact to produce behaviour.

6.8 Function and Content

Can the problems clustered around misrepresentation and ambiguity be cured by looking upstream from the formation of the concept rather than, or as well as, downstream to its causes. Surely there is some plausibility in the idea that **cow** is a cow concept rather than a cow-appearance concept or a cow-or-thin buffalo concept because of the way it is used in the cognitive system. We can and should appeal to *what the concept is for.* 'Two-factor' theories of content have been quite popular in the literature on the mind, having been defended in various forms by Field, Lycan, McGinn and Devitt. They take content to be fixed by some combination of causal relations between mind and world, and functional relations within the mind. Unfortunately there are important problems in recruiting two-factor theories to this problem.

Firstly, in their normal formulation two-factor theories are irrelevant to the misrepresentation problem. For it is typically argued that there is not a single notion of content but two independent notions. One is the truth-referential notion that is the focus of this chapter. We need this notion of content to explain why believing truly is usually more adaptive than believing falsely, to capture generalizations individualistically unstatable, or whatever. The second notion is functional. It explains the cognitive role of an intentional state in the mental economy of an agent. A man is looking in the direction of a pane of glass. He sees a man sitting on a chair; under the chair is a snake. He thinks to himself 'that poor bastard is about to be bitten'. Unbeknownst to him, the pane of glass is not a window but a mirror. He is that man, so the referential content of believing that he himself is about to be bitten is the same as believing that poor bastard is about to be bitten. But wouldn't they be beliefs with different contents? Lois Lane believes that Clerk Kent is decent but bumbling. Isn't that a different belief from believing that Superman is decent but bumbling? The point of the functional notion is to explain the sense in which Lois Lane's beliefs about Kent aren't the same as beliefs about Superman even though they have the same truth conditions as beliefs about Superman. As they stand these theories are irrelevant to problems about referential content for they take referential notions for granted. Field (1978) and Lycan (1981b) take referential semantics and functional role to be independent vectors; if so, functional role is no use in eliminating indeterminacies of reference.

Second, functional theories of content, with a few exceptions (Devitt, Millikan), concentrate on the inferential role of intentional states, with only an occasional nod to the role of inputs and outputs. This is a point that Devitt and Cowie particularly enjoy making. A concentration on inferential role is bad news for those who want to recruit functional considerations in explaining why **dog** refers to dogs. For:

1   An inferential role theory of content lumps us with a holistic theory of content. For the inferential productivity of an intentional state depends on the other intentional states of the system. The belief that wombats are ferocious prompts the belief that the moon is full if you happen also to believe that wombats are ferocious when the moon is full. Holistic theories of content make content idiosyncratic; people never act the same way because they believe the same thing, because they never do believe the same thing. Indeed, it is hard to see how I (or anyone) could explain an agent's behaviour by reference to belief content at all. For to do so I have to attribute intentional states to the agent. To do that, if inferential role determines content, I have to know the inferential role a belief has in the mind of the agent in whom I am interested. That, manifestly, is something I am not within a bull's roar of knowing about any agent but myself.

2   Perhaps this problem is not decisive. It may be possible to formulate a principled restriction on the kinds of inferential connection that are content relevant. If so, an inferential theory of content need not be a holistic theory of content. Even so, an inferential theory does not help solve the *qua*-problem. For that is a problem about the reference of concepts, and concepts do not have inferential roles. Only sentences, or sentence-like representations, have inferential roles. There is an old dispute in the philosophy of language between atomic and molecular theories of meaning. Defenders of atomic theories hope to derive an account of sentence meaning from their account of word meaning, together with their account of the language's syntax. Molecular theorists think that misguided. In their view the fundamental semantic notion is sentence meaning; their slogan is 'only in the context of a sentence does a word have meaning'. Causal theorists of meaning, both of language and thought, are the contemporary defenders of semantic atomism. Inferential role theories of content are the translations into the mental realm of molecular theories of meaning.

Almost all appeals to internal function in theories of content are inferential theories, or include a major inferential component. It is not an accident that theories emphasizing inference play down the role of input. It is very hard to give a functional picture of the join between input and belief. For it is at this point that everything the agent believes about her world is of potential relevance. If Fodor is right, part of the point of having a central processor is so we do not automatically believe what we perceive. Suppose your perceptual module delivers a snakish representation. It is by no means obvious that its normal function is to induce the belief that there is a snake present, or that it typically does so. Lots of people know that they are apt to false alarms about snakes, especially at night or in dense bush. For those who concentrate on the functional role of intentional states, the percept-belief transition is one locus of the notorious 'frame problem' (see chapter 10). No wonder input is downplayed in their account of functional role; no one rubs salt in their own wounds. But the upshot of all this for those defending a causal theory of content and looking for an additional filter to sort content relevant from content irrelevant causal relations, is that functional role theories are of exactly the wrong sort.

6.9 Back to the Future: An Empiricist Theory of Content

Not quite all appeals to functional role emphasize inferential role; Devitt's (1989) is input oriented, though it presumes a solution to, rather than solves the holism problem. I think input systems are the place to look if we want to recruit functional considerations to a theory of content. So I think Devitt is right to look to input. But not for his reasons. The crucial point is that input systems are, I am betting, Fodorian modules. Such modules have crucial properties that enable us to appeal to functional considerations.

Input systems are innately specified. That enables us to side-step the problems of holism, and the worst problems of the appeal to teleology. Consider first teleology. The structures that form modular representations do have a selective history to call their own; they are isolated and autonomous, at least by comparison to the intentional states our central processors form. Our perceptual modules are relatively froglike. Selective history licenses us to say that frogs have fly detectors, and that a black spot on some frog's retina is its representation of a fly because it's produced by a Normally working fly detector. Equally it licences us to say that humans have, for example, face detectors, and that some neural assembly is Eric's representation of Melanie's face, because that representation is produced by a modular mechanism with a determinate function, face recognition, operating Normally. Of course functional considerations alone will not tell us it is *Melanie's* face, but we do not need them to. Causal facts have a role to play too. Modules, unlike perhaps minds, do have predictable outputs in virtue of which they can be selected.

What of holism? Modular mechanisms, and the architecture of our modules, are invariant across our species. A problem with holistic theories of content is that holistic content is idiosyncratic content. Functionally defined modular representation need not be idiosyncratic.

For the internal states appealed to in the functional definition ought not be other *representations in the module*, but its *standing mechanisms*. The functional role, for example, of the symbols on the primal sketch should be defined *not* by the relations between the symbols on a sketch, but by the relations between a symbol and the mechanism that built the symbol, and the mechanisms that use it. Appealing to the standing mechanisms avoids idiosyncrasy. For those mechanisms are universal. So we can appeal to the *role* of a representation in determining its content if we appeal to its relations to those standing mechanism of the mind that have a determinate biological function and which are typical of the species. That is, we can appeal to role in considering representations formed by modules.

How might all this help in constructing a theory of content? In effect, I have in mind a modification of the hierarchical proposal Devitt and I made (Devitt and Sterelny, 1987). The semantic base consists, in this new view, of concepts that are formed from modular input systems. I propose to abandon a Kripkian account of the semantic properties of the representations the modules construct. I propose to replace it with a teleological account. The structure produced by the firing of a group of cones in our retina represents a colour, not a shade of colour or a particular intensity of light. Even though it is caused by some particular shade and some particular intensity. For the biological function of the cones, our colour vision receptors, is the representation of a stable and useful fact about our environment, namely the colour of surfaces. For colour vision, like many other modules, is serviced by constancy mechanisms. Perceptual representation is stable over dramatic changes in incoming stimuli. As I noted in discussing Dretske, the world does not appear to change colour when the sun comes from behind the cloud. Perceptual processing works to keep track of invariances in the world, not the varying stimulations from it. Teleology solves the depth *qua*-problem. I think it solves the breadth problem too. Our colour constancy mechanisms are not perfect; they do not work in dim light or in Abnormal illumination. A Granny Smith apple does not look green in starlight or under sodium lights. But our greenness detectors form the concept **green**, not **green or grey**. They simply aren't working in the dark. So when something green looks orange under sodium it is misrepresented. For the token concept is not formed by conditions of the same kind as those selectively responsible for the existence of the type. Base-level concepts are modular concepts.

Above the base, the story stays much the same, but not quite the same. Devitt and I gave a 'descriptive-causal' account of, for example, natural kind concepts like **tiger**. Eric has the concept of tigers partly in virtue of his causal contact with a tiger specimen, and partly in virtue of his descriptive knowledge of tigers. Both are required for possession of the concept. Causal contact without any descriptive knowledge is not sufficient, for the *qua*-problem is not solved. Descriptive knowledge is not in general enough, for very often people have concepts of kinds when they are seriously ignorant of, or badly mistaken about, those kinds. Mostly we do not have identifying knowledge of the referents of our concepts. So we had to suppose people had just enough knowledge of what they think about to solve the *qua*-problem, without attributing too much knowledge to concept owners. For it is just not true that you need to know a lot about something to have a concept of it. Think how little the Greeks knew about the heart, yet they had a concept of it. So we were fairly coy about just what knowledge was required in order to have a tiger concept. I can now be a little less coy. Given what I have just said about modules, the descriptive elements of **tiger** possession are not beliefs or intentional states, but the perceptual *Gestalt* of tigers. Marr argued that animals can be represented as a hierarchy of generalized cones, with a major cone representing the trunk of the body, others representing the head and major limbs attached to it and so on. This particular proposal may be wrong of course, but there will be (unless the modularity hypothesis is wrong root and branch) some coarse-grained purely perceptual representation of tigers. That representation, of course, has nothing like enough information in it to specify the necessary and sufficient conditions of being a tiger. Some tigers will not fit it; three-legged or otherwise nonstandard ones will not. Something could fit it without being a tiger. So the causal link with actual tigers is still necessary for possession of a **tiger** concept.

So, there are modular representations. There are concepts we can form on the basis of causal links and modular concepts. That provides, I think, enough cognitive background for the rest of the machinery Devitt and I posited. Other descriptive-causal concepts, and fully defined concepts, can be acquired on these foundations.

This view has much in common with a traditional philosophical program, concept empiricism. That program took sensory concepts to be fundamental, and given by our innate perceptual equipment. Other concepts, in particular, nonobservational ones, were to be defined directly in sensory terms, or indirectly via a chain of intermediaries. The similarities with my view are obvious. That similarity is a bit worrying, for no one ever succeeded in finding sensory definitions of nonsensory terms. But there are two very important differences between my program and traditional concept empiricism.

First, the properties modules represent are not sensory properties. I have laboured the point that constancy mechanisms in our perceptual systems give us excellent reason to claim that the modules represent objective features of the world, not features of our *experience* of it. But at least on some versions of concept empiricism, sensory properties were experiential properties. Even setting that aside, modular representation extends beyond the representation of shape, colour and the like. There are, likely enough, modules for the recognition of faces and phonemes. The candidates for modular representation are features of the world that (a) were biologically important to our ancestors, (b) are reasonably reliably detectable by an encapsulated special purpose mechanism. I do not know what those features are, but they certainly go well beyond sensory properties.

Second, it is not in general true that nonbase concepts are defined in terms of base ones. Perhaps some concepts do serve as abbreviations in the language of thought. Such concepts' semantic properties would depend entirely on those of the concepts they abbreviate. But many nonbase concepts' referential properties depend in part on causal links between concept and referent. I am not looking for definitions of the nonbase concepts, so I need not worry about the fact that there are so few of them.

In short, I think we need a conceptual foundationalism without definitions, and in which we give a teleological account of the content of base concepts. That's my best guess at a theory of content; in section 7.4 I will argue that it sheds light on acquisition, too.

Suggested Reading

Sections 6.1–6.3

Both Putnam and Schiffer reject the representational theory of mind largely because they think there is no naturalist explanation of meaning to be had. See Putnam's *Representation and Reality* (1988), especially the first two chapters, and Schiffer's *Remnants of Meaning* (1987), especially chapter 4. Neither work is easy though.

Kripkian causal theories of reference hit the streets in Kripke's *Naming and Necessity* (1980) and Putnam's 'The Meaning of "Meaning"' (1975b), a paper that extended the theory from names to natural kind terms and artifact terms. Devitt's *Designation* (1981) is rather dense, but develops causal theories for singular terms carefully and in detail; more importantly, Devitt, unlike Kripke, shows how causal theories fit into a naturalistic picture. I made my first attempt on the *qua*-problem in 'Natural Kind Terms' (1983) and again in *Language and Reality* (Devitt and Sterelny, (1987).

Section 6.4

The first major statement of indicator semantics is Dretske's *Knowledge and The Flow of Information* (1981), updated in his 'Misrepresentation' (1986a) and 'Aspects of Cognitive Representation' (1986b), and again in *Explaining Behaviour* (1988). A precis of *Knowledge and The Flow of Information* was published in *Behavioural and Brain Sciences* together with various critical responses, and his reply. Stampe is another early defender of this species of causal theory; see 'Towards a Causal Theory of Linguistic Representation' (1979), and 'Verification and a Causal Account of Meaning' (1986). Fodor presents his version in *Psychosemantics* (1988a), and updates it in *A Theory of Content I & II* (forthcoming). The best overview of these issues is Godfrey-Smith's *Misinformation* (1989), but Fodor's *Semantics, Wisconsin Style* (1984b) is a useful first response to Dretske.

Sections 6.5–6.7

Papineau tries out his teleological account in 'Representation and Explanation' (1984), and revises it slightly in 'Reality and Representation' (1987). Millikan's *Language, Thought and Other Biological Categories* (1984) is very dense. But fortunately her papers are very readable. Most salient are 'Thoughts Without Laws; Cognitive Science With Content' (1986), 'Biosemantics' (1989a) and 'Truth Rules, Hoverflies and the Kripke–Wittgenstein Paradox' (forthcoming a). She responds to Fodor on teleology, and gives his views a passing thump, in 'Speaking Up For Darwin' (forthcoming b). Dennett enters these muddy waters in a paper, 'Evolution, Error and Intentionality' (1987), in *The Intentional Stance* airing his scepticism about whether there really are hard facts about content at all. The Godfrey-Smith paper cited above, again, is a good overview. He argues, as does Millikan in 'Biosemantics', that teleological theories are not indicator theories in *Indication and Adaptation* (forthcoming).

Sections 6.8–6.9

Field's 'Mental Representations' (1978), Lycan's 'Towards A Homuncular Theory of Believing' (1981b) and McGinn's 'The Structure of Content' (1982) all offer 'two-factor' theories in which inferential role is the key component of functional role. Stich defends a multifactor theory in *From Folk Psychology to Cognitive Science* (1983) and 'On The Ascription of Content' (1982), but again inference plays a major role. Cowie points out how input considerations are played down and jumps on holism in *Three Kinds of Meaning Holism* (forthcoming); Devitt's 'A Narrow Representational Theory of the Mind' (1989) and chapter 3 of Fodor's *Psychosemantics* (1988a) are good on these issues too. For a very different appeal to teleology in giving an account of perceptual representation, see Matthen's 'Biological Functions and Perceptual Content' (1988).

7

Eliminativism

7.1 The 'Received View' of Propositional Attitudes

In the last two chapters, general methodological issues about the representational theory of mind have been fought out. In chapter 5, I argued that the appeal to mental representations plays an essential role in psychology; in chapter 6, that representation can be explained in more fundamental terms. In this chapter I focus on a range of sceptical views about the explanation of behaviour in terms of an agent's thoughts.

But first let me review the 'received view' of propositional attitude psychology. The received view is not everybody's view. Rather, it's an account of propositional attitude psychology attempting to meet three demands: (a) to allow propositional attitude psychology to be integrated within theoretical cognitive psychology; (b) to throw light on the semantics of propositional attitude ascriptions, i.e. to sentences like 'John believes that pigs are wingless' or 'Max hopes that snow will remain white'; and (c) to do reasonable justice to the way we actually use propositional attitude psychology in day-to-day life. Lycan, Field and Fodor (amongst others) have argued that we can satisfy all three demands by seeing propositional attitudes as a relation between an agent (the individual who has the thought in question) and a sentence token of the agent's language of thought. To believe that pigs are wingless is to token in a functionally appropriate way within your 'central processor' a sentence in your language of thought that means that pigs are wingless (sections 2.2–2.3). Filling out this idea is, as we have already seen, no trivial task. The last chapter was devoted to the construction of a theory of meaning for the language of thought. The Field–Fodor–Lycan theory requires for its completion an account of meaning. It also requires a theory of how an internal sentence can be a belief rather than a hope, a fear, a desire, an assumption, and so on. We need to know the difference between believing, desiring, hoping and so on. The 'received view' has quite a lot going for it.

1   The language of thought hypothesis integrates propositional attitude psychology with cognitive psychology. In sections 2.2 and 2.3, in particular, I reviewed the psychological case for the received view. We can explain the systematicity and productivity of thought, and its parallels with language, if thought tokens are a species of sentence tokens. Moreover, important facets of cognitive processing fall naturally into place if we think in mentalese. For the role that beliefs and desires play in the causation of behaviour will be explicable in terms of the computational relations amongst the inner sentence tokens, and, more generally, in terms of the functional relations between inner sentences, perceptual inputs and behavioural outputs.

2   Lycan and Fodor emphasize the virtues this view has for giving an account of the semantics of propositional attitude *ascriptions*. If so, that's a major advantage. A theory of beliefs, desires, and the like ought to make it unmysterious how we can talk about them. Some theories of propositional attitudes fail to meet this criterion, for they hold that propositional attitudes are attitudes not to psychological objects but to abstract objects, propositions. It is not at all clear what propositions are, but on every view of them, they are weird; sets of 'possible worlds', for example. Abstract objects, by definition, are not located in space and time and have no causal relations to any object (such as a person) who is so located. It is hard to understand how we can talk about thoughts, if thoughts are relations to such mysterious things.

Propositional attitude ascriptions have some striking semantical features. First, note that anyone who understands propositional attitude attributions at all understands an indefinitely large number of them. You will understand not just

John believes that pigs are wingless

but as well indefinitely many other ascriptions of belief to John. Take any freestanding indicative sentence that you understand; prefix to it 'John believes that' and you will understand the resulting belief attribution. This fact demonstrates that 'believes that pigs are wingless', 'fears that worms have teeth' and so on are not primitive, undefined predicates. They are unlike 'green' or 'punchy' in this regard. For if they were undefinable predicates, there would be an indefinitely large number of them, all semantically unrelated, and, in consequence, they would have to be learned one by one. Since there would be indefinitely many, that's not possible, for the language of propositional attitudes would be unlearnable in finite time. Since we learn it in finite time, the complex 'believes-that- pigs-are-wingless' is semantically composite. How could it be so? A natural suggestion is to take a propositional attitude ascription not to attribute a simple property to John, but to state a relation between John and some other entity: an entity indicated by the clause 'that pigs are wingless'. Lycan, for example, suggests that we see the logical form of a propositional attitude sentence as something like

Tom believes one of those. Worms have no fangs.

Propositional attitudes, thus, are 'construed as a dyadic relation that a person bears to a linguistic or quasi-linguistic token that falls into a certain category' (Lycan, 1981b, p. 142) The view that thoughts are mental sentences could scarcely fit better with this account of their ascriptions. Moreover, there is a famous puzzle about propositional attitude sentences that this view helps to solve. For such sentences yield so-called 'opaque' contexts. Ordinarily, the substitution in a sentence of one co-referential term by another preserves truth. Thus

Uranus' orbit lies between Saturn and Neptune

is true, and substituting for 'Neptune' the phrase 'the planet discovered by Herschell' we get another true sentence. But from

Toby believes that Uranus' orbit lies between
Saturn and Neptune

it by no means follows that

Toby believes that Uranus' orbit lies between
Saturn and the planet discovered by Herschell

for Toby, keen amateur astronomer but utter ignoramus about the history of his subject, wouldn't know Herschell if he was bitten by him. This fact about propositional attitude ascriptions has posed theorists of language deep problems. The 'that clause' is semantically structured, so its semantic properties are a function of (a) its syntactic structure, and (b) the semantic features of its elements. But it is hard to reconcile the view that the meaning of 'that the orbit of Uranus lies between Saturn and Neptune' is a function of the clause's structure and elements with the fact that the semantic role of one of the elements ('Uranus') seems to have changed because it's in a clause which ascribes a belief. We can't build the semantics of whole out of the blocks, if being in that particular whole alters the blocks.

This problem has funded a small, but high-tech industry in philosophy. Seeing propositional attitudes as inner sentences suggests an intuitive solution to it. For, as Fodor points out, we can see the opacity of propositional attitude ascription as like the opacity of quotation, about which there is no mystery. From the fact that Edith wrote

Churchill was a fascist reactionary

on the blackboard, and the fact that Churchill was the greatest British leader of the century, it by no means follows that Edith wrote

The greatest British political leader of the century was a fascist reactionary

on the blackboard. Chances are, she didn't. Now, if propositional attitudes are relations to sentence tokens written on a mental blackboard, of course it won't follow that because Toby has written one token on his board, he must also have written on it another token semantically related to the first. The opacity of propositional attitudes becomes as unproblematic as the opacity of quotation, if the idea that attitudes are relations to inner tokens can be got to work.

3 How well does the language of thought theory of propositional attitude psychology comport with the intuitive data? Do we in fact take people to have the beliefs, desires and other attitudes that this theory predicts? On this issue, there is a good deal of controversy. Dennett, for example, has argued (Dennett, 1982, and elsewhere) that the language of thought view imposes unreasonably strict conditions on the identity of propositional attitudes; Putnam (1988) seems to have similar views. Dennett argues that it is a consequence of the 'received view' that two individuals can only believe the same thing if they token instances of the same sentence in their (common) language of thought. Dennett (1981b) tells a little story to illustrate the implausibility of such a strong requirement:

Jacques shoots his uncle dead in Trafalgar Square and is immediately arrested by Sherlock. Tom reads about it in the *Guardian* and Boris learns of it in *Pravda*. Now Jacques, Sherlock, Tom and Boris have had remarkably different experiences, to say nothing of their earlier biographies and future prospects. But they all believe that a Frenchman has committed murder in Trafalgar Square. They did not all say this 'to themselves'; and even if they had, doing so would have had entirely different import for Jacques, Sherlock, Tom and Boris. Yet they all believe that a Frenchman committed murder in Trafalgar Square. Dennett gives other examples making the same point; namely that an intentional identity between agents is compatible with arbitrarily great design differences. Dennett believes that the received view incorrectly ties intentional commonalities between agents to design commonalities.

Dennett could equally well have made his point in terms of those standbys of functionalist science fiction, the sentient Martian, or the genuinely intelligent computer. We can reasonably assume that they do not think in human mentalese, in virtue of the Martian's and the computer's differing internal organization. Yet surely we, the computer, and the Martian can all hope that the sun doesn't go nova. In short, we can see Dennett as advancing a familiar charge: the language of thought view of propositional attitude psychology is chauvinist. In defining the essential conditions of having a certain thought too concretely, it denies sentience of a certain type unwarrantedly.

Dennett's worry can be met. I have claimed (section 2.3) that intentional states are realized by relations to sentences in a language of thought. Like other functional states, they can be multiply realized. We sometimes count thoughts as the same if they have the same truth conditions. In that sense, at least, sentences in different languages of thought can realize the same type of belief, for sentences in distinct varieties of mentalese can have the same truth conditions. Perhaps if human, Martian and Hal-ish mentalese are very different, there is some sense in which their thoughts are all different. But they could each token a sentence, in their different languages of thought, with the truth condition: 'Oh dear, the sun's going nova.' Hence they could all believe that the sun is going nova.

Let's summarize. The idea is to take thoughts to be realized by relations to sentences of mentalese. I have claimed three significant advantages for this view of the nature of propositional attitude psychology (a) it enables us to fit propositional attitude psychology into a decent general theory of the nature of the mind, (b) it enables us to tell a sensible story of how propositional attitudes are ascribed, (c) it has reasonable fidelity to our intuitive, commonsense views of who has what thoughts when. Let me turn now to objections: both to this view of propositional attitude psychology, and, more generally, to the view that propositional attitude psychology is worth preserving.

7.2 Is Folk Psychology a Degenerating Research Program?

Paul Churchland, in a vivid and forceful paper (P. M. Churchland, 1981), has argued that once we see clearly that folk psychology is a theory, we ought to see that it is quite likely to be a radically false theory. Consequently it is likely that there are no intentional states. Churchland is inclined towards *eliminativism*, the view that the central terms of intentional psychology – 'belief' and 'desire' – are empty; they apply to nothing. Three elements go into Churchland's eliminativism.

Firstly, Churchland emphasizes the Quinian rating of a theory, and downplays its merely empiric virtues. Thus (as we shall shortly see) Churchland heaps calumny upon intentional psychology on the grounds that it fits badly into the rest of our picture of our mind, and because it fails to guide research. Churchland does not really dispute the claim that intentional psychology is predictively powerful, and is so in a domain of human activity, deliberate action, in which it has no real rivals. But this merely empirical virtue does not outweigh its alleged systemic vices; the fact that intentional prediction saves our life on the road is not enough to make it a well-confirmed scientifically credible theory.

Secondly, Churchland's ontological conclusion, namely that there probably are no beliefs or desires, is partly fuelled by his semantic views. Churchland holds that the meaning of a term derives from its theoretical role. Thus, for example, the term 'gene' derives its meaning from a bundle of laws about reproduction and inheritance of traits across generations. The term applies to those objects of which gene-theory is more or less true. This semantic theory promotes eliminativism because a badly mistaken theory is true of nothing, hence its distinctive vocabulary is empty. Churchland (1979, pp. 16–25), for instance, discusses a slightly idealized version of the caloric theory of heat according to which heat is a fluid. Different types of material pass this fluid at differential rates and can absorb different amounts of it. Churchland asks us to imagine a society in which the caloric theory is accepted wisdom, and takes it to be intuitively clear that 'heat' as used by caloric-thinkers is empty. When they use the word 'heat' they refer to nothing. I think Churchland is wrong about this; when a Caloric speaker explains a burn by saying she touched 'an object through which much caloric was flowing', she speaks truly. For 'high caloric pressure' in Caloric refers to a high mean molecular kinetic energy. We can refer to objects whose nature we importantly misunderstand. Astronomy provides an obvious example. Ptolemaic astronomy badly misunderstood the nature of the planets and the stars. But defenders of geocentric astronomy were wrong *about the planets* in writing that they moved around the earth; in writing that, they were not writing of nothing. In moving from geocentric to heliocentric astronomy, we changed our mind about the nature of the planets, rather than starting to believe things about them for the first time. Defenders of theoretical role semantics have great difficulties saying anything plausible about examples like this, and consequently great difficulties in giving a coherent account of scientific progress. If, for example, Newtonian theory is importantly false, then 'mass', 'force' and the other terms of Newtonian physics refer to nothing. How then can we see it as the vast improvement it is over the neo-medieval views it replaced. The solution to these problems is to downplay the importance of theoretical role in our account of meaning in giving some kind of causal theory of the reference of natural kind terms, (sections 6.1–6.3) Those accounts explain how we can refer to entities and kinds of entities of whose nature we are ignorant. It follows that even if Churchland is right in thinking that intentional psychology is badly flawed, the eliminativist moral does not follow. We might stand to beliefs and desires as the Greeks stood to planets and stars: right in recognizing their existence, but wrong about their nature.

Thirdly, Churchland thinks that there are important alternatives to the view that the mind is a sentential machine, accounts of cognition and representation much more closely tied to the neurosciences. I will consider one of those alternatives in the next chapter.

Let's return to Churchland's reasons for thinking intentional psychology is deeply flawed. He thinks it is a degenerating research program: it's a view of the human mind that is failing to deliver new insights; failing to solve new problems. On the contrary, in a flash of splendid rhetoric he urges:

A look at the history of FP does little to allay such fears, once raised. The story is one of retreat, infertility, and decadence. The presumed domain of FP used to be much larger than it is now. In primitive cultures, the behavior of most of the elements of nature were understood in intentional terms. The wind could know anger, the moon jealousy, the river generosity, the sea fury, and so forth. These were not metaphors. Sacrifices were made and auguries undertaken to placate or divine the changing passions of the gods. Despite its sterility, this animistic approach to nature has dominated our history, and it is only in the last two or three thousand years that we have restricted FP's literal application to the domain of the higher animals.

Even in this preferred domain, however, both the content and the success of FP have not advanced sensibly in two or three thousand years. The FP of the Greeks is essentially the FP we use today, and we are negligibly better at explaining human behaviour in its terms than was Sophocles. This is a very long period of stagnation and infertility for any theory to display, especially when faced with such an enormous backlog of anomalies and mysteries in its own explanatory domain. (pp. 74–5)

Its failure to progress is not all that Churchland urges against folk psychology. It is in his view an exceedingly limited theory as well: failing to provide insight into a range of central features of human psychology. Churchland instances in this connection: sleep, mental illness, visual perception, sensory-motor coordination, learning. There is much about our mental life on which our folk theory is silent.

Furthermore, and perhaps most important of all, folk theory fails to integrate with the rest of our self-knowledge. The physical sciences (including everything from particle physics to evolutionary theory and neuroscience) are close to an integrated theory of the human animal; an integration which has no room for folk psychology.

What should we say of a theory which is limited; which has failed to provide new insight in living memory; one which is theoretically isolated from the best of our systematic knowledge, the natural sciences? Surely we should say that the theory is probably false. But how just is this critique of propositional attitude psychology?

The justice of Churchland's critique depends on the relationship between propositional attitude psychology and cognitive psychology. For consider this obvious defence of folk psychology:

P1   Folk psychology is a central part of cognitive psychology: endowing cognitive psychology with a budget both of theoretical tools, and theoretical problems.

P2   Cognitive psychology is not stagnant, and is much less limited than folk theory as Churchland pictures it. Nor does it fail to integrate with the physical sciences, for cognitive processes must be neurally implemented.

C   So folk psychology is probably appoximately true.

The first of these premises is in fact quite controversial: there is a good deal of debate on the exact nature of the relations between folk and cognitive psychology. Fodor and Pylyshyn both at times suggest that cognitive psychology's central role is to explain how intentional processes are computationally implemented; to explain, for instance, just how humans reason in the ways folk theory says they do. That is to see folk psychology as a major chunk of the ecological theory of the human mind. Others (Stich for one) have thought cognitive psychology can and should be divorced from cognitive psychology. But the Churchlands are in no position to take this line, for they are sceptical about cognitive psychology in part because it is infected with the theoretical suppositions of folk theory.

In any case, to run a defence of folk theory along these lines, I need only defend a moderate thesis. I need only claim that the domain of cognitive psychology includes and incorporates folk psychology. A folk psychology incorporated within cognitive psychology is unlikely to be unchanged: doubtless any folk theory needs to be cleaned up and made precise in various ways. For instance, the folk theoretic notion of implicit belief might drop out of a theory which identified beliefs and desires with explicit memory and motivational states in our central processor.

Suppose, then, that folk theory can be made a part of cognitive psychology. What would Churchland's discussion look like then? It would look much less convincing.

First, folk theory would look more progressive. For it would have played a role in the development of theories that do address perception, memory and language use. For example, propositional network theories of memory borrow their central notion – a thought – from folk psychology. For the same reason, folk psychology will look less limited. Cognitive psychologists try to say things about memory, learning, perception and the like. If what they say is worth saying, and if it draws on notions provided by folk psychology, then Churchland's claim that 'On these and many other mental phenomena, folk psychology sheds negligible light' is false.

Furthermore, we should remember that cognitive psychology is a multi-level theory of the mind. We can discuss the mind at many levels: folk theory is the most abstract of these. The homuncular ground plan of an intentional system (section 1.3) is simple, abstracting away from many details of our psychological organization. So we would expect there to be many mental phenomena on which folk psychology is silent. All those facts about our mental life that depend entirely on *how* propositional attitudes are stored, and *how* reasoning is implemented, will be facts about which propositional attitude psychology has nothing to say. For its point is to abstract away from implementation.

What of integration? Defenders of cognitive psychology regard it as part of the very naturalistic synthesis that Churchland embraces. Cognitive processes must be neurally implemented. An implementation thus serves as the bridge between the theories of cognitive science and the theories of materialist neuroscience. Cognitive psychology is no kind of dualism. If a cleaned-up propositional attitude psychology is part of cognitive psychology, it is not dualist.

What might Churchland say to all this? His resistance, I think, is likely to be on two fronts. He might endorse Patricia Churchland's charge that cognitive psychology is an inadequate theory of mind because of its reliance on a sentential model of mental representation. As shall shortly be seen, Patricia Churchland thinks that there are a bundle of arguments to show that the central mode of mental representation is not sentential. So she agrees the language of thought hypothesis is central to propositional attitude psychology, but that very assumption shows the empirical inadequacy of folk psychology. Folk theory is true only if there is a language of thought. There is no language of thought, so folk theory is not true. To the extent that Paul Churchland relies on this argument against a cleaned up propositional attitude psychology, his argument collapses into hers.

Churchland has an independent argument against the picture I have offered in defence of intentional psychology. I have argued that that psychology is abstract; it is uncommitted to details of the format and transformation of sentential representations in the brain. But Churchland thinks that there are good reasons to be deeply suspicious about abstract, functional descriptions of psychological processes. For he thinks that functionalizing a theory can be an obscurantist dodge; a ploy to escape refutation. He gives a very nice example: alchemy could have been insulated from refutation by going functionalist:

Being 'ensouled by mercury,' or 'sulphur,' or either of the other two so-called spirits, is actually a functional state. The first, for example, is defined by the disposition to reflect light, to liquefy under heat, to unite with other matter in the same state, and so forth. And each of these four states is related to the others, in that the syndrome for each varies as a function of which of the other three states is also instantiated in the same substrate. Thus the level of description comprehended by the alchemical vocabulary is abstract: various material substances, suitably 'ensouled', can display the features of a metal, for example, or even of gold specifically. For it is the total syndrome of occurrent and causal properties which matters, not the corpuscularian details of the substrate. Alchemy, it is concluded, comprehends a level of organization in reality distinct from and irreducible to the organization found at the level of corpuscularian chemistry. (1981, p. 80)

Churchland's warning is well made. But it can surely be no more than a warning that vacuously functionalizing a theory is both tempting and inadmissible, and that is a point I conceded in section 1.2. We cannot reasonably take Churchland to have produced an argument against all theories whose central kinds are functional. As Lycan loves to point out, 'neuron' itself is a functional term. Further, one that is multiply realized: there are different kinds of neurons, and they differ in their biochemical bases. There are different chemicals that function as neurotransmitters, taking excitation or inhibition (again: these are functional concepts) across the synoptic connections that link different neurons. Another brutally biological functional term is 'heart'. Hearts are objects functionally defined: they come in different designs (for example, in the number of chambers) but they have in common a function: the circulation of blood. In my view, most of biology deals with functional kinds (section 1.2), so biological theories are functional theories.

So the charge against propositional attitude theory or cognitive psychology cannot be: it is illegitimate to traffic in functional notions. It must rather be: some functional theories are no good; going functional merely disguises their emptiness. What reason have we for thinking folk theory is not one of these? But to this sceptical question there does indeed seem to be an answer. The first chapter of Fodor's (1988a) is a hymn of praise to the predictive virtues of folk psychology. Even if we suspect Fodor of gilding the lily a trifle, we can predict (and some of us can manipulate) the behaviour of others via the attribution to them of intentional states. Typically, in these situations we have no other means of prediction and control. But, after the rise of atomic chemistry, that was simply not true of Churchland's hypothetical functionalized alchemy. So folk psychology has predictive power that functional alchemy lacked; that's a difference we are entitled to think significant.

Jackson and Pettit (in their (forthcoming)) make even stronger claims about the epistemic strength of folk psychology. They agree with the Churchlands and Fodor that folk theory is, indeed, a theory, in particular, a functionalist theory. But they regard it as particularly secure, holding that it hardly outruns its empirical base. They offer the following analogy. Suppose you punch 4 on your pocket calculator, then 7, and 11 appears on the screen. You adopt the functional hypothesis than when you punch n, the calculator stores n. Of course, this hypothesis goes beyond the evidence, but after a few trials the hypothesis would be overwhelmingly credible, however much doubt remained about *how* n was stored. Now it is true (they concede) that the functional hypotheses of folk psychology are much more complex than the one concerning number storing, but they have been tested much more often. In their view, folk psychology is functionalist, and is hence uncommitted to claims about physical implementation, and is equally uncommitted on many of the details of psychological organization. So it is particularly secure. It competes, they think, only with the idea that it is a matter of chance that people behave as if they had beliefs and desires. The chance hypothesis is, as they say, incredible.

I think folk psychology is empirically well supported. But I think Jackson and Pettit overstate the case. Return to the calculator. There are alternative pictures of the functional organization of the calculator. On these alternative pictures it is not a fluke that the calculator appears to obey the simple principle 'if n is punched, n is stored'. For over a certain range of inputs, the alternative picture predicts the same behaviour as the simple picture. Perhaps the calculator obeys the principle 'on the first m trials, if n is punched, store n; on the $m + 1$th trial, store $n + 1$; on the $m + 2$th trial, store $n + 2$; . . .'. We mostly can eliminate a principle like that because we know that calculators are designed, and there would usually be no point in designing such a malicious instrument. (It might have a use in a psychology lab, however). Now consider, for example, various folk theoretic laws of thought. Perhaps one of these is that we typically apply *modus ponens* 'If an agent believes p, and believes if p then q, the agent will tend to come to believe q'. There are alternative accounts of our functional organization that will coincide with this hypothesis in restricted domains, and will hence explain why we seem to obey this principle without actually doing so. Perhaps we obey these principles only if p, q are about certain domains. The *modus ponens* principle takes inference to be context independent. If it truly describes us, how we reason is unaffected by what we are reasoning about. If that is not so, folk theory will *appear* to be true of us; it will not be just chance that its predictions are often true. But none the less, it will misdescribe our functional organization.

So folk theory, like other theories, does outrun its empirical base. It also has empirical failures. Further, even when we predict right, those predictions are rough and qualitative. My students can predict what I shall talk about, but they cannot predict the words I will use. Still, its empirical virtues are unchallenged by any rival in the same domain. Without positive reason for suspicion, there is no reason to conclude that folk theory is fundamentally false, or is a vacuous functional theory. Churchland's moral is a serious one: it is important but difficult to rule out vacuous functional theories. But he has no case for taking folk psychology to be vacuous, and his case for thinking it false rests on two insufficiently argued thoughts (a) propositional attitude psychology cannot be integrated with cognitive psychology, or (b) cognitive psychology is (likely to be) empirically worthless.

7.3 Is Folk Psychology Parochial?

Stich has argued that the kinds of intentional psychology are not the kinds required for a genuine theory of the mind. Stich agrees with Putnam and Burge that the kinds of folk psychology are not individualist. Two beliefs are of the same type only if they have the same (or similar) content. Content, as we saw in chapter 5, is not an individualist notion. But Stich's bad news is that content is gradient, multidimensional, pragmatic and parochial.

Let me outline Stich's theory of belief attribution. Suppose I attribute to Igor the belief that doves are timid because they have no teeth. What would make this attribution true? First, Igor's belief must be similar to some possible belief of mine. Namely the belief state that would typically cause (or would play some distinguished role in the causation) of an assertion by me of 'Doves are timid because they don't have teeth.' When we attribute a belief we identify it via a kind of mime: it's the belief that would be the cause of an assertion of the that-clause, were I to utter it.

So, on Stich's view, belief identity is an attributer-relative notion. I attribute beliefs to others on the basis of an implicit comparison with myself. That's already bad news for the notion of content. But there is worse to follow. For Stich thinks the implicit comparison is (a) a similarity notion, and (b) multi-dimensional. Different belief tokens count as beliefs of the same type not in all being the same, but in virtue of all being similar. That might already be a problem. Tokens of gold – a paradigm natural kind – are all exactly alike in atomic number; all stars, without exception, are alike in generating energy by fusion. Admittedly, the members of a biological species are not all alike; nor is there any guarantee that they all share a property that is also peculiar to them. But, first, there is some doubt that species are natural kinds, and, secondly, species don't shade into one another. Each dog is more like every dog than like any bear: there are no intermediate bear-dogs. So at least species clump together, even if they share no identifiable defining characteristic. If belief tokens are typed in virtue only of the similarities they have to each other, will they clump? It may be that Igor's belief is intermediate between the states I would express by 'Doves are timid because they don't have teeth' and 'Doves are timid because they don't have fangs'. So what belief should I attribute to Igor?

Stich thinks the problem is not just that I attribute beliefs to others on grounds of their similarity to some possible state of mine. The similarity in question is multi-dimensional. Stich identifies three bases of similarity: internal functional role, doxastic surround, truth conditions.

One dimension along which the belief of another can be like a belief of mine is in similarity of internal functional role, in particular, inferential role. The importance of this ingredient in belief ascription is most plausibly seen when it fails. So Stich invites us to consider a sequence of Daves, Dave I to Dave IX. Dave I has a relatively minor inferential deficit: he has lost transitivity. He will not infer from $[a \rightarrow b$ and $b \rightarrow c]$ to $[a \rightarrow c]$. By the time we get to Dave IX, even *modus ponens* has gone. We are invited to share two views. First, by the time we get to Dave IX we are disinclined to ascribe to him any beliefs. Dave IX is perfectly prepared to announce that Gorbachev is the premier of USSR. But does he believe it? For, even though he also announces that if Gorbachev is the premier, then he is Russian, he cannot draw the conclusion that Gorbachev is Russian. Second, we are invited to share Stich's view that there is no clear point in our sequence of Daves where Dave N is no believer that Gorbachev is premier, but Dave $(N - 1)$ is. So, Stich concludes, inferential role plays a role in belief identity, but only in a graded way.

Doxastic surround, the other beliefs of the person, can also play a role. One of Stich's illustrative examples has now become very well known; I too will discuss it. It's a somewhat idealized version of a real case.

Mrs T is a woman, now old, who in her youth was deeply impressed by the assassination of McKinley. For most of her adult life, Mrs T incontrovertibly believed that McKinley was assassinated. But in her old age Mrs T became senile, and progressively lost her memory. No doubt in senility there are other cognitive losses as well: the idealization comes through Stich's asking us to suppose that this form of senility affected only memory. So Mrs T's beliefs started to fade away: the sentences in her language of thought begin to be erased. At first only a few go: she forgets the name of McKinley's wife; of the then Vice-President. At this stage, surely she still believes that McKinley was assassinated. But more goes, until ultimately only 'McKinley was assassinated' is still written in her brain. She no longer even recalls, Stich points out, that the assassinated are dead. All she can do is mouth 'McKinley was assassinated'.

Surely Mrs T now no longer believes that McKinley was assassinated. But, *ex hypothesi*, the inferential potential of her mental token is unchanged. For we have joined Stich in imagining Mrs T has suffered only a memory loss; her inferential and other cognitive capacities are unchanged. But on Stich's view it's the *potential* causal role that is relevant to our first dimension of content similarity. For Stich wants to say that the sentence token 'All politicians are liars' doesn't have a different inferential role in the head of Paul Churchland than it has in mine, because I know, and Churchland doesn't, that David Lange is a politician. So it follows that the inferential role of Mrs T's token belief 'McKinley was assassinated' is unchanged. So if all that mattered to belief identity were inferential role, Mrs T would still count as believing McKinley was assassinated.

Stich concludes that doxastic surround is also important. The sadly decrepit Mrs T contrasts with her earlier self in now having a very different (and much impoverished) doxastic surround. That's why we no longer count her beliefs as the same. This conclusion is crucial to Stich's ultimate scepticism about belief. For doxastic surround is clearly a similarity notion at best; no two people will ever have the same doxastic pattern. Further, the role of doxastic surround in content determination makes it impossible, in Stich's view, for us to attribute beliefs to exotics, to those with very different beliefs and desires. Consequently, if doxastic surround is important to intentional identity, intentional psychology is limited to people like us. It is parochial.

Finally, the referential properties of intentional states are relevant to their individuation. In showing this, Stich makes points that are familiar from the Twin Earth literature, but without using extraterrestial examples. In view of the discussion in chapter 5, we can quickly grant his point here: two individuals can have similar, or even identical, internal psychological organizations, yet, in virtue of their different histories, not be in the same intentional states.

So intentional states are tokens of the same type if they have similar contents. But there is not one but three ways in which belief tokens might be similar. Worse, which way counts depends on pragmatic features of the local context of belief attribution. Do I and a physicist have the same belief in believing that some quarks are up quarks, and others, down quarks? For some purposes, Stich urges, yes. 'For $1,000,000, which particles have the properties up or down?' For other purposes, it is not so. If you want an explanation of those properties, don't come to me.

Let's suppose that Stich is right about all this. To preserve intentional psychology, we need an account of intentional taxonomy: of when token thoughts are tokens of the same type. Stich undertakes to provide us with such a taxonomy. Intentional identity requires content identity; content identity (really, content similarity) factors into three elements. Intentional ascription requires the ascriber to produce a content sentence (the that-clause) that is (a) similar in content to the thinker's belief state, and (b) is the sentence the ascriber would assert if he had that same belief. If Stich is right about the taxonomy of intentional states, he is surely right about the bleak prospects for incorporating intentional psychology within cognitive psychology. No science needs notions taxonomized not just in virtue of similarities, but similarities in three independent vectors whose importance varies according to context. No science needs kinds that can be ascribed only if the investigator and the subject are sufficiently similar.

Much of what Stich says about his examples is plausible. It is not clear what, if anything, Mrs T (senile) or Dave IX believe. So I need an account of intentional identity that, by and large, agrees with Stich's judgement on the cases, but which offers an alternative account of them. In particular, belief attribution must not be observer dependent. If Stich is right about that, he really has struck a fatal blow against the idea that intentional psychology is good protoscience. For the kinds of science are not observer dependent.

I think Stich's views about the nature of intentional kinds can be resisted. Some of his examples are not problems of content; they are not problems of saying *which* belief an agent has. Rather, they are cases where the agent has no belief at all; they are too dysfunctional to be intentional systems. In other cases, the theory of content defended in the last chapter shows how to accommodate Stichian intuitions while resisting his account of content. Two intentional states have the same content if they have the same structure and are composed out of the same concepts. Structure derives from the mechanisms that build complex representations. But what of concepts? In considering them, a difference in grain emerges. We can count concepts as the same if their referents are the same, giving us a coarse account of content identity. We get a finer filter if we count concepts as the same only if the mechanisms of reference are also the same. Let's consider how all this bears on Mrs T and the others.

For Mrs T to believe that McKinley was assassinated she must have the concept of assassination. At the limit of her breakdown, she does not. In section 6.9, I argued that many concepts are descriptive causal, or descriptive. Very likely it is not possible to have the concept **yacht** without having the concept **boat**. I think it equally likely that there is no having a concept of assassination without concepts of killing and death. But Mrs T has lost the link between **assassination** and these concepts. So Mrs T (senile) is functionally different from Mrs T (compos). Whatever the shape of the symbols on her VDU, she is conceptually impoverished. She no longer has an assassination concept, so irrespective of her inferential powers, she no longer has any beliefs about assassinations. She has no mechanism of reference for **assassinate**, so even our coarse filter does not count her as believing that McKinley was assassinated. The same point can be made about other examples.

Mrs T, deep in her senility, no longer has any beliefs, *ergo* not the belief that McKinley was assassinated. She is no longer an intentional system. An eight-year-old who can say '$E = mc^2$' certainly has plenty of beliefs. But it is reasonably plausible to say that the child is not expressing a belief (but merely parroting a phrase) or, at least, not expressing a belief about energy, mass and the relationship between them. Perhaps the kid is expressing a belief about what adults say given certain verbal cues. Similarly, Dave IX is in such poor cognitive shape that he too is out of the intentionality business altogether. His mental states do not have the functional profile shared by all beliefs. They have next to no inferential role at all. If, as many think, perceptual recognition involves inference, Dave IX will not even be able to learn from perception.

It is important to find alternative accounts of Stich's examples. For his assessment of them is often very plausible. The alternative on offer is importantly distinct from Stich's theory, for it is not ex officio a parochial theory. In ascribing an intentional state to another, we are not automatically though implicitly comparing that other to ourself. It's parochiality of content identity that would make content so unsuitable for scientific psychology.

Let's consider some of Stich's other cases. He makes great play of our inability to ascribe beliefs/desires to very alien cultures, to prelinguistic children, and to adults. Evans-Prichard reports that in certain circumstances the Nuer are prepared to claim that a sacrificial cucumber is an ox. Stich emphasizes that it is at least very misleading to report the Nuer belief with a simple that- clause: the Nuer believes that some cucumbers are oxen. Analogous problems arise for prelinguistic children and animals. It can often be compellingly plausible to ascribe a belief to an animal, but, equally, there seem real indeterminacies in which belief to ascribe. Consider a fearful chimp, having caught wind of something dangerous in a tree. Does it believe that there is a leopard in the tree; some carnivore in the tree; something dangerous in the tree? Does it have a concept of a tree, or just of treelike things? All things considered, can we just report the chimp as believing that *p*, for any particular *p* that *we* can express?

These examples are harder to meet than those concerning Mrs T and her ilk. For it is very difficult to specify the truth conditions of exotic intentional states, and thus hard for this account of intentional identity to get a grip. What are the truth conditions of the Nuer's beliefs, or the chimps? It clearly won't do to say the Nuer have no beliefs at all. But what are the truth conditions of their belief expressed by (the Nuerese equivalent of) 'Some cucumbers are oxen'. The chimp case is also difficult. It is, I suppose, tenable to say that the chimp has no beliefs, but only rather belief-like states, hence our psychology need not extend to chimps. But it doesn't seem very plausible, so, we are confronted with a Nuer-like problem. Is the chimp's belief true if there is a twin leopard, or a dummy leopard in the tree? If it is no tree but only a tree-like construction?

Perhaps the appropriate response is to say that the puzzlement generated by these problems is empirical. It's not generated by our having different, equally valid, ways of taxonomizing beliefs. It's not generated, as Stich believes, by the ascriber-relativity of intentional ascription. It's generated by our profound, but contingent and empirical, ignorance of Nuer and chimp psychology. Our uncertainty about the truth conditions of the chimp's beliefs is generated by our uncertainty of the range of application of the chimp concepts. (For the great empirical diificulties in getting a grip on the extension of primate concepts, see Premack (1986).)

We can, and need to be able to, resist Stich's view that we can in principle only describe the intentional states of those who are intentionally like us. But that is not the whole of Stich's scepticism about the suitability of intentional psychology as scientific psychology. He argues that belief tokens share only *similarities* in content, not *identity*. Again, Mrs T is deployed. When does she cease to believe that McKinley was assassinated? At no *point*, Stich urges: her loss is gradual. Similarly, Stich thinks that it is arbitrary to pick a particular point on the sequence of Daves as the point where the belief that Gorbachev is premier is lost. Fodor responds that Stich only shows that our belief epistemology is gradient: we don't know when to stop saying that she has that belief (Fodor, 1987, p. 62 and the footnote to that page). I think this is a mistake, for I see no discovery that would enable us to be more determinate. I think Mrs T's loss of belief is gradient. But not because content identity ought to be replaced by content similarity, but because the functional signature of *being a belief* comes in degrees. There is a continuity of cognitive capacity from us to cockroaches and beyond. Creatures insufficiently sophisticated to have intentional states can yet be close or less close. Mrs T ends up not very close at all. But her loss of capacity, we can grant, is gradual. Hence I agree, with Stich, that there is no point at which we can say: here she loses the belief that McKinley was assassinated.

But does this matter? There is no point at which, in the development of a photosensitive patch of membrane to the vulture's eye, we can say: here is the first, most rudimentary, eye. Yet eyes are natural kinds of physiology. The conditions on being a belief can be gradient without threat to the status of intentional states within cognitive science. The threat would come if being a belief, or a particular belief, was multidimensional and pragmatic. We can defuse that possibility. A functionalist account of the difference between having intentional states and not having them, together with a denotational account of content serves to explain our intuitions on Stich's cases without requiring his account of content and its attribution.

7.4 Is Knowledge Sentential?

Patricia Churchland has argued vigorously against the sentential paradigm of information processing. (Though she does not argue that there are *no* sentential representations.) In Churchland (1986), which synthesizes and extends her earlier work on this subject, she offers three arguments against sententialism. I think that they fail. In the next chapter I will discuss the merits of an alternative, nonsentential account of mental representation.

7.4.1 The Infra Linguistic Catastrophe

Not all thinkers are users of a public language. The behaviour of animals is often strikingly intelligent: they are capable of both innovation and social learning. There are species of birds (mainly tits) that have learnt to exploit the food source of bottled milk, left on doorsteps, by penetrating the cap. The pioneers of this have passed it on to their descendants. Japanese macaque monkeys have learnt to wash sand off their food; primates have learnt to use simple tools; and so on. These feats are quite sophisticated. Similarly, prelinguistic children are capable of sophisticated perceptual processing and learning: indeed, their learning of their first language is an extremely complex cognitive achievement. (Though, of course, once they have learnt some part of their language this may be part of their cognitive resources for learning the next.)

How do these facts bear on a sententialist view of cognition? There are two options. One might claim that there is a major division between adult human cognition and the rest. Important chunks of adult human cognitive processes, it might be said, are sentence-crunching processes, but no animal or prelinguistic human cognitive processing is sentential. Patricia Churchland rightly points out that this claim is *grossly* implausible. Not only is there no evidence (apart from the capacity to speak a language) of this in- principle gulf; it would make the evolution of our linguistic capacities mysterious.

So the better sententialist option is that defended by Fodor. At least some animals and prelinguistic children have a language of thought. So some of their cognitive processing is sentence-crunching. Against this option, Churchland urges two claims:

1   It's an evolutionary anachronism to see animal cognition as sententialist. For sentences are a recent and special evolutionary invention

If we think of linguistic behaviour as something that evolved because it provided for a quantum jump in the information available to organisms by allowing for complex exchange between individuals, then the enthusiasm for cognition as sentence crunching seems insensitive to evolutionary considerations. (1986, p. 388)

If humans invented the sentence for communication, then indeed it is implausible to think orangutans, monkeys and toddlers have a language of thought. Adaptations, however, often involve the exploitation of a preexisting structure for a new purpose. For example, it is widely accepted that feathers began life as insulation and only later became part of a mechanism for flight. If that is right, then feathers are a 'preadaptation' for flight. If, in the evolution of public language, organisms exploited a preadaptation, a kind of representation already in use for internal purposes, then there is no implausibility in supposing that nonlanguage users think in their own version of mentalese. Since we can only guess on this question, she has not much of an argument here.

Language does pose an evolutionary problem, that of understanding how a system as complex and sophisticated as language could evolve in gradual steps, each of which was adaptive. How could a productive, systematic symbol system evolve from one intrinsically limited, or one without genuine syntactic structure. The insistence of Chomsky and other transformational linguists that natural language is different in kind to any animal communication system makes this worry more acute. But the point to notice here is that this problem is unchanged whether we see it as arising as a problem about the cognitive evolution of all mentally sophisticated animals, or as a problem special to the social evolution of our species. (For a first pass at this problem, see Brandon and Hornstein (1986).)

2   Patricia Churchland thinks that Fodor himself has produced a *reductio* of sententialism. For he has argued not just that we and other animals have a language of thought, but that we have a rich innate conceptual repertoire. On Fodor's view, we have innately such concepts as **tiger** and **xylophone**. Now, Fodor's view is indeed bizarre, and if sententialists were committed to it, then perhaps sententialism would be self-refuting. However, if the theory of content defended in the last chapter, or any similar theory, is right, then sententialism is not committed to an innateness hypothesis nearly as strong as this. For bizarre nativism arises (see section 2.3) from Fodor's view of concept learning. He thinks it requires the learner to formulate a mentalese hypothesis that specifies the extension of the concept in question. Thus you can only learn **nerd** if your built in conceptual stock is rich enough to define the concept. On my view (and on Fodor's!) the mechanism of reference of a concept is not a specification of that concept's extension. The mechanism for many concepts (causal-descriptive ones) involves some descriptive elements, but also a causal network as well. Since *possessing* a concept requires no such definition, nor does *acquiring* the concept. Some base concepts, if the teleological suggestion of section 6.9 is on track, are innate, hence unlearned. But natural kind concepts, artifact concepts and the like are those for which causal descriptive theories of some kind are appropriate. Hence they are not innate. Sententialism is not committed to bizarre nativism. Here, if nowhere else, Patricia Churchland is insufficiently critical of Fodor. The 'infralinguistic catastrophe' is avoided if nonlanguage using animals have a language of thought. There is no reason to reject this possibility.

7.4.2   Tacit Knowledge

Many of the sceptics, and at least one of the friends, of the language of thought hypothesis think that one of its problems is the problem of tacit belief (and other attitudes). Take, for example, Boris. Let us suppose Boris has an average stock of beliefs and desires. Does Boris believe that worms have no beards? Does Boris believe that his chair will not turn into a snake and bite his bum? It is very likely that Boris has never for a moment entertained these possibilities. So Boris does not house within inner sentences that mean that worms don't have beards, and that chairs won't turn into snakes. Now, if Boris is like most of us, he can speedily respond if asked about worm's beards. He will not struggle to tell us that they are beardless. This has left philosophers like Dennett, Lycan and, apparently, Patricia Churchland most unhappy with the straightforward denial that Boris believes that worms are beardless; this she calls the 'austere' view of implicit belief. She emphasizes the speed and ease with which some beliefs which are not explicitly stored can none the less become conscious. She concludes from this consideration that 'the austere solution looks unacceptable' ((1986) p. 391).

But the alternative to the austere solution is undoubtedly messy. For how obvious do the consequences of our explicitly stored beliefs have to be for them to count as part of what we believe? None of us believe all the logical consequences of our explicit beliefs. There is no principled intermediate place to stop. Even if there were, we sometimes fail to draw even the obvious consequence of our own beliefs.

So is there anything really wrong with the austere line? I think not. First, the austere line loses no explanatory power. In so far as intentional states enter into the explanation of behaviour, they will be explicitly represented, though not necessarily conscious. Second, there is no major clash of intuitive judgement with the austere theory. If worries about hairy worms, or the dangerous transformation of chairs, really *never* have crossed Boris's mind, then we have no clear inclination to credit Boris with these thoughts. Perhaps denying that Boris believes that worms are beardless does minor violence to our pretheoretic judgements. But no one planning to integrate folk psychology with serious theory has supposed that folk theory needs no revisions whatever. This problem of tacit attitudes really is no problem for the language of thought thesis.

Churchland links this problem with another. She rightly points out that much of our knowledge, prima facie, is not sentential. It's knowing how, not knowing that. This claim is enormously plausible for physical skills, for instance those involved in batting. I am inclined to accept it for many cognitive skills as well. It seems unlikely to me that the skills involved in being a good chess player reduce to a corpus of sentential information. For example, pattern recognition seems very important. But the point here is no different from the one made earlier by Paul Churchland: that there are cognitive capacities on which intentional psychology will shed little light. I agree, but diverge from the Churchlands on whether this is rightly to be seen as an objection to intentional psychology. Of course, if too many cognitive capacities turned out to be based on nonsentential cognitive processes, intentional psychology would be marginalized. Churchland's claim that cognitive processing is predominantly nonsentential would then be vindicated. Our judgement here turns importantly on the assessment of nonsentential accounts of problem solving, memory and the like. The leading alternative to mentalese is the focus of the next chapter.

7.4.3 The Frame Problem

The 'tacit knowledge problem' is not one. That cannot be said about the frame problem. Humans and other beings have striking informational capacities. The subtlety of these capacities has become evident to those who wish to design a robot capable of acting in the world. What kind of capacities for knowledge representation would a robot have that can manage ordinary activities. We are not talking here of metal genius but of humdrum acts like finding your way downtown, or managing in a bank or restaurant. The frame problem arises in trying to specify the informational demands of unsophisticated activity. It turns out that there are at least four different problems.

1 One difficulty that will confront our robot is *update*. As Igor moves through his office, his representation of the relative position of its contents must change, for changes in relative distance have consequences for what Igor can do. Such changes are usually unproblematic for us. Moreover, if Igor does anything – for instance, moves his chair – he will not just change the relative position of the chair to the other objects. He will change what he can do. Some actions previously feasible will no longer be options: standing on the chair to change the light. But much *won't* change. Moving a chair is unlikely to change its colour. If we want to make a metal Igor, we need to solve two tough problems. (a) Which of its representations of its environment and its possible actions need to change after which actions; which can be left untouched? (b) We will need efficient methods for updating those representations which need it.

2 We solve problems all the time; we find our way to the bank or the bookshop; we succeed in making ourselves coffee. Because these tasks are easy for us, they do not present themselves as problems. It does not follow that it would be easy to design a robot that could cope with these activities of daily life. Humans have an enormous amount of information, implicitly or explicitly. In solving problems, we almost always extract painlessly and efficiently just the *relevant* information and *ignore* the rest. It's as certain as anything in psychology can be that in finding the kettle for my coffee I do not have to survey my data on the stripes of zebras, or my mother's birthdate to determine its irrelevance. Most of what I know I do not have to look at at all, not even to judge it

as irrelevant. But whether my caffeine-addicted colleague is in – that is relevant, and that I can get at right away. So how can we leave so much unsurveyed, extracting just what we need? A robot needs this capacity too, or it will spend all its days calculating what it knows and determining that almost all of it is irrelevant to its planned activity.

3   If a robot is to exhibit the everyday competences we routinely display, background knowledge needs to be made explicit. For only thus can it be made part of the robot's data.

4   There is a problem about inference. We rely on many nondeductive inferential procedures: inductive and probabilistic inferences, inferences from the best explanation, default reasoning of many kinds. At the very least, it is very hard to formalize such reasoning.

Now, Patricia Churchland (again, in somewhat curious near-agreement with Fodor) thinks that the frame problem is more-or-less insoluble. But she also thinks that it's an artifact of sententialist models of representation. If she were right, then she would indeed have a powerful argument in favour of nonsentential theories of mental representation. But I think her views on this issue are premature. I claim in section 10.5 that nonsententialist 'solutions' to the frame problem have just the same case by case *ad hoc* character that is rightly complained about of 'sententialist' theories in artificial intelligence. She declares that 'specifying the knowledge store in sentences is a losing strategy', and goes on to write:

Somehow, nervous systems have solved the problem of knowledge access. Once that solution is understood, we may be amazed at how different it is from what we had imagined, and we may find that we had even misconceived the problem. (1986, p. 394)

It's hard to disagree with this modest thought. Somehow we overcome the various frame problems. Perhaps the inferential aspects of the frame problem result from taking representation to be sentential. But I doubt that, for example, the relevance problem and the update problem are artifacts of sentential representation. Surely, however we represent information, we have vastly more than we use for any given problem. So the selection problem arises. So does the update problem, for as we change and move around the world some facts about the world and our relation to it stay constant, but not all. Somehow we keep track of the constancies, work out the differences. Perhaps a different format, a different system of representation would drastically simplify these problems. But I am yet to see how. I will return to this problem in sections 10.2–10.5. The frame problem poses a huge problem to cognitive psychology. But not, as far as I can see, to *sententialist* cognitive psychology in particular.

7.5 Conclusion

In this chapter I have been assessing the claim that intentional psychology, as part of an overall psychological theory, has crippling drawbacks. I think the arguments adduced in favour of this claim are not compelling. Moreover, we ought to regard the predictive success of intentional psychology, imprecise and fallible though that success is, as reason to believe that intentional psychology is approximately true. That success is not overwhelming; if we had strong positive grounds for believing intentional psychology to be false, that support would be undermined. But I do not think those strong grounds have yet been provided.

Suggested Reading

Section 7.1

For the psychological plausibility of the received view, see the readings for section 2.4. For its importance to a theory of belief/desire ascriptions, and their semantics, see Fodor's 'Propositional Attitudes' (1978), Field's 'Mental Representations' (1978) and Devitt's 'Thoughts and Their Ascription' (1984b). Dennett's scepticism about the fidelity of the received view to our untutored judgements is scattered through his work, but is especially pressed in 'Beyond Belief' (1982) and 'Three Kinds of Intentional Psychology' (1981b).

Section 7.2

Paul Churchland's scepticism about intentional psychology is prepared in *Scientific Realism and the Plasticity of Mind* (1979), where the underlying semantic and epistemological theories are developed. The scepticism is pressed in 'Eliminative Materialism and the Propositional Attitudes' (1981) and, less strongly, *Matter and Consciousness* (1988a). Both the Churchlands have drawn plenty of fire. Two responses that, while notionally directed mainly at Patricia Churchland, are relevant to the issues of section 7.2 are von Eckardt's 'Cognitive Psychology and Principled Scepticism' (1984) and Patricia Kitcher's 'In Defense of Intentional Psychology' (1984). Von Eckardt takes up the link between cognitive psychology and folk psychology; Kitcher takes up the alchemy analogy. Direct defences of folk psychology are Jackson and Pettit 'In

Defence of Folk Psychology' (forthcoming) and Horgan and Woodward's 'Folk Psychology is Here to Stay' (1985). Horgan and Woodward reply to Stich as well, whereas the Jackson and Pettit piece is especially concerned to show the unlikeliness of neuroscientific data undercutting folk theory. I agree with the eliminativists that folk psychology is a theory, hence it is at least a *candidate* for eviction on the grounds of utter falsity. A number of philosophers have argued that there is something self-defeating or incoherent about the eliminativist idea: see Rudder Baker *Saving Belief* (1987) or Boghossian 'The Status of Content' (forthcoming). Devitt argues that nonempirical defences of content fail in 'Transcendentalism about Content' (forthcoming).

Section 7.3

Stich's views on folk psychology are developed in 'Autonomous Psychology and The Belief-Desire Thesis' (1978a), 'On The Ascription of Content' (1982) and the first six chapters, in particular, of *From Folk Psychology to Cognitive Science* (1983). Most of the critical response to Stich has concentrated on his scepticism about the explanatory importance of nonindividualist properties. The equally damaging suggestions that intentional notions are holistic and observer dependent have received much less attention. But Fodor reacts vigorously to the holism in chapter 3 of *Psychosemantics* (1988a), as does Devitt in 'A Narrow Representational Theory of the Mind' (1989).

Section 7.4

The antisententialist view of knowledge has been developed by both the Churchlands. Important papers of Patricia Churchland are 'A Perspective on Mind-Brain Research' (1980) and 'Language, Thought and Information Processing' (1981). Most of this is synthesized in her book, *Neurophilosophy* (1986). In addition, there is their joint paper, 'Stalking the Wild Epistemic Engine' (1983), and a paper from Paul Churchland, 'On The Nature Of Theories: A Neurocomputational Perspective' (1990). See the readings for sections 8.1–8.3 for connectionist inspired antisententialist accounts of knowledge, and those of sections 10.3–10.5 for readings on the frame problem. For my earlier thoughts on the problem nativism poses for the mentalese hypothesis, see 'Fodor's Nativism (Sterelny, 1989). For an even more mad dog nativism, see Piattelli-Palmarini's 'Evolution, Selection and Cognition' (1989).

8

Connectionism

8.1 An Alternative to the Language of Thought?

Jerry Fodor (1975) quotes the famous LBJ remark 'I'm the only president you've got' to illustrate his view that the representational theory of mind was the only serious theory of cognitive processes extant. That claim can no longer be made; there is now a *connectionist* account of cognition that is more or less explicitly opposed to the language of thought hypothesis.

Connectionists offer a rival view of the architecture of the mind, the nature of mental representation, and the nature of operations on these representations. The classical cognitivist defends a set of linked theses on these questions. Representations are syntactically complex. Mental operations are defined with respect to that syntactic structure. This view of representations and their transformation brings with it commitments about the overall organization of the mind. Complex representations require complex systems (homunculi, modules, a central processor) to house and use those representations. Hence the elaboration within classical cognitivism of homuncular functionalism in its differing forms: with processors nested within processors, eventually analysing very complexly functioning homunculi as systems of processors simple enough to be directly implemented in neural material. This picture goes by various names: classical cognitive psychology, classical artificial intelligence; the 'rules and representations' view of cognition;

the language of thought model of cognition; and even GOFAI, standing for 'good, old fashioned artificial intelligence'.

Connectionists offer a picture which seems to contrast sharply. Connectionists see the mind (or subdomains of the mind) as networks These networks consist of large numbers of multiply interconnected nodes. The nodes are simple, numerous and interact without supervision from a central processing unit. In the limit, all the nodes are connected; even if the limit is not reached each node is connected with many others.

Paul Churchland uses a pattern recognition network to illustrate the basic ideas of the approach (Churchland, 1988a, p. 159). Its particular function (when suitably ensouled in a submarine) is to determine, from a sonic echo whether an object is a rock or a mine. Like many networks it is arranged into three layers or banks. The first layer consist of input nodes. We can think of these nodes as transducers: each is tuned to a particular frequency of sound, and will fire more strongly (rather than less strongly or not at all) as that frequency is represented in the total incoming signal. Each input node is connected to all the 'hidden nodes'; these are connected to the two output nodes. So incoming signals first excite the input nodes which in turn excite some, and inhibit others, of the hidden nodes in the second bank of cells. They in turn ultimately excite one of the output nodes, and inhibit the other. We want the network to be so arranged that one of these output nodes fires when there is a mine that the echo bounces off, and the other when it's a rock.

Another standard example is a word recognition network. In this network, the input nodes detect line segments in various orientations. Consider, for example, the letter 'N'. N-detection might well involve the decomposition of 'N' into two types of line segments, vertical segments and oblique segments. A connection network incorporating that idea will have an input unit which fires if the input being scanned contains an oblique stroke. The hidden units, in this network, represent letters, and the output units represent words (see Rumelhart et al., 1986, p. 22).

Let me list the basic properties of these networks:

1 Connections between the nodes differ in type and in strength. Some are inhibitory; others excitatory. Node A might be connected to both B and C yet B plays a greater role in A's behaviour, for the connection from B to A may have a greater weight than that from C to A.

2 Whether a node fires (and how strongly it fires) is a function of

the sum of the incoming stimulations and the state of that node. In many networks, nodes have threshhold values: they will fire if the sum is above that threshhold, otherwise they stay turned off.

The important point to remember here is that the node is under local control. What it does depends only on its state and its immediate environment, not on any global properties of the system.

3   The network's information is encoded in the weights between the nodes. Typically, these weights are modifiable. The network's capacity to learn (and, in effect, its memory) depends on this modification process. Learning proceeds by slight modifications of the weights between nodes. This is known as 'training' a network.

Let me give an intuitive sketch of training the mine/rock recognizer. Initially, the connection's strengths are set at random. The input nodes are then presented with a series of teaching stimuli. Consider the first of these. Some of the input nodes will fire strongly, others weakly, others still, not at all. In the next cycle, these reach the hidden nodes; stimulating some, inhibiting others. These begin to inhibit or excite both other hidden nodes and the output nodes. Many nodes will get and give both excitatory and inhibitory signals, as will the output nodes. Gradually, as these stimuli are transmitted back and forth, the network will begin to settle into a stable state: it's a striking fact about these networks that, though they have an enormous number of states, only a few are stable. Eventually the network will settle into a stable state with 'yes mine' node on or the 'yes rock' node on.

Suppose the 'yes rock' detector came on but the signal was from a mine. There is an automatic teaching procedure that works like this. The excitatory connections between the hidden units and the 'rock' node will be slightly lowered in their weights, and the inhibitory connections will have their weights slightly increased. We do the opposite for the connections between the hidden units and the 'mine' node. In effect, we (or rather, the teaching procedure) examines the network to see who voted right, and who voted wrong. Those who voted right have their various weights increased slightly; those who voted wrong, a slight decrease. Then the next member of the training set is presented, and so on. Very strikingly indeed, such networks can thus be trained not just to eventually get the classification of the teaching set right, but to generalize beyond the teaching set. Networks can thus (amongst other things) be trained to recognize patterns. Of course, they cannot do this by themselves; they need an outside agent – something outside the network – to correlate the teaching stimuli with their correct classifications. But granted that, nothing outside the network is needed to supervise the gradual changing of the internode weights.

4   There is no automatic commitment to the view that particular intermediate nodes in a network stand for any identifiable element or feature of the environment. In this respect, the word recognition network, in which intermediate nodes represent letters, is not entirely typical. Hence it's often claimed that representations in these systems is distributed. The representational properties are carried by the networks as a whole (or some part of the network) rather than by individual nodes representing particular features of the environment.

5   When the nodes are taken to have representational significance, they are representationally simple. They are simple both in what they represent, a simple feature or 'microfeature', and in the nodes having no syntactic structure.

6   For any real cognitive task, the networks have to have very large numbers of nodes. As the number of nodes grows, the number of connections grows exponentially, not linearly.

7   The connections between the nodes are understood causally rather than as a system following a sequence of rules. For note:

(a)   The transactions between the individual nodes are local and simple: so simple that there is no need for even the dumbest homunculi to reside in the nodes.

(b)   The behaviour of the whole network is just a complex probabilistic sum of the behaviour of its atoms. Hence there is no interesting intermediate layer of descriptions between an account of the behaviour of the network as a whole, and an account of the behaviour of its nodes. There is no control or executive orchestrating the network's behaviour. There is no homuncular breakdown of a connectionist network after the style of Lycan and Dennett. It's striking that connectionists' favoured metaphors aren't computational but thermodynamic: when a network is running, it is settling down ('annealing') into one of its few stable states.

8.2 The Prima Facie Case for Connectionist Models

The basic charge (repeated in many different forms) against language of thought based cognitive architectures is that they are biologically implausible. They fail to offer a plausible account of creatures who do their thinking with a brain. I will outline a few of the main currents of thought here.

1 A famous connectionist argument is the '100 step' argument. It goes like this. Neural transitions are very slow by comparison with electric ones; about 1000 times as slow. None the less, we perform many cognitive tasks, especially those concerned with perception and recognition, very quickly: in under a second. Consider one of those tasks; say, recognizing that the object you are about to put your foot on is a snake. Recognizing a snake on classical AI is a computationally complex process. A machine vision program would have to carry out well over a million primitive computational operations in order to do it, if it could do it at all. On such a system, recognizing a snake is assembled from a million substeps, each done one at a time. That's fine, if the physical structure that implements your computational processes can carry out a million separate steps in less than a second. IBM machines can do this, but human brains cannot: neurons can go through somewhere between 100 and 1000 states in a second, not a million. So that if our recognizing a snake is a cognitively complex process assembled from simpler ones, arranged in sequence, there can be only a hundred or so in that sequence.

There is a stronger and a weaker conclusion to be drawn from this point. The weak conclusion is that, however our capacities for visual recognition work, our brains don't run the same programs as those written in the machine vision labs at MIT. Surely that must be right. The strong conclusion is that cognitivist theories of perception must be wrong. Theorists like Ullman and Rock have taken perceptual processing to be a species of inference, and hence perceptual representation as complex and mediated by many intermediate representations. They are language of thought models. Are those refuted by the '100 step' argument? No. Two issues are being conflated. We must distinguish between complexity and sequence. There are language of thought based parallel models: some versions of the 'Marcus parser', which models sentence comprehension by incorporating a Chomskian transformational grammar, use parallel procedures.

Moreover, the '100 step' argument may only show that if perceptual recognition is computed serially, the primitive steps from which it is assembled are not small. Conventional machine languages (from which higher-order operations are assembled) carry out only tiny steps at a time. For example, they compare the number at one address with the one in the workspace for a same/different judgement, or they add one to a number at an address. You need lots of these primitive operations to even add two numbers, let alone recognize a snake. Serial processing working real time in the human brain would need a more powerful array of primitive operations. But for all we know, it may have such an array.

The '100 step' argument doesn't establish much of a case either for a connectionist architecture or against a classical one.

2   Humans are good at what (conventional) computers are bad at, and vice versa. We are good at pattern recognition; we recognize, for example, faces, words, objects and scenes quickly and quite often from degraded information. We are good at relevantly accessing information from large information stores. When you recall facts about your best friend, you do not have to sort through a list of all your friends, or all your facts. We seem to access that information directly, apparently we have 'content-addressable' memory. That is, we can directly access our memory by subject matter. We can even do so from inaccurate prompts ('Kerry? You must mean Terry.').

Conventional computational devices are not good at these skills. In this regard, the difference between the way strong humans and strong programs play chess is both striking and illustrative. Programs running on large mainframes can now play good chess; they are of at least strong international master standard. But these programs are brute-force devices. That is, they calculate all possible variations to a certain depth. They then have a crude evaluation of the resulting position. Human players calculate far fewer possibilities: many legal moves are not considered at all. But good players are fast, sophisticated and accurate at evaluating positions. The pattern of errors in human and computer chess is very different.

Connectionists think that this is symptomatic of deep differences between cognitive processes in us, and the analogous processes in classically organized computers. In contrast, in their view connection networks and humans are good at the same types of tasks. It is even claimed of some networks that their patterns of learning duplicate the same symptomology of errors of human learning.

It's hard to know what to make of this argument. The pattern-recognition capacities of networks is very striking, and is good ground for an interest in connectionist models. The lack of success of pattern recognition in other approaches is equally striking. The diagnosis of those failures is less clear. Do they fail because they attempt to treat perceptual recognition (hence pattern recognition) inferentially? If so, that does seem strong grounds for scepticism about classical architecture. But it may not be so. The difficulty of providing classical AI devices with content-addressable memory for the machine language, and their efficiencies in calculation, may be consequences of the machine languages out of which complex representations in AI are assembled, and of the physical design of standard computers.

3   Defenders of connectionism often begin by suggesting that human problem solving is characterized by 'multiple soft constraints'.

For example, in his introduction to connectionism, Tienson points out that speech understanding involves many different factors: analysing physically continuous noise into a sequence of phonemes; recovering the syntactic structure and the semantic properties of the utterance; exploiting the social, physical and linguistic context to disambiguate, fill in elisions and to interpret indexical elements like 'I' or 'that idiot'. Yet these factors are 'soft'. Mispronounced utterances can be understood. So too can sentences deformed by ungrammaticalities, spoonerisms, mischosen words ('you mean 'disinterested', not 'uninterested', cretin'). Contextual inappropriateness embarasses, but unfortunately does not block understanding.

Tienson and the others do not suggest that language of thought based theories of cognition are *refuted* by the fact that the constraints determining a solution to a problem can yet be violated. But the all or none nature of the rules that transform one complex representation into another make it hard to account for the violability of the constraints. After all, as Smolensky points out, the basic transformation is an *inference*. An inferential step is either a valid step or it's fallacious and forbidden; hard to see where the softness could get in.

I must confess to failing to see the force of this argument; it just seems to me to be a confusion of the ecological level, specifying the task domain, and the computational level, specifying the procedures via which those problems are solved. A bundle of algorithms can explain how a problem solver succeeds in solving problems subject to multiple soft constraints. Consider that classic of artificial intelligence, chess. The best programs are now better than all but a few hundred strong grandmasters; they rank higher still in forms of chess with fast time limits. They run relatively simple brute force algorithms; procedures which definitely apply or fail to apply to the representation of the position being transformed. Yet to play decent chess, let alone excellent chess, one must solve problems while subject to multiple soft constraints. Consider the problems faced by a player in the opening. She must develop her pieces; try to keep her king safe; begin to carry out some kind of aggressive plan; defend herself against the threats of her opponent; avoid weakening her pawn structure, occupy the centre and so forth. None of these constraints are mandatory; indeed, they tend to cut across one another. It is always a matter of delicate judgement which to ignore, and to what extent. The constraints are many, and soft, yet a machine running exhaustive search and evaluate algorithms none the less obeys them.

4   Classical architecture is not robust. For example, conventional mechanisms are extremely sensitive to damage or noise – a small fault

in the central processor, or a typo in the program, and the whole system is likely to crash. That's not true of the human mind: our capacities – by and large – degrade gracefully. If the language centres of the brain are damaged, there is no complete, abrupt and final loss of linguistic abilities. There is some loss; its extent and duration will be variable, but will more or less correspond to the degree of damage. We cope well with noisy inputs: for example, with ungrammatical utterances. Strikingly, connection networks are resistant to damage in the same sorts of ways. Normally, if a node is removed, the network won't crash, but its discriminatory capacities will be a little less accurate; increasingly so, as other nodes go too. Like humans, networks can use noisy data: they can recover patterns from inexact or distorted inputs. As distortion increases, the error rate goes up, but no abrupt halt occurs. Both humans and networks are flexible in other important ways, too. Our performance does not crash when time and memory constraints are exceeded; under time pressure, our performance of cognitive tasks deteriorates, but does not abruptly cease.

Classical architectures are insufficiently attuned to the fact that our brains are built of neurons. Connectionists think that cognitive theory should start from the fact that cognitive functions are carried out by banks of neurons. They suspect defenders of language of thought models of cognition paying only lip service to physicalism, for the constraints of neural implementation play too little a role in their theorizing. This complaint is certainly true of some. Chomsky, for example, is hardly interested in psychological information on response time, error profile, or comprehension, let alone neural information. But they does not seem to apply to Ullman or Marr (see section 4.4). Nodes and networks, by contrast, are supposed to reflect the properties of neurons and their connections.

In summary, connectionist networks are held to be biologically plausible models of cognition, respecting the speed of neural activity, the abilities and disabilities of our actual cognitive capacities, and the properties of neurons and neural assemblies.

8.3 Rival or Implementation?

How are connectionist models related to sententialist accounts of cognition? On this important issue, there is nothing like a consensus, or even clarity. There is a central ambiguity in connectionist writings. A radical thesis is in the air: connectionist models refute and should replace classical models. For connectionist models show that the appeal to rules, to complex sentential representations, hence complex processors, is not needed. So, for example, it's alleged that a connectionist model can explain the productivity of past tense morphology without positing a rule operating on abstract phonological representations to yield a past tense representation. Linking connectionism to an eliminativist view of propositional attitudes and of cognitive psychology is more explicit in some philosophical commentators on connectionism than its hard core practitioners, but it is found there too.

There are two modest theses as well. One is to take connected networks as implementations. They explain the implementation of computational processes by a brainlike physical architecture. For they show how networks of simple interconnected processors can carry out basic computational tasks: in particular, pattern matching and transforming. For training a network to yield certain outputs given inputs implements both a matching and a transformation; they turn the input into the output. So construed, connection networks support classical cognitivist models of the mind. In some ways, this is a very natural view of connectionist models, for they are more easily seen as descriptions of neural processes that abstract away from some of the details of real neural nets than as high level theories themselves requiring neural implementation. After all, if a node is not an underdescribed neuron but rather a bank of neurons, and a connection isn't a synaptic connection but rather a complex chain of cells, then the '100 step' argument does not even begin to tell in favour of connectionist theories. A trained connectionist network recognizes words in a few hundred machine cycles. But that is a biologically realistic pace only if nodes are neurons.

There is an alternative modest understanding of connectionism. We might hope to institute a division of labour. Perhaps pattern recognition and some types of retrievals from memory are carried out by connectionist networks. But problem solving, language understanding and the planning of behaviour are the domain of sentence crunching devices. There is, after all, no reason to suppose that there is only one type of information processing device in the mind.

Connectionists often seem to hover uneasily between the radical and the modest. Typically, they claim that classical, higher-level cognitivist stories are shown by connectionist models to be approximations, often good approximations of psychological truth. None the less, connectionist models offer a more exact account of mental processes than alternatives. So for example, in the Rumelhart and McClelland bumper books of connectionism, there are connectionist attempts to mimic the possession of concepts and of other 'high-level' cognitive processes. These mimicries are clearly not intended as mere implementations of the apparatus for a language of thought, but nor are they refutations either.

The claim that a connectionist model is more accurate than a language of thought alternative does not take us far. If connectionist models do no more than implement cognitive processes, they will be more exact than high-level stories. For there will be failures (from breakdowns) inexplicable at the higher-level that are explicable at the implemention level. Only at the most fundamental physical level are laws exceptionless. Exceptions at one level are explicable at lower levels. So, for example, in population genetics, exceptions are mutations. A copied gene ends up unlike its parent. Mutations are not explained within genetics; the rate of mutation is something it takes as given, and to be explained at a more fundamental biochemical level.

So the programmatic writings of connectionism do not come clean on the degree to which they see themselves as offering a revolutionary alternative. It is clear that they don't *just* see themselves as offering an implementation theory. They are offering a theory of psychological phenomena: memory, language learning, concept acquisition. Connectionist theories are psychological theories. I will return to these issues in section 8.6.

8.4 Is Mental Representation Structured?

We will see that the debate between connectionists and their critics turns on disagreements both about the nature of sentient minds, and the power of connectionist theory. Critics emphasize, and connectionists downplay, the unbounded character of our capacities for mental representation. Connectionists argue, against the claims of their critics, that connectionist mental representation can be rich and structured. In this section, our focus will be the mind. How rich a theory do we need? In particular, is a bounded system of mental representation *in principle* an inadequate theory of human sentience? In section 8.5, I concentrate on the alleged limitations on connectionist representations.

The connectionist challenge has not gone unanswered. For example, Pinker and Prince (1988) trash one of connectionism's flagship examples, a connectionist network that appeared both to learn the past tense form of English verbs, and to go through the same learning stages that a child does. Children go through a period in which they use both regular and irregular pasts correctly, though only for a small number of verbs.

They then appear to overgeneralize a morphological rule, and produce 'runned' rather than 'ran'. The mature output throttles back on the general rule, so 'ran' reappears. Very strikingly, Rumelhart and McClelland designed a network whose learning exhibited the same developmental stages. Furthermore, it did so without the explicit representation of any morphological rules at all, and without having to build in a distinction between regular and irregular forms, or knowledge of particular past tense forms one at a time.

Pinker and Prince argue convincingly that the developmental realism of this model is an artifact of the learning set on which the network trained. Moreover, they argue that the connectionist account of language learning fails for reasons intrinsic to connectionism. In a connectionist network, the representation of an entity is nothing but the set of microfeatures (and their connections) that encodes that representation. It is thus hard to distinguish structural relations between representations from similarity relations between them, or even to properly represent structural features at all; even ones as simple as order and number. Rumelhart and McClelland's network represents the stem form of verbs by recourse to 'Wickelphones', which are ordered triples of ordinary phonemes. The verb 'try' for example would be represented as the activation of {ry#, #tr, try}, i.e. of the three Wickelphones it instantiates. This weird recourse is needed because the microfeatural representation of a word does not have order built into it in the way that, for example, sentential representation does. More importantly, Pinker and Prince argue that a connectionist account of language learning has too many free parameters. One dispute between connectionists and their critics revolves around the requirements on good psychological explanation. The critics of connectionism insist that there are essential aspects of cognition. A theory of cognition is no good if fundamental aspects of cognition emerge as mere byproducts of particular problem solving procedures, or of the neural implementations of those procedures. If you think, for instance, that consciousness is essential to cognition, you will reject a theory according to which it is possible for a cognitive agent to lack consciousness. On such a theory of cognition, consciousness is a 'free parameter'. So, for example, linguists have always wanted not just an account of the languages people do learn, but also of those we do not. Thus, in no human language, do we form a question from an indicative simply by reversing the word order. There is nothing a priori wrong with such a procedure; indeed, it is simpler than the ones we do seem to use. Yet it is surely obvious that a reverse-the-order language would be literally inhuman. Our account of language and its learning ought to exclude reverse order languages. It ought not come out as an accidental idiosyncrasy of English, and French, and Swahili, and Police Motu and ... that they are none of them reverse order languages. Pinker and Prince argue that the connectionist account of language learning fails to meet this constraint; it could as easily have learned a reverse-order past tense output, producing 'nur' when given 'run', 'tae' when given 'eat' and so on. So the dispute is not just over what features cognition has, it is also over which features are essential rather than accidental.

Pinker and Prince's paper raises most of the critical issues about connectionism conceived of as a radical replacement for language of thought based theories. They argue that connectionist representations are insufficiently rich, and that attempts to make them more adequate result in implausible and *ad hoc* microfeatures. They argue that cognitive theories must recognize structural relations between representations, not just relations of causal association or overall similarity. They argue that the theoretical virtues of an account of cognitive processes based on rules operating on representations are understated by connectionists.

In an important paper, Fodor and Pylyshyn (1988) take up these ideas and apply them more generally. They argue that connectionist models of mental representation and mental processing are impoverished; so impoverished that they can, in principle, offer no satisfactory explanation of central features of cognition.

They characterize connectionist theory as follows. First, connectionist mental representations have no constituent structure. They are not built from elements that themselves represent. Second, mental processing is 'associationist'. The only psychologically relevant relations between mental representations are those of excitation or inhibition between nodes. So, the picture is: simple representations, simple processing. Sentementialist theories, on the other hand, require complex representations, and recognize richer structural relations between representations: relations that are relevant to cognitive processes.

These differences matter. For, according to Fodor and Pylyshyn, simple representations and associationist relations between them are *too* simple. Buying mentalese buys us quite a bit. If mental representation is complex, we get a natural account of the differences between thinking that someone hates everyone, and thinking that everyone is hated by someone. The difference in meaning is a consequence of the difference in quantifier scope, a structural property of *complex* representations. Similarly, granted a theory of content, we can distinguish between thinking that Thatcher is unrepentant, and thinking that the first female English prime minister is unrepentant, even though Thatcher is that person. For a mentalese name is syntactically simple; not so the mentalese equivalent of 'the first female English prime minister'. Hence two cognitively distinct representations are involved. We explain how it is possible to both believe and fear that Thatcher is unrepentant. Language of thought theories allow the one representation to be accessed by quite different mental processors. It is not at all clear that a doctrine of simple representations with simple associations between them can accommodate these putative facts of our mental life.

One standard argument for a language of thought is the alleged productivity of thought. There may be no psychological principle that imposes an upper bound to the number of representations we can form. Perhaps the restrictions are a consequence of the physical implementation of our cognitive mechanisms. If so, then no system of primitive, structureless mental representation suffices. Productivity requires compositionality. A system of primitive representation is *ipso facto* a bounded system.

There are many who are unconvinced both of the theoretical robustness of intentional psychology and the allegedly productive system of representation that realizes it. So Fodor and Pylyshyn see clearly the desirability of an argument that does not trade on productivity. While they themselves think that 'an idealization to an infinite competence' has earned its keep, they recognize that others do not. Further they think they do have an alternative to hand.

The crucial idea is that mental representation is *systematic*, or, in their alternate terminology, that mental life is not *punctuate*. They do not make a serious effort to specify systematicity; rather they attempt to give us an intuitive feel for the notion through examples. Systematicity consists in the intrinsic connection between the ability to have certain thoughts. Their favourite examples are relations; you can't think that aRb unless you could think that bRa. 'You don't find people who can think the thought that John loves the girl but can't think the thought that the girl loves John' (Fodor and Pylyshyn, 1988, p. 39). If you can think that tigers are beautiful, and have the concept of leopards, you can also think that leopards are beautiful. These examples help, though it is unclear how the notion extends to nonrelational examples; embeddings, for instance. Suppose Igor thinks that if it's Tuesday, then Granny will be drunk. Can Igor thereby think that if it's Tuesday or Wednesday, Granny will be drunk or hung over? Is his mind punctuate if he cannot manage this further, more complex, thought?

Let's agree that we have a clear enough intuitive idea of systematicity, and ask: Could connectionist representation be systematic? On the face of it, a network can be exactly as systematic as you like. If your network can represent X, and if the demands of a 'nonpunctuate mental life' require, in your view that Y and Z also be representable, then just dedicate a couple of nodes to those tasks. No problem. Fodor and Pylyshyn agree, and maintain that this *is* the problem.

Their argument is as follows:

P1 Cognitive representation is systematic.

P2 Systematicity of representation is an automatic consequence of languagelike representation.

P3 The systematicity of representation isn't a free parameter in a theory of mental representation.

P4 The systematicity of mental representation isn't guaranteed by the basic architecture of connectionist theory, though in any particular case it can be wired in by hand.

So

C Connectionist models offer no explanation of the systematicity of cognitive representation.

I have two reservations about this argument. I think Fodor and Pylyshyn have missed alternative explanations of systematicity. Furthermore, their claims about mental representation depend too heavily on accepting folk psychology. Let me begin with the first of these worries.

Let us agree that systematicity is a fundamental fact of our cognitive life. It is not, for example, like space limitations on short-term memory. Many experiments in cognitive psychology converge on the claim that humans can stack about seven unrelated items simultaneously in short-term memory. That evidence is quite robust; none the less, no one would want to claim that it is a fundamental feature of our cognitive organization. No one would be surprised if it turned out to be a consequence of the amount of neural tissue dedicated to short-term memory. Individual variation, and variation across closely related species, would not surprise. By contrast, systematicity could hardly be an accidental byproduct of implementation, or a mere byproduct of the particular procedure we happen to use for solving some local problem. If our minds are systematic, then that is a functional feature of our mental organization. However, it does not follow that the explanation of systematicity must be architectural: a consequence of our basic mental organization.

It is easy to slide from the claim that systematicity is a functional, rather than an implementational, feature of our mental life to the idea that it is to be explained by the basic architecture of our cognitive system. But it is a slide that can be resisted, as Braddon-Mitchell and Fitzpatrick (forthcoming) point out. They agree that it is a functional fact that mental representation is not punctuate. But they offer a diachronic rather than a synchronic explanation. Punctuate mental lives are bad for your reproductive prospects. For a punctuate mind is incapable of having some thoughts, including, perhaps, survival and reproduction enhancing ones. So natural selection will tend to build a nonpunctuate mind. Minds are typically systematic. That is no accident, but the explanation is selective rather than architectural. A connectionist does not have to believe that the systematicity of intelligence is a chance byproduct, an idiosyncrasy.

Now, it is reasonable to have one's doubts as to whether this kite will fly. Natural selection may not fine-tune mental organization in the way this suggestion supposes. We should expect only a rough approximation to a nonpunctuate mind; the approximation getting rougher as we move topic away from the famous four Fs (feeding, fleeing and fighting). Those who believe that natural selection optimizes, should expect it to build a nonpunctuate mind elegantly, by building a language of thought, rather than a klugy network which has systematicity wired in a step at a time by Mother Programmer.

This sceptical reaction is fair. None the less, their point is important and principled. It is one thing to require that systematicity be explained; it is quite another to insist that that explanation devolve from the basic computational architecture instantiated in the brain.

Mental representation may not be systematic. If propositional attitude psychology is serious theoretical psychology, the appeal to systematicity is compelling. But there are many who doubt that propositional attitude psychology is an approximately true theory of the causal bases of intentional behaviour. Do they have reason to accept the view that cognitive representation is systematic? Fodor and Pylyshyn consider a related question in considering whether nonverbal minds, and the nonverbal parts of our minds, are systematic. They reckon so:

It is not, however, plausible that only the minds of verbal organisms are systematic. Think what it would mean for this to be the case. It would have to be quite usual to find, for example, animals capable of representing the state of affairs aRb, but incapable of representing the state of affairs bRa. Such animals would be, as it were, aRb sighted but bRa blind since, presumably, the representational capacities of its mind affect not just what an organism can think, but also what it can perceive. In consequence, such animals would be unable to learn to respond selectively to bRa situations. (So that, though you could teach the creature to choose the picture with the square larger than the triangle, you couldn't for the life of you teach it to choose the picture with the triangle larger than the square.)

It is, to be sure an empirical question whether the cognitive capacities of intraverbal organisms are often structured that way, but we're prepared to bet that they are not. (1988, pp. 39–40)

They overstate their case. I rather doubt that animal representation is systematic, though, given the imprecision of the notion and the murky data, it is difficult to be sure. But let's consider a few examples. Chimps fear leopards; they think that leopards are dangerous. Some have the concept of a banana. But it is not obvious that they can think that bananas are dangerous, and apt to kill them. *We* can have utterly bizarre thoughts; I have known someone to think that musical instruments were alive and conscious. We (perhaps via our public language) have achieved a separation of form and content, so some of our mechanisms for constructing thoughts are independent of domain, independent of what they are about. We have no grounds for assuming other creatures have achieved the radical separation of form and content that is a necessary part of systematicity. (Dennett (forthcoming) airs a similar worry.) We do not have to rely just on intuition; there is an established body of data on 'one trial' learning relevant to this issue. Rats, for example, if offered food with a new taste will not eat it again if it makes them ill. They can form an immediate and aversive association between taste and illness. But only with taste. If, for example, they become ill after eating food while hearing new sounds they will not avoid that food or those sounds in future. They can learn to think that things that taste like *that* make you sick, but not things that sound or look like *that* make you sick.

Premack and Woodruff (1978) argue that chimps can have thoughts about thoughts. They can have thoughts like 'that chimp wants to take my banana' rather than just 'danger to banana'. For example, they can engage in deceptive practices, which only have point if they can think about others' minds. But are they capable of more complex embeddings? Can a chimp think 'that chimp wants me to believe that he is not hungry?' If Premack and Woodruff are right, chimps have the constituent concepts out of which such a thought could be constructed. Could they have still more complexly embedded thoughts? These are difficult empirical questions, especially as the degree of complexity attained is likely to be different for different primates. But at some quite early stage, cognitive capacity will give out. It gives out for us. It's a consequence, then, that either the capacity to have thoughts about thoughts is punctuate, not systematic, or Fodor and Pylyshyn will need to treat this form of punctuateness as a mere performance limitation, a consequence, perhaps, of limitations on short-term memory, or some such. But the move to systematicity from productivity was precisely an attempt to avoid reliance on questionable idealizations of this kind.

Perceptual representation also raises worries about systematicity. The ethological literature is crowded with examples of behaviour patterns that are, apparently, released by perceptual gestalts of some kind. Most famously, ducklings new-born imprint on anything that moves. But there are many other examples. Fodor and Pylyshyn acknowledge these counter-examples to systematicity, but regard them as rare and relatively peripheral.

It's difficult, in the absence of an explicit definition of systematicity, to assess this guess. But there is a problem not just about perceptual gestalts, but about grain as well. It's not at all clear, for example, that the bats' perceptual representations are systematic. Bat echo location can tell the bat that a moth is moving 1 cm/second faster than it (the bat) is, but not that it is moving 87 cm/second faster as opposed, say, to 90 cm/second faster. That is, outside certain crucial ranges of relative velocity, there is a dramatic drop in perceptual gain. Bats can represent some relative velocities but not others. Their perceptual abilities are punctuate.

Time to sum the state of play to date. Fodor and Pylyshyn remind us of the reasons for buying a language of thought hypothesis in the first place. Mental representation is prima facie a productive and compositional symbol system. If so, it's language-like, and a connectionist theory of representation is not adequate. Reply: the view that representation is productive and compositional is purchased only via a questionable idealization, and by buying into folk psychology as explanatory psychology. Both commitments can be resisted. Counter to this counter: you can resist productivity, if you will, but not the evident fact that representation, even representation that has nothing to do with the propositional attitudes of language users, is systematic. Connectionist theory yields no explanation of why mental lives are not punctuate, for connectionist architectures can be arbitrarily punctuate. I've just considered a final move. It's not obvious that only an architectural explanation of systematicity will do; furthermore, those sceptical of intentional psychology have little reason to accept that mental representation is systematic.

Structure is important not just to the issue of what we can represent, but to mental process as well. Unstructured symbols foreclose important options about mental process. For on the standard view, (many) mental processes are structure sensitive: they apply to symbols in virtue of their syntactic structure. Deductive inference is the standard example: the operation of simplification (*P&Q&R&S so P*) applies to a conjunction and yields a conjunct in virtue of the syntactic structure of the premise. It doesn't matter how many conjuncts there are, or what they say: simplification remains a valid rule of inference. If representations have no constituent structure, this theory of inference must be abandoned, and it seems to have no replacement. Of course, as Fodor and Pylyshyn concede, a particular network can be connected so that its transitions mimic simplification. If a node that represents a conjunction is active, it can excite nodes that represent its conjuncts. But this requires a case-by-case treatment for every node, network and inference rule: a general theory of deduction is being lost in a myriad of subcases.

Though persuasive, this argument is, as usual, not decisive. For one thing, the limits of the ability of connection networks to learn patterns aren't known; perhaps a network could learn simplification, and other logical principles, by learning to recognize very abstract patterns in valid arguments, given a suitable learning set, and feedback learning. Moreover, it's perhaps questionable that the human mind – human mental processing – involves much fully general, context independent, reasoning. There is in the psychology literature a mountain of sceptical results, seeming to demonstrate the contextuality of human reasoning.

However, even when all these reservations are taken into account, structureless representation gives away our only general theory of an important class of mental processes. But are connectionist representations structureless? I attempt to answer this question in the next section.

8.5 *Connectionist Mental Representation*

Fodor and Pylyshyn argue that connectionist representation is structureless. Consider a three node network in which a root node, representing the conjunction *A&B* is connected to two daughter nodes representing each conjunct. Activating the root node excites each daughter node, thus this 'network' implements simplification. Contrast this with a mentalese story. If Igor thinks, in mentalese, that today is Tuesday and Granny is drunk, his conjunctive thought has subparts with the content that today is Tuesday and that Granny is drunk. The content of his complex thought is determined in a regular way by its constituent elements, and the behaviour of his cognitive machine responds to that constituent structure. But none of this is true of the network. This 'network' spreads activation from the root to two daughter nodes. These are causally connected to the first node, but are not part of it. The connectionist representations are semantically and syntactically structureless.

The claim that connectionism deals only with simple representation is both critical and controversial. It is critical because it's the lack of constituent structure, and hence of complex representation, which makes connectionism implausible as a general theory of mind. It is that lack which seems to force a connectionist to take a deflationary view of human cognitive capacities. It is controversial, because it seems to be true only of local representation. In local representations, a single node represents some facet of the problem domain. But connectionist representation is often distributed, not local. The representation of a face, or a room, or a word is distributed over many nodes, each of which represents some 'microfeature' of the domain. There are distributed representation of rooms. These are 'schemata'; descriptions of average or typical rooms. The distributed representation of, say, the standard bathroom consists of elements which themselves have semantic significance. These elements will represent the presence of a toothbrush, a soap dish, and so on. The nodes in a distributed representation are not just physical parts of that representation, they are semantically significant parts. What more could constituency require?

Hinton, for example, discusses a system of distributed representation, intending to contrast the representations for chimpanzees, gorillas and apes. How are beliefs about chimps and gorillas to be contrasted with belief about apes in general? His idea is to have gorillas and chimps both represented by patterns of connections in a single network. The representation of apes would be a proper part of both patterns, which would thus have a chunk in common. Ape-general belief would be encoded in the connections in this chunk; gorilla-specific belief in the connections between the gorilla-unique part of the pattern (Hinton et al., 1986, 81–4).

Thus it seems that the distributed connectionist representations envisaged by Hinton are not simple. They have parts which (a) are semantically significant, (b) play a role in causal transitions in the network, and (c) contribute to the semantics of the complex representation systematically. The nodes which compose these distributed representations code so-called 'microfeatures' of the problem domain. Many connectionist input nodes, for example, represent quite precise physical features of the incoming signal. In the word-recognition network often used to illustrate connectionist networks, hidden nodes represent letters, a 'microfeature' of a word. In Rumelhart's connectionist simulation of schemata, the state of the network as a whole represents a category of room (bedroom/office/kitchen, etc.), and nodes represent room-features; the presence or absence of a telephone, and the like (Rumelhart et al., 1986b).

It seems as if distributed representations incorporate the traditional empiricist view that our concepts for the everyday macroscopic objects of our world are derived, constructed from more elementary microconcepts. I do not think that is their view, but it turns out to be very difficult to say just what it is. For there are very serious problems buried in the connectionist notion of a distributed representation.

1 Many writers on connectionism emphasize that distributed representation does not give you an invariant, context independent representation. How coffee is represented will depend on at least: (a) the other representations coded in the network, (b) the initial weights on the connections between nodes in the network, and (c) its particular learning history. NETTALK, for example, is a family of networks that take as input an inscription of a word, and give as output its phonological representation (Sejnowski and Rosenberg, 1988). Each network performing this task turns out, on analysis, to draw a consonant/vowel distinction. But individual learning histories will result in different combinations of nodes being active in different networks when a vowel is being pronounced. (I owe this example to Andy Clark.) This is not a peculiarity of NETTALK. Smolensky makes a similar point, though for slightly different reasons.

If you want to talk about the connectionist representation of coffee in this distributed scheme, you have to talk about a family of distributed activity patterns. What knits together all these particular representations of coffee is nothing other than a family resemblance. (Smolensky, 1988b, p. 148)

None of this variation would matter if distribution had no semantic significance, if the distribution of a representation over a number of nodes was merely a fact about its physical implementation. For then it would be just another example of the multiple realization of a functional kind. But if a distributed representation is one with constituent structure, the relation between nodes and representation is not one of physical implementation. But then variation undercuts the *point* of positing concepts. We posit concepts to give a compositional theory of meaning for complex representations. The idea is to explain the meaning of complex structures by appeal to primitives, to the concepts that make up those complex structures. That requires that concepts have semantic properties that are constant across the different symbol structures in which they find themselves. We cannot reduce the meaning of a complex containing **coffee** to the meaning of **coffee** (and its other constituents) if we have to explain the meaning of **coffee** by appeal to the context in which it finds itself.

2   It is not clear that a distributed representation is a representation *for the connectionist system* at all. We, looking at the network, notice that (say) a certain subset of the nodes are active when and only when there is a word-final 'th' in the lexical input to NETTALK. From our perspective we can say that this is a distributed representation of word-final 'th'. But this set of active units will play no role, *as a whole*, in the workings of the net. Individual units from that collection will, but the distributed representation of 'th' is not any entity in the system at all, any more than a random collection of nodes is. Given that the influence of node on node is local, given that there is no processor that looks at groups of nodes as a whole, it seems that seeing a distributed representation in a network is just an outsider's perspective on the system. It is at most a useful heuristic. I should point out that this worry is no relative of individualism. An individualist looks at a state of a cognitive system and demands to be told the explanatory point of its alleged representational properties. I am demanding to be told why I should regard distributed representations as states of the system at all.

3   The relationship between distributed representations and the microfeatures that compose them is deeply problematic. Suppose we think that they *define* the concept. But then we have returned to a theory of the componential analysis of concepts: the concept **lemon** abbreviates {**tart, yellow**, . . .}, a theory that has desperate and unsolved problems. Perhaps we might see the relationship as like the relationship between names and descriptions according to cluster versions of description theories of names. According to such theories, a name, for example 'Aristotle', does not abbreviate a single definite description of Aristotle but rather a cluster of descriptions, a cluster that might vary somewhat from speaker to speaker and which might even include a few descriptions that do not apply to Aristotle at all. But if the cluster is thought of as giving the meaning of the name, more complex versions of the problems that infest componential analysis emerge for the cluster theory. If the cluster does not give the meaning of the name it is attached to, the relationship between name and the descriptions in the cluster is a mystery. (For the problems for the cluster theory, see Devitt and Sterelny, 1987, sections 3.2 and 3.3; on componential analysis see section 6.1.)

Perhaps the relationship between distributed representation and microfeatures is *epistemic*. Some connectionists interpret the passing of activation from one node to another as indicating epistemic support for the representational content of the excited node from the content of the exciting node. But if the relationship is merely epistemic, then micro-features are not constituents of distributed representations.

Furthermore connectionist distributed representation has all the usual problems of holist theories of content. So we can add three more problems to the three above.

4   Since the stable pattern I acquire depends in part on the state of the system when my learning started, my pattern will be unique to me. No one else will have my concept: common content, hence a large part of the theoretical point of content, vanishes.

5   There is no distinction drawn between learning more about chimpanzees, and changing my concept of a chimpanzee. This holism is likely to have its usual paradoxical consequences, seen in the bizarre epistemologies and metaphysics of holism everywhere. My thoughts are incommensurable, hence rationally incomparable, both with others and with those of my earlier and later selves.

6   There is no distinction drawable, even in principle, between functional and nonfunctional connections. A positive linkage between two nodes in a distributed network might mean a constitutive link (e.g. **catlike**, in a network for tiger); a nomic one (**carnivore**, in the same network); an accidental, inductive one (**asian**, in the same network), or a merely associative one (in my case, a particular football team that play in black and orange).

It is admittedly hard to be certain in one's judgements on this issue, for connectionist models are still in a very early stage of development. But I suspect that the notion of a distributed representation merely muddies the water; I think Fodor and Pylyshyn may be right in arguing that connectionist representations are structureless. But even if they are wrong, I suspect that a distributed representation of (say) coffee is *so* unlike the concept **coffee** that distributed representation cannot explain how cognitive representation could be systematic and productive. Smolensky in effect admits this in his reply to Fodor and Pylyshyn (Smolensky, 1988b, p. 149). I think a thorough-going connectionist should deny that cognitive representation is productive and systematic, and should appeal to some diachronic story to explain the illusion that it is.

Thought is complex in two ways. Some concepts are, or seem to be, structured. The concept of aged and alcoholic grannies contains the concept of grannies as a constituent. Despite the doubts I have just aired, distributed representation might shed light on the connectionist treatment of this facet of complexity. But there is a second facet. How does a network represent 'Chimps like gorillas' rather than 'Gorillas like chimps'? For it's not enough that the patterns of activation that stand for chimps, liking and gorillas all be active.

There seem to be only two ways of dealing with this problem. One is to slice the representational pie thinner and have, instead of chimpanzee or ape patterns, distinct patterns for chimpanzee-as-subject, chimpanzee-as-object, and so on. There seem to be two strong objections to this proposal. First, it threatens to proliferate microfeatures beyond control. For we would need a separate feature for every syntactic role recognized. That's a large number of roles, for consider:

> Chimpanzees like apes;
> Gorillas that like chimps like apes;
> Baboons that like gorillas that like chimps like apes;

and so on, for the degree of recursion the overall cognitive system is capable of attaining.

Second, the proposal raises in sharp form an issue that is already problematic for connectionist theory. In virtue of what do these representations have their representational properties? In virtue of what does some distributed network represent chimphood? We saw in chapter 6 that the task of explaining representational properties is far from trivial, but one might hope it is no worse for connectionists. Perhaps a pattern of activation represents apeness in virtue of being reliably present when an ape caused the stimulus. A connectionist might think that indicator theories, or teleological theories, of content go as well with connectionist accounts of mental life as with language of thought accounts. I have already mentioned problems with that idea; one might be able to give an indication theory of microfeatures, but it is much harder to give a coherent connectionist account of how we can represent words, or rooms, or even vowels; in short, of the features of our world that we can routinely recognize. But once we move to the claim that a certain distributed network represents chimps *qua* subject, the problems of giving a connectionist account of representation get much worse. For what is it for an activation pattern to correlate with *chimp qua subject*? A subject-chimp is not a special kind of chimp, like a female chimp or a pigmy chimp. It is a way of representing chimps. Language of thought theories at least have a sketch of what's involved in saying that a certain concept, or structure of concepts, has some particular syntactic role. For such theories recognize structure-dependent processes. It's in virtue of its role in those processes that a representation has the syntactic properties it has. The syntactic property of conjunctivity, for example, will play a role in a considerable variety of inferential processes. But connectionist theories recognize only local processes; no process operates on a (distributed) representation as a whole. So it offers no equivalent story of how an extra microfeature in a representation could make a chimp-representation be a representation of chimps as the subject of some thought.

An alternative is to suppose that there aren't nodes dedicated to specifying the subjecthood of chimp, when active, but dedicated to simply representing various constituency relations. This is the alternative embraced by Hinton (see Hinton et al., 1986, p. 83 and p. 107). This suggestion avoids the proliferation of microfeatures. But the problem raised above reapplies: in virtue of what is a dedicated node the **subject-of** node? There is still no hint of an account of the representational properties invoked. Here connectionism shows its roots in artificial intelligence in which the representational properties of cognitive models are simply stipulated. But the representational properties of our mental states are not the result of some theorist's stipulation.

Let me summarize the state of play. The critics of connectionism claim that both connectionist representation and processing are of very restricted kinds. They then argue that humans (and nonhumans) have representational resources much richer than those encompassed by connectionism, and that those richer representations make possible complex, structure-dependent operations. So there is no adequate connectionist theory of those representations and processes. The connectionist response is tripartite. In part, they have a deflationary view of our representational capacities: thus connectionists and their allies are sceptical of appeals to productivity and to linguaform representation. In part, they claim that the critique understates the representational structure they can admit: so there are various connectionist attempts to incorporate, or mimic, constituent structure in representation. I have been most sceptical of this response. Third, there is the beginnings of the attempt to mimic complex processes by simple ones: that's the message of connectionist attempts to deal with 'high-level' cognitive processes like language, conceptual schemas, and the like.

8.6 Connectionism and the Language of Thought

What then should we make of connectionism? In particular, to what extent does it undermine the representational theory of mind? On these questions it would, of course, be idiotic to be dogmatic. It is still early days for connectionism. Even so, some tentative conclusions are in order.

1 We should be very cautious about drawing radical conclusions from connectionist models. First, like virtually all work in artifical intelligence, we get, at best, accounts of tiny fragments of human cognitive capacities. We get no account of how we recognize words, but rather a model of the capacity to recognize some English four-letter words presented in a standard typeface. We get no account of how we use language but an account of the ability to produce the past tense form of the verb, given the infinitive. Hinton and Rumelhart both investigate our capacity to encode information in a quasi-sentential way, but model only minuscule chunks of the information any human has, and say even less about the ways we can use that information. It is not just connectionists who do this; everyone in the AI community does. The hope of course is that these models of small chunks of an ability will generalize to something like the whole ability, a hope that so far has been conspicuously disappointed. It may not be in this case, but there is no argument to connectionism as a global theory of the mind from its demonstrated success in dealing with some major portion of it.

Second, if we consider these fragments, it is often hard to tell exactly what chunk of human cognitive capacity they are supposed to be modelling, and what we could count as success. Marr began by giving an account of the precise nature of the competence he hoped to explain. Whatever the other failings of his project, that methodology at least enables us to evaluate his success. Now let's consider, for example, schemata. These are a hypothesized form of mental representation alleged to underlie much of our recognition, categorization, and similarity judgements. A schemata of a bird is not a *definition* of a bird, for it does not specify the necessary and sufficient conditions of being a bird. Rather, it is a specification of a *typical* bird: a specification that particular animals might fit exactly, reasonably well, or not at all. A seagull, the idea runs, will fit the schemata snugly; an emu, not very well; a snake, not at all.

Rumelhart, not surprisingly, thinks there is something to the idea of schemata, for it has the 'softness' – the more-or-lessness – beloved of connectionists. So he gives a sketch of connectionist schemata. The networks in question represented rooms. Each node (of which there were 40) represented a room-feature; say, the presence or absence of a coffee pot. Of the enormous number of states of the network, only five were stable: these correspond to the stereotypes of a kitchen, bedroom, bathroom, living room and office. The network was 'run' by fixing a few of the nodes as 'on' (say: fridge-node and telephone-node) and waiting for the network to then settle into one of the stable states.

Now, it's entirely unclear to me what psychological process this story is a story of. Is it, for example, supposed to be a preliminary model of recognition? If so, it's not a very plausible account. Do we recognize a room by first noticing a few features, then a few more, then still more, and so on? Further, we routinely recognize cross-functional rooms: bed-sitting rooms; office bedrooms, kitchen-dining rooms, and so on. If Rumelhart's model were on the track of an account of recognition, it seems to predict that such rooms would be difficult or impossible to recognize. Is it then supposed to be an account of memory? It's hard to see how. What memory process is represented by the settling into the stable state from the fixing on of some of the feature nodes?

Consider another example. In Ramsey et al. (forthcoming) a network is described that is supposed to capture the information that is held in a cluster of propositions about cats, dogs and fish and their putative possession of fur, fleas, legs, fins and scales. The network is structurally of a fairly standard type, with three layers of input, hidden and output nodes. But the bank of input nodes are quite unlike those with which this chapter started. In the mine/rock detector and the word recognizer, the input nodes are transducers. Not so in the Ramsey network; nor do they represent anything else. So what *is* the input; where is it from? Moreover, the output is odd: the output nodes are just true/false nodes. The output is blind to the particular proposition up for judgement; it cannot evaluate 'Dogs have fleas' as true, and thus yield as output 'Something has fleas'. If this network were part of a larger system, it would act on that system in only two ways. So what fragment of human competence is this a first pass at? It seems to be the beginnings of a quiz module.

Third, in considering the idea that connectionism should replace language of thought based accounts of cognition, we should bear in mind not just the analogies between connectionist and human processing, but the disanalogies as well. To take just one example, connectionist learning is slow, proceeding as it does by the gradual adjustment of internode weights. Some human learning is slow. It takes a long time to learn the chess positions in which you should swap a bishop for a knight. But some learning is very quick; you can find out where the knight is just by looking. Lots of human learning is quick; there is a lot of one-shot learning from perception and language. Connectionist learning looks a good model for skill learning, but not for information gathering.

2 Still, despite the reservations above, and all the trumpet blowing

that seems epidemic in this field, it is clear that the connectionists are on to something. Pre-connectionist AI was extrodinarily unimpressive in its attempts to construct devices capable of pattern recognition, sample-to-whole recognition, and recognition from degraded or distorted inputs. Despite all their limitations, relatively simple networks seem surprisingly good in these areas. The damage resistance and graceful degradation under overload of networks are a genuine strike in their favour. But all this can be conceded without seeing connected nets as replacements for language of thought based theories of cognition.

How modest should the claims on behalf of connectionism be? I suggested in section 8.3 a division of labour; we should look for connectionist accounts of pattern recognition, the acquisition of skills, and the like whilst still looking for essentially inferential accounts of many other cognitive capacities. It is rash to second guess the future, but that still seems right to me. Should we also see connected nets as implementing rule and representation based accounts of, for example, language understanding? Remember, we can think of nets as implementation theories; either as neural theories, with irrelevant detail stripped away, implementing cognitive processes, or as lower-level cognitive theories implementing higher-level ones.

The suggestion that networks are implementations raises issues too murky for me to resolve. I will no more than mention three of these. First, it is not obvious that nets that implement complex representations retain the properties that make nets attractive accounts of elementary cognitive processes in the first place. Is damage resistance inherited up, or brittleness passed down? Second, it may be that nets are not good implementations of complex representations. Kirsh has argued (Kirsh, 1988) that nets are a very clumsy and expensive implementation of representations that contain variables. Natural language is rich in variables, for anaphoric pronouns are the natural language expression of bound variables. In 'three policemen who got drunk shot themselves', the relative pronoun 'who' and the reflexive 'themselves' are anaphors bound by 'three police'; that is, the interpretation of the anaphors is parasitic on 'three police'. If mentalese is rich in variables, or if Kirsh's argument generalizes to other syntactic structures, then nets look unlikely implementations of mentalese. Thirdly, Ramsey et al., in the paper mentioned earlier, argue that connectionism as a *cognitive* theory is incompatible with intentional psychology. If so, then the language of thought is not implemented by more fundamental, but still cognitive, connected nets. I am unpersuaded by their particular argument, for I think it depends on the acknowledged simplifications of their model. Nevertheless, the problems of distributed representation suffice to show that there are real problems in seeing connectionist *cognitive* models as implementations of a language of thought.

No one can tell yet whether connectionism is a 'new paradigm' for studying the mind. But if it is, it is a deflationary one. For I argued in section 8.5 that distributed representation is not an adequate connectionist stand-in for the complex representations of mentalese. So if connectionism replaces language of thought based views of cognition it will do so in part by lowering our estimate of the powers of our cognitive engine. But I pointed out in section 8.4 that so long as the connectionist is willing to turn a sceptical eye on intentional psychology, and seizes on to diachronic accounts of partial systematicity where it is found in the mind, the pessimistic opinion of our powers may be defensible. There is a tradition, after all, in psychology of 'explaining' our general, context-independent intelligence by denying that we have any such capacity. I suspect the radical connectionist ought to join this club.

Suggested Reading

Section 8.1

It has been widely argued that connectionism enables us to accept the representational theory of mind without accepting the view that the mind is a symbol processor. Both Churchlands argue this; see the readings for chapter 7. See also Hatfield and Kosslyn's 'Representation Without Symbol Systems' (1984), Hatfield's 'Representation and Content in Some (Actual) Theories of Perception' (1988) and Nadel et al., 'The Neurobiology of Mental Representation' (1986).

Section 7.5 of P. M. Churchland's *Matter and Consciousness* (1988a) is a clear, enthusiastic and nontechnical introduction to connectionism. Two other good introductions are Tienson's 'Introduction to Connectionism' (1988) and Horgan and Tienson's 'Settling into a New Paradigm' (1988), both in a special issue of the *Southern Journal of Philosophy*. Andy Clark's *Microcognition* (1989) is a lively and readable book-length treatment of all the issues in this chapter, defending a sophisticated form of the idea that connectionist and language of thought theories of the mind can cohabit. The first four chapters of Rumelhart et al. (1986a) present the connectionist case in reasonable detail, with nothing technical that cannot be skipped. An alternative somewhat earlier presentation is Feldman and Ballard's 'Connectionist Models and their Properties' (1982).

Sections 8.2–8.3

Broadbent argues for an implementational interpretation of connectionism in 'A Question of Levels' (1985). An important overview is Smolensky's 'On the

Proper Treatment of Connectionism' (1988a), though this is a rather murky and difficult paper; it came out, together with commentaries and a reply in *Behavioral and Brain Sciences*. A number of connectionist papers that emphasize the neural plausibility of connectionism are collected in *Neurocomputing*, a recent anthology edited by Anderson and Rosenfeld (1988). See also Dan Lloyd's *Simple Minds* (1989) which discusses connectionism in the course of developing a theory of representation informed by, and sensitive to, the facts of neural organization.

Sections 8.4–8.5

A massive counterattack on connectionism appeared in a special issue of *Cognition*; the two main papers are Pinker and Prince's 'On Language and Connectionism' (1988) and Fodor and Pylyshyn's 'Connectionism and Cognitive Architecture: A critical analysis' (1988). Smolensky replied in his 'The Constituent Structure of Connectionist Mental States: A Reply to Fodor and Pylyshyn' (1988b). Fodor in turn has replied. See Fodor and McClaughlin (forthcoming) 'The Rutgers Chainsaw Massacre II'. See chapter 9 of *Microcognition* (Clark, 1989) for a judicious summary and assessment of these debates.

Dennett is sceptical of the alleged systematicity of animal mental representation in 'Mother Nature versus the Walking Encyclopedia' (forthcoming). Millikan too is sceptical; her 'Biosemantics' (1989) is good on the differences between human and near-human representational systems and more basic ones.

9

Reduction and Autonomy

9.1 Autonomy Revisited

Many physicalists defend the 'autonomy of psychology'. Functionalism, as an account of the mind, is designed to reconcile autonomy and physicalism. These issues were raised in the first three chapters; I will now return to them in the light of what has already been said. In particular, I shall consider the bearing on autonomy of Churchland's anti-functionalist arguments, the connectionist models discussed in the last chapter, and Fodor's own speculations on modularity.

There is, in fact, no single autonomy thesis. Rather, there are at least three autonomy theses; metaphysical, methodological, and epistemic. Fodor, Lycan, Putnam and Dennett have all explicitly or implicitly defended a metaphysical thesis: namely that the natural kinds of psychology are not identical to those of the neurosciences or any other reducing discipline. Every instance, or token, of a psychological state is, sure enough, identical to some neural state. Every psychological kind is realized by neural kinds. But, it is said, nothing like type–type identities are available, a claim buttressed by familiar appeals to actual and possible variation in the physical implementation of single psychological states. So our first version of the autonomy of psychology is:

The natural kinds, and hence laws, of psychology are not identical to the natural kinds and laws of any other discipline. Hence the discovery of the physical realizors of these kinds will not show, even in principle, that the special kinds, laws and explanations distinctive to psychology can be discarded.

A second version of the autonomy thesis is methodological; it can be extracted, in particular, from the work of David Marr. We saw in chapter 4 that he defended a distinctive methodological strategy for those investigating the workings of the mind. First, specify as precisely as possible the information processing competence of the system under investigation. Only then try to find computational processes adequate to that competence, and neural implementations of those computational processes. From this idea we get the following methodological maxim:

> When constructing psychological theories, do not get bogged down in the details of implementation, either computational or neural.

The upshot of this methodological maxim is that psychological theorizing can proceed, especially in its early days, independently of neuroscientific theory. Only when the nature of psychological competence is accurately specified, and one or more computational models adequate to that competence have been developed, will the neurosciences play a pivotal role in psychology.

A third version of the autonomy thesis is epistemic. To what extent is neuroscientific data relevant to psychological theory? In the opinion of at least some of those defending autonomy theses, neuroscientific data are of little significance. For example, no one working within the transformational movement makes much appeal to neural evidence when defending their favoured theory of linguistic competence. No one claims that neuroscientific data are *in principle* irrelevant to psychology. Scepticism is much more limited than that. It has a number of sources. One is principled: neuroscientific data bears *directly* only on the implementation of psychological functions. Yet you cannot tell from looking at an implementation just what function is being implemented. You cannot tell noise from message, or error from success. A single physical process can be implementing a word processing command on my Mac one minute, a chess command ten minutes later. But much of the scepticism about neural data has more mundane sources: above the level of single cells, we know too little about the functional mechanisms of the brain. There is not enough reliable neuroscientific evidence at the right scale for the neurosciences to play an evidentially central role in psychology. So perhaps we can formulate our third version of autonomy as:

Expect psychological theories to be confirmed or disconfirmed essentially by psychological evidence. That is, evidence about learning curves, reaction times, error patterns and the like.

All three theses are limited and partial. Psychology can never be completely independent of the neurosciences, for there is an ontological dependence of psychology on those sciences. Psychological functions and processors must be physically realized by neural matter, not wonder tissue. A psychological theory requiring functions realizable only by wonder tissue is *ipso facto* a false theory. Even the most devoted follower of Marr's methodological maxims expects only a partial and temporary independence of psychology from its physical base. Marr's own work on early vision treated the constraints of implementation very seriously; he always looked for algorithms that were plausible candidates for neural implementation. So it's never thought that psychology is evidentially entirely independent of the neurosciences; even as staunch a defender of autonomy as Fodor stoops to appealing to those sciences in defending his modularity thesis.

Patricia Churchland (1986) expresses her scepticism about all these autonomy claims: epistemic, methodological, and metaphysical.

9.2 Against Autonomy

Patricia Churchland characterizes the antireductionist as accepting all of the following four claims:

1 The categories of folk psychology are essentially correct.
2 These categories define intentional states, and hence logical and semantic relations between those states.
3 These categories fail to reduce to neurobiological ones.
4 Not only does neuroscience fail to reduce; the neurosciences are largely irrelevant to folk psychology.

Churchland identifies two central ideas behind the autonomy thesis so conceived. First, information processing is reasoning, so the brain is a sentence cruncher. I discussed her reasons for rejecting that idea in section 7.4. Second, psychological kinds fail to reduce to neurobiological ones because they are multiply realized.

Churchland grants the multiple realizability of psychological kinds, but denies that this blocks reduction. If psychological kinds reduce to neural ones, then metaphysical autonomy, at least, is undermined. So let's consider her line of thought. Her basic idea is that 'reductions may be relative to a domain of enquiry' (p. 357). She gives the nice example of temperature, which is mean molecular kinetic energy. More exactly, the temperature of gases is mean molecular kinetic energy. But when we speak of temperatures at the heart of stars, for example, we are not talking of that, for there are no molecules to be found at the heart of a star.

The property of temperature is multiply realized by more fundamental physical properties. But it by no means follows that temperature is irreducible. What are we to say to this? It might explain how pain-in-chimps and pain-in-humans reduce to neuroscientific concepts, albeit in somewhat different ways. But it does not seem a good model for explaining the physical difference between my and Patricia Churchland's thinkings-about-Paul-Churchland. For one thing, humans and chimps fall into different domains, so it is fine for different reduction laws to apply to chimps and humans. Similarly, gases and solids are distinct kinds, so distinct reduction laws can reduce the physical property of temperature. But Churchland and I both have our human moments, so, since we do not belong to different natural kinds, the same laws, including reduction laws, had better apply to us both. Secondly, many functionalists argue for more than the multiple realizability of intentional kinds. They further suggest that the set of realizors is arbitrarily large and messy. If that is right, there is a disanalogy between intentional states and temperature and, perhaps, between intentional states and pain as well. It is likely that temperature and pain have a small and closed set of realizors.

Moreover, we need an explanation of why pain-in-chimps and pain-in-humans are both instances of a more general phenomenon. It is hard to see how that explanation could be neuroscientific. Consider a biological analogy, the widespread phenomenon of mimicry. Some species protect themselves from predators by an evolved resemblance to a distinct dangerous or foul-tasting species. Consider two cases: a harmless snake mimicking a venomous one, and a tasty-to-birds moth mimicking a foul one. Obviously, there are 'domain specific' reductions of mimicry. There will be explanation, in genetic, developmental, and metabolic terms of how the distinctive patterns, in virtue of which snakes and moths mimic their respective models, grow and are maintained. But these explanations do not tell us why and how these patterns are important to the animal, nor will they explain how the snake and moth instance a general phenomenon. Equally, a case-by-case reduction will leave out the psychological and biological import of pain to the organism, and why the two sorts of pain are examples of something more general. That is so, even if the realizing kinds are a small and tidy set.

It is important at this point not to get down in verbal issues about the meaning of 'reduction', a notion far from clear. The central claim made by defenders of metaphysical autonomy is the *no-replacement* thesis; see, for example, the introduction to Fodor's *The Language of Thought* (1975). That is, the identity of each instance of a psychological kind with some instance of a more basic physical kind does not allow us to replace psychological theory with a theory of the more basic physical level without loss of explanatory power. If the analogy with mimicry is good, the existence of domain specific reductions of psychological kinds does not allow replacement without loss. The reduction of Kepler's laws of planetary motion to Newton's more general laws of mechanics did permit just that, as does, apparently, the reduction of some chemical properties (e.g. valency) to physical ones.

Suppose the no-replacement thesis is true of psychology. That certainly does not establish the epistemic and methodological irrelevance of the neurosciences to psychology. I think these ideas have been defended only in a limited way. Nevertheless, I think Churchland is probably right in refusing to allow even a limited independence, and insisting on the methodological and epistemic interdependence of different theoretical levels. None the less, the 'co-evolutionary strategy' she endorses is perfectly consistent with psychology's not being replaceable, even in principle, by the neurosciences. This is the sense of autonomy functionalists have been most concerned to defend.

In part, I think that Churchland and the archfunctionalists are talking past one another. For the notion of autonomy that she is most moved to attack, the methodological and epistemic independence of psychology, is the one they are least moved to defend. Churchland makes many acute points demonstrating the epistemic relevance of the neurosciences to psychology. For instance, in the early chapters of her book she outlines some fascinating data on cognitive deficits: impairment of cognitive function due to brain lesions. Much of this data, though clearly of interest, is not easy to interpret. In part, that is because some of it is so weird; for example, blindness denial (pp. 228–30). It is hard to imagine the intentional states of someone who has gone blind without realizing it; surely it must be obvious that you can no longer see. Not always, it seems. People blind from damage to the visual cortex, rather than the eyes, sometimes deny, sincerely, that they are blind. Blindness denial and other similar denials clearly bear on psychology, but their nature is so obscure that it is hard to decide exactly *how* they bear. Interpreting neurological data is complicated by a second factor: there is no straightforward inference from a deficit caused by a lesion to specific neurons to the conclusion that those neurons have the function of subserving the lost function. If removing a segment of DNA from a human chromosome turns legs into stumps, it does not follow that the function of those genes is turning stumps into legs.

Churchland is right on the epistemic point. The neurosciences are evidentially relevant to psychology. Equally, I think she is right to be sceptical that any strong notion of autonomy can be founded by appeal to Marr's levels, and an associated structure/function distinction. The caricature defender of autonomy thinks of psychology as the study of various information processing algorithms that compute ecologically significant functions. The realization of those functions is a concern only of the neurosciences, whose domain is implementation. But that is just the plumbing; psychology proceeds breezily independent of such messy details.

I doubt that anyone holds a methodological independence thesis as nakedly as this, though Putnam once might have. Certainly, no one ought to. For, as Lycan has often argued, and as Churchland argues here, there is no absolute structure/function, or function/realization, distinction. Rather, the kinds that realize a functional property are themselves functional kinds which must in turn be realized. So, for instance, being the template of a face in a memory store may be realized by an array of points in a matrix. But matrices and arrays are functional kinds. There is no general division of labour according with the motto: 'psychologists study functions, neuroscientists their realizations', because there is no general function/realization distinction.

9.3 Reduction and Elimination

If the kinds posited by folk psychology or cognitive psychology cannot be physically realized then they ought to be eliminated. Churchland argues for the stronger view that if no type–type reduction is possible, then 'a fragmentation and reconfiguration' (p. 365) of the unreduced theory is appropriate. Thus Churchland imposes strong constraints on physicalist theories of cognition: high-level theories need to be (a) reduced to lower-level theories, or (b) to be 'reconfigured' until they can be reduced, or (c) eliminated. Since it is widely accepted that the prospects for the reduction of intentional kinds are not good, an acceptance of Churchland's constraint greatly strengthens the case for eliminativism.

She makes her case for necessity of reduction through two, non-cognitive examples. I will discuss the most important of these, the relationship between classical population genetics and molecular genetics, in some detail. For I want to draw exactly the opposite conclusion from it. I shall argue that natural kinds need not be reducible to ultimately physical ones, though they must all be realized by ultimately physical ones.

In classical genetics, genes are the units of hereditary transmission, mutation and recombination. For many years after the founding of classical genetics, the molecular basis of the gene was unknown. The discovery of the double helix structure of DNA in 1953 began the unravelling of this mystery. It turned out that the basic coding of genetic information is very simple. The most primitive elements of the code are four bases, adenine, thymine, cytosine and guanine, that can occur in any order on a strand of DNA. Each group of three bases specifies one of 20 amino acids; these are the basic elements out of which proteins are built. So the primitive information in the genetic code is information about proteins.

Thus, the basic code is very simple. But the relationship between this code and the inherited characteristics of mature organisms turned out to be incredibly complex. (a) A given chunk of DNA material in some particular organism typically has more than one effect; for example, the gene responsible for albinism in humans also turns out to cause peculiarities in the structure of the human optic nerve. (b) Many chunks of DNA that are biochemically just like others seem to do nothing at all; to make no causal contribution to the organism. This so-called 'junk' or 'parasitic' DNA is not physically different from functional DNA. (c) There are many repetitions; apparently redundant sequences in the genetic material. (d) The one trait – shortness, or dark skin – can have quite different genetic bases. We have already seen part of the reason for that; the base to amino acid code has redundancies; the same acid can be specified by more than one base triple. So different base sequences can underlie the same proteins.

These facts mean that there is no simple, one–one relationship between the classical notion of the gene and the molecular structures which realize its biological functions in replication and development. There are two ways one can read this set of facts. First, a functionalist might see here an argument for the relative autonomy of population genetics. Molecular genetics would then be seen as an implementation theory rather than as a theory that could, in principle, replace population genetics.

Churchland rejects this line ((1986) p. 364). She grants that classical genetics is not reducible as it stands. But some more complex descendant theory is. We can get a one–one reduction 'so long as the micro half of the relation is permitted to include things beyond the DNA configuration, things like the biochemical milieu' (p. 366). Why does a simple one–one reduction between 'classical' genes and 'molecular' genes fail? It fails because of the effects both of the other genes on the chromosome and of the biochemical situation in the cell in which the gene works. The surround makes a difference to (a) whether and when the gene does *anything* – to whether it is 'switched on' and thus synthesizes a protein, and (b) what that protein does. So if the reducing kind is a strip of DNA plus genetic surround plus cellular environment, the relationship between classical and molecular properties is tidier.

Churchland thus rejects conventional wisdom. An 'evolved macrotheory', classical genetics as revised in the light of biochemical information, is reducible to a suitably sophisticated microtheory.

I think Churchland's reading of this example is questionable, and think there are two strong considerations against it. First, classical genetics continues to be relatively independent of molecular genetics in just the ways defenders of the autonomy of psychology would expect. I will make this point with two brief examples. Consider, first, altruism. It's obvious that altruistic behaviour, behaviour that benefits group mates and cost to self, is good for the group in which an animal lives. But how could such a behaviour evolve? Vampire bats live in colonies that share food; an unsuccessful hunter will solicit blood from a luckier hunter. This mechanism is very important to the survival of colonies, as bats cannot go long without food, and individual hunting failures are not rare. But why are such groups not subverted, or prevented from forming, by cheating mutations; bats that solicit aid but who refuse to give it, thus gaining the benefit of social living but not bearing the costs. Sewell Wright suggested one possibility. Suppose the population of a species is divided into small subgroups, with breeding within the group, so there is little or no gene flow between groups. In small groups, random factors can play a large role, so a chance mutation for food sharing could become universal within a small group. The cooperative group would be less likely to go extinct in a bad season, and thus it and any daughter groups it founded might survive ecological crises in disproportionate numbers. Perhaps we could even reach a situation in which all the surviving subpopulations were descendants of an original altruistic group.

I will give one more example. In humans, and many other animals, the sex ratio at birth is close to $1:1$. Why? In the thirties, Fisher gave the following explanation. Suppose the ratio in some species was not $1:1$. Imagine that the female dragon:male dragon ratio is one:three. What kind of offspring should a female dragon produce, assuming that females and males are just as easy to make? In these circumstances, she should produce females, for on average only one in three of her sons will mate. So she maximizes her grandchildren by making daughters. That is to say, once the ratio slips away from equality to a pre-ponderance of males, natural selection will favour (all else equal) a gene that makes bearing females more likely. If females become more common, natural selection will favour a male producing mutation. The stable ratio, if costs are the same, is $1:1$.

The point about these examples is, first, that their force is indepen-dent of implementation details. The precise molecular machinery for sex determination is irrelevant. That machinery is under the influence of natural selection, and through natural selection the $1:1$ ratio is stable in very many animal groups. Evolutionary theory is full of similar cases of cost benefit analyses that assess the likely fate of a gene 'for' a certain trait; analyses that do not stand or fall on the molecular details.

Second, I think it is quite wrong to suppose that a classical gene can be identified with a microtheoretical kind that includes the genetic and biochemical environment of the DNA chunk. For classical genes are first and foremost units of heredity. An organism passes some of its genes to its offspring; that is the explanation (in part) of parent–offspring similarities. The biochemical and genetic environment is not passed on; a child, gaining 50 per cent of its genes from each parent, will have a distinct biogenetic environment for its inherited chunks of DNA. So no microtheoretic kind that includes genetic neighbours or cellular environment is identical to a classical gene or can play the same explanatory role as the classical gene.

So I think that classical genetics does not reduce to molecular genetics, though classical genes are realized by chunks of DNA, in particular biochemical and genetic surrounds. Genes are implemented by chunks of DNA, but classical genetics is not in principle replaceable, and it does have a modest methodological and epistemic independence. So we can draw an important conclusion from this tour through biology. Physicalism does not require that every good theory be reducible, ultimately, to physical theory. So the fact that folk psychology, and much of cognitive psychology, is unlikely to reduce to the neurosciences does not commit us to their 'reconfiguration' or elimination.

9.4 Autonomy and Modularity

Churchland acknowledges but downplays the significance of the multiple realizability of computatational processes. But is it so obvious that the information processing mechanisms of the mind are multiply realized? We can explore this question through a hypothesis we have already discussed: Fodor's modularity hypothesis.

The defence of autonomy we have been considering is guided by a methodological principle, namely that theories are warranted by their explanatory power. So a theory is justified if it gives us 'access to generalizations' unstatable within rival frameworks. Functional theories of a given level of abstraction are justified if they deliver lawlike generalizations, generalizations unstatable in less abstract terms. Systems heterogeneous in their physical constitution and workings turn out to exhibit, at higher levels of abstraction, homogeneities. Let's suppose, for instance, that recognizing 'Paint it Black' isn't a neurophysiological kind. Our actual neurophysiologies, and other possible neurophysiologies, differ too much for us to be able to specify a neural property that is recognizing 'Paint it Black'. So recognizing 'Paint it Black' isn't a neural natural kind, but it's a natural kind of some variety. For we can give explanations, and state generalizations by appeal to such properties that would otherwise escape us. Functional kinds in general, and computational kinds in particular, are justified by their explanatory value. Otherwise we get hyperinflation of computational theory. It's wrong to see a rock as following a rather boring program (following the command 'erode slowly' in response to most inputs); it's wrong to think of planets computing their course around the sun (see section 1.2). These weeds can be excluded if we admit only those computational theories that pay their way. We licitly abstract away from physical detail only to purchase a more unified or general theory.

But if the modularity hypothesis is right, it's not obvious that our perceptual modules are sufficiently neurally idiosyncratic to fund a generalization argument. Will my phoneme recognition centre or face recognizer vary so sharply from other English speakers that only at the computational level will commonalities emerge? If our minds do have a modular organization, in particular if those modules are serviced by dedicated wetware, individual differences in neural organization may not be so enormous after all.

Fodor and other defenders of the modularity hypothesis regard modules as *computational* subsystems of the human mind. However, it is far from obvious that we should follow their lead here, particularly bearing in mind the distinction between the ecological and computational levels. The modules have representational functions: they function to recognize faces, to detect phonemes, to tell the mind the direction from which a sound has travelled, and so on. But these job descriptions are silent on mechanism; in particular they do not commit us to the view that, for example, the face recognizer recognizes faces by rule governed symbol processing.

If the perceptual mechanisms are modular, a computational description of their workings may well be redundant. We are confronted again with a problem we met in sections 1.2 and 3.5. Consider, for example, Ullman's 'Correspondence Problem'. If you want to be able to infer the distance from you to an object from either the apparent motion it causes on the retinal image, or the disparity of the position on the two retinal images of its representation, you need to be able to reidentify its representation from image to image. That's the Correspondence Problem (See sections 4.3–4.4). Ullman very reasonably wanted his computational solution to that problem to be biologically plausible. So he shows it can be solved by a 'simple network': a locally connected network of simple processors (1979, pp. 87–91). Without venturing into details, he suggested that there is no principled difficulty in the neural implementation of those simple processors. Marr is similarly motivated. He suggests that there is no neurophysical implausibility in positing mechanisms that register discontinuities in the intensity values on the retinal image and that thus detect edges. However, if these processes can be implemented in a simple, local and uniform way in wetware, then a worry becomes very pressing. Why go beyond a *wetware* explanation of their processing? A computational symbol processing description of their behaviour seems as otiose as describing the digestive system as counting calories. You *can* describe a digestive system that way, but it helps not at all in explaining digestion.

Let's consider another example. 'Priming' is the acceleration of comprehension in 'semantically predictable' circumstances. People are a little faster in recognizing the word 'dog' in the context 'Beware of the savage ...' than the context 'Sweet and sour ... is delicious'. This phenomenon has often been seen as an example of the effect of background knowledge on perceptual processing. Fodor, on the contrary, argues that it is best explained as the result of associative links, not background knowledge. He may be right in denying that priming is a counterexample to his modularity hypothesis, but if so, there is no reason to regard priming as the result of inference or anything at all like it.

A problem for the autonomy of psychology thus looms. Adoption of the modularity hypothesis opens the door to a straightforwardly neuro-scientific account of the best understood psychological mechanisms, the perceptual mechanisms.

If so, that chunk of psychological theory does reduce. The ecological level, specifying the jobs that psychological mechanisms perform, reduces to ethology and evolutionary biology. The neurosciences explain the operations of those mechanisms. No essential role for cognitive psychology remains. There are four possible reactions to this line of thought. (a) One can accept the argument, and conclude that inferential and other computational models of cognitive processes have only a temporary or heuristic value, useful intermediaries in the development of a satisfactory neuroscientific account of mechanism, but no part of the final truth about how our mental processors operate. (b) We could accept that we ultimately do not need a computational theory of per-ceptual processing but will still need such a theory of the central pro-cesses. (c) We could abandon the modularity hypothesis. (d) It may be that the 'access to generalizations' methodology is too restrictive. Perhaps symbol processing explanations play an essential explanatory role even when the symbol processing device is uniformly realized. Let me say a little about this last option.

There are at least two ways of defending a symbol processing account of a uniformly realized mechanism. Perhaps the invariant realization of the device is a mere accident. Mutation or an unusual development sequence *might* have built an alternative implementation. For example, Berwick and Weinberg (1986) have argued that our capacities to understand complex sentences are just what you would expect if our built-in transformational grammars prohibited too much change between deep and surface structures. In particular they have in mind a constraint on movement called the *subjacency constraint*. They argue that if elements could radically change position, as surface structure is transformed into deep structure, it would be very difficult to decode speech. The interpretive possibilities become unmanageably large and complex. Since we can decode speech, the grammar we have built into us in virtue of which we can speak and understand includes the subjacency constraint, *however that grammar is realized*. That is so, even if there happens to be only realization. The Berwick–Weinberg argument does not explicitly appeal to multiple realization. But it still depends on implementational diversity. For why should we talk of internal grammars at all if there is a single physical mechanism common and peculiar to language understanding? True, there *might* have been another mechanism. But if there is only one mechanism, then it is hard to see what a neurophysical explanation leaves unexplained.

There is an alternative way of downplaying the significance of multiple realizability. An intuitive idea is that a purely neuroscientific account of mental mechanisms collapses an important distinction between our mental capacities and the capacities of very simple animals and inanimate devices like thermometers. Our perceptual mechanisms are special, because they are rule governed rather than lawlike. Our perceptual processing is intelligent; it is like inference or like problem solving. If the modularity hypothesis is right, it is problem solving from a restricted data base, but it is inferential none the less. (See, for example, Fodor (1983), Rock (1983) especially the introductory overview, and the introduction to Pinker (1985).) Our abilities to recognize artefacts contrast with the output of a thermometer. The reading on a properly constructed thermometer is simply and fully explained by physical laws. Not so our capacities. We have no difficulty in recognizing certain shapes as tables. Now, table to table stimulus to table percept interactions are realized by lawlike physical processes, but there are no table–table stimulus–table percept laws; laws characterizing all/only such interactions. For tables are not natural kinds. So there are no laws about tables *qua* tables; hence, in particular, no table–table percept laws. Now, of course, in some sense each instance of perceiving a table is a law-governed process. But if we were satisfied by such case-by-case accounts, we would miss a phenomenon that can be captured by a computational account.

Fodor has defended this view because he thinks there is a difference in kind between the abilities of higher animals to respond adaptively to their environments and the ability of, for example, single-cell animals to respond adaptively to their environments. No one believes in an autonomous psychology for the *E. Coli*, despite their adaptive response to lactose. Many believe in an autonomous psychology of humans and chimps. Perhaps the difference is that *E. Coli* respond not just to fewer kinds than we do; they respond only to natural kinds. In virtue of housing within symbol manipulating mechanisms, we respond as well to nonnatural kinds. Selective response to nonnatural kinds distinguishes symbol processing systems from those that merely react causally to environmental stimulation, and thereby distinguishes those systems for which an autonomous psychology is appropriate.

This idea has a lot of intuitive plausibility. There really does seem a difference in kind, not just degree of complexity, between the ability of an ant to recognize a nest-mate, and our ability to recognize caricatures of Reagan. But it is hard to make Fodor's suggestion work; that is why in section 3.5 I emphasized the flexibility and adaptability of a system rather than relying on Fodor's suggestion.

Consider first the idea of a natural kind. If we construe this idea tightly, then too many creatures have autonomous psychologies. Fodor and Pylyshyn (1981) took natural kinds to be those needed for formulating the laws of the physical sciences. But if we follow this path, we will need an autonomous psychology of, for instance, bees. They respond selectively to the dance and movement of other bees, for that's how one bee transmits information about food sources to others. But bee motion ain't no natural kind of physics. Of course, if we are generous about what counts as a natural kind, then we will all become antlike. If a kind is natural merely by figuring in counterfactual supporting generalizations, then just about all kinds are natural kinds. 'Table' will name a natural kind: 'If I have my eyes open, and in good light, and if there is a table in front of me, then I will see a table' is true, counterfactual supporting generalization.

Suppose this worry can be defused. 'Table' doesn't name a natural kind. So, the idea runs, our regular and stable capacity to recognize tables isn't a manifestation of a law of human perceptual nature. To capture this phenomenon, we must appeal to the rule-governed transformation of symbols. That is, it's a *computational* process. There is a problem with this argument; it depends on a false dichotomy.

Consider artefacts, or natural designed systems like stomachs. Car keys aren't natural kinds either. So in some *strong* sense of law, there are no key–engine laws. So one might say that a car's starting when the engine is turned on doesn't express, in this strict sense, a nomic regularity. But we certainly wouldn't conclude from that that the engine starts by recognizing some symbolic input. For the relationship between key turning and engine firing is decomposable into a chain of events, each pair instancing a straightforward law of either mechanics, electricity, or chemistry. In a broad sense, the key–engine regularity, while not exceptionless, is counterfactual supporting and sustained by laws. Consider a natural mechanism. What happens when we eat an apple? There are apple–chemical energy regularities; regularities that are mediated by a very complex mechanism of ingestion and digestion. There are no *strict* apple–chemical energy laws; the mechanism can break down or fail to operate in the usual way for a myriad of reasons. Regularities of digestion are at least sustained by laws if they are not themselves laws. In both of these cases we can and do give functional explanations. If we wish, functional explanations that abstract away from many of the physical details of the processes. Why think perception is different? Manifestly, it decomposes into a chain of events, which really are connected by nomic regularities. We can give functional stories here too, and these need not be obsessively detailed. Neuroscientific explanation is, as Lycan tirelessly reminds us, functional explanation. We need some reason to move beyond a functional explanation to a computational one. It is true that perceptual systems are tuned to nonnatural kinds. But many merely functional systems react selectively to nonnatural kinds; for example, engines respond to the insertion and clockwise motion of a key.

The modularity hypothesis undercuts the autonomy of perceptual psychology by undercutting the claim that psychological devices are multiply realized. That is not the only basis for claiming that psychology is irreducible to the neurosciences. I have considered alternatives here and in section 3.5. But it was the most convincing basis.

9.5 Autonomy and Plasticity

We require explanatorily important computational generalizations to contrast with ecological specifications in being genuinely about how the cognitive system works. We require them as well to be unavailable to the neurophile who refused to traffic in notions like representation and rule. It is not obvious that there are any such generalizations.

I think it is very plausible to suppose that the perceptual modules have a good deal of innate structuring. If so, there will be neuroscientific generalizations covering (say) human speech perception. A neural theory doesn't have to be a description of what every neuron is doing at all times. The neurosciences can accommodate a good deal of plasticity and individual variation from person to person. For they can advert to structural and functional commonalities across our different brains. In this respect neurosciences are just like the other sciences of the structure and function of organs and organisms. It is possible to give a theory of the human circulatory system despite a good deal of variation in the fine grain of the capillary network and in the degree of clogging and general decay from person to person.

Suppose we abandoned the modularity hypothesis. After all, the data supporting that architecture is drawn mostly from vision and speech perception. These are our most highly developed senses, each having a mass of dedicated and specialized hardware. The deliverances of our other senses may not manifest the informational encapsulation perhaps characteristic of these two. There is some anecdotal evidence for that; it's said that if you touch the skin of a person expecting heat with a piece of ice, the initial sensation is of heat. There's some nonanecdotal evidence as well: namely, in the *dominance* of visual information over the tactile transducers, in case of conflict. (On this phenomenon, known as visual capture, see Rock (1983, pp. 70–1).

So we may be idiosyncratic at the level of brainware, not just in detail and locally, but globally and structurally. If so, perhaps no brainware generalizations about how we all perceive our world are available. (Though I do not really believe this likely.) Why expect a *computational* level of similarity, between physical heterogeneity and common ecological function? If our cognitive mechanisms are idiosyncratically organized through drawing on flexible and multipurpose wetware, then perhaps we maintain relatively similar capacities by different means. If so, there may be no uniformities about how this mechanism works; neither uniformities statable by talk of neural assemblies and the connections between them, nor uniformities statable by talk of representations and transformations upon them. Classical cognitive psychologists believe that the organization of the brain is plastic; too plastic for there to be any theory of cognitive functioning statable solely in the language of neurons, connections and assemblies thereof. But the appeal to plasticity may cut deeper than they want. Paul Churchland has argued, after all, that *the mind* is also plastic; cognitive procedures are not fixed once and for all across the species. It is possible that both are right. If so, the explanation of psychology's rather halting progress is that *there are no laws to discover about mental processing*. We have been asking the wrong questions. Don't ask: how do people recognize their house or plan their dinners? Ask: how do multitudes of different procedures for house recognition and dinner planning develop into roughly comparable competences?

This is a decidedly spooky conclusion. Psychology disappears either by reducing to the neurosciences or by dissolving into myriads of special cases. We are not forced to this conclusion, but it is not so easily escaped. The defence of autonomy requires the acceptance of two hypotheses.

1 *Cognitive uniformity*: Our representational structures, and the procedures that access them, are near enough identical across the species.
2 *Neural diversity*: The physical implementation of those structures is enormously varied.

The appeal to neural plasticity is supposed to warrant the assumption of diversity, and hence require (granted hypothesis 1) a move to a level of theorizing that abstracts away from physical implementation, and which is therefore irreducible. What we need now is a reason for believing hypothesis 1. A defender of hypothesis 1 needs to show that interesting features of cognition are explicable by appeal to some hypothesized computational model, *not* by appeal to the way that model is implemented. There are some very striking features of human perception: for instance, we are terrific at recognizing faces in normal orientation, even from obscured photos, line drawing, or caricatures. But we are awful at recognizing upside-down presentations. Suppose we had (a) a computational model of face recognition that predicted exactly those features of our ability, and (b) evidence for very wide divergence in the neurophysiology of our face-recognition routines; suppose for instance that the capacity was recoverable from strokes and lesions. Then surely we would have good reason to accept that computational theory of the mechanism of face recognition.

Evidence of this type is going to take some finding. A good place to look is at the central processes. Variation in the physical implementation of central processes may well preclude reduction to the neurosciences. So what might a look at central processing show? One candidate, of course, is intentional psychology itself. If anything in this whole area is uncontroversial, it is that if there are intentional states, they are diversely implemented. But that is a big 'if'. For intentional psychology to underwrite cognitive psychology, intentional states must be causally salient and computationally similar inner states of sentient organisms. I believe that the moon is roughly spherical. So do you. But do we token syntactically similar sentences in our languages of thought? Do we process those sentences in similar ways? If we do, and if intentional psychology is explanitorily indispensable, then intentional states realized by sentences in the language of thought constitute one domain of autonomous central psychology.

Can we defend autonomous psychology from less controversial premises? It would be good to appeal to the results of cognitive psychology itself here. But most is irrelevant. Much cognitive psychology is perceptual psychology, and we certainly cannot assume wildly divergent implementations of perceptual processes. Some of the psychology of cognition, as distinct from perception, is vitiated by a failure to distinguish claims about what is represented from claims about the medium of representation. That distinction is crucial in this context, for what we need is an argument that our minds use similar means, not that they perform similar jobs. There has been, for example, in both cognitive psychology and artificial intelligence a good deal of discussion as to whether, in addition to sentential representation, there are as well special structures for representing somewhat larger chunks of information. There are many different ideas and terminologies around, but most are concerned with the problem of explaining our great capacities for default reasoning, our ability to infer what will usually happen in a wide range of meagrely described circumstances. To explain these capacities, different theorists have posited schemas, prototypes, scripts and frames. These discussions are often horribly muddy: prototypes, for example, are sometimes described as though they are subsentential structures – fuzzy concepts – and sometimes as though they are built of sentences. But even more typical in these discussions is a failure to distinguish between the domain represented, and how we represent that domain. So, for example, the discussion of scripts sometimes amounts to the claim that we have representations of typical social interactions, and sometimes to the quite different and much stronger claim that we have special structures for those representations.

However, there is one group of studies that seem to be just what we need. There is a substantial body of work on human reasoning, and in particular, on the characteristic error patterns in that reasoning. Distinctive patterns, especially but not only in probabilistic reasoning, stand out. Human susceptibility to various forms of the gambler's fallacy is notorious. We are very apt to infer from a previous run of good cards that our streak will continue. We are all equally apt to infer that we are 'due' for a good hand; if the past has been sad, the next deal is especially likely to be kind to us. We have these beliefs even when we are quite sure the deal is fair, but of course those beliefs are quite irrational. If the deal is fair, there is no causal connection between past and future hands. This inferential tendency is just one of many pathologies of reasoning. Another is a well-documented resistance to change known as the 'belief perseverance effect'. Suppose you come to believe, say, that Lindy Chamberlain, not a dingo, killed her child on the basis of evidence of blood stains in the Chamberlain car. Even if you afterwards come to believe that evidence to be quite unreliable, there is a strong tendency for the inferred belief to persist. The similarities in the way things go wrong across the population suggest that we carry out inferential processes in the same way. Yet these are not modular processes, so quite likely there is no dedicated neural mechanism common to the population. So perhaps one good home for autonomous psychology is that of central processor reasoning. Unfortunately, we will see in the next chapter that it is very hard to come up with a good theory of intelligent reasoning.

Time to summarize. I want to draw three morals from this chapter. First, the notion of autonomy is quite ambiguous, and some, at least, of the debate this idea has generated depends on this ambiguity. The differing views are less far apart than they seem. Second, there remains an important disagreement. Intentional psychology, and probably a chunk of cognitive psychology, is irreducible to the neurosciences. Churchland argues that this shows that intentional psychology needs to be at least revised so that it is reducible. I deny this, claiming that population genetics, and I think many other areas of biology, are not reducible to any more basic science but are none the worse for that. Physicalism requires that all natural kinds be physically realized. But it does not require all kinds to be reduced to physical kinds. Third, I argue that the domain of autonomous psychology is likely to be much narrower than many of its defenders suppose. In particular, the best-developed psychology, perceptual psychology, is quite likely not autonomous. For the most important underpinning of the theoretical independence of psychology, the multiple realizability of psychological states, gets at best an uncertain grip in perceptual psychology.

Suggested Reading

Section 9.1

Well-known defences of the autonomy of psychology are the introduction to Fodor's *The Language of Thought* (1975), and two of Dennett's papers, 'Intentional Systems' (1971) and 'True Believers' (1981a), reprinted in *The Intentional Stance* (1987). Earlier defences are Fodor's *Psychological Explanation* (1968) and two papers of Putnam, 'Minds and Machines' and 'The Nature of Mental States', both chapters of *Mind, Language and Reality* (1975). Pylyshyn also argues for the irreducibility of psychology in the first two chapters of *Computation and Cognition* (1984), but that is much tougher going. Fodor and Pylyshyn certainly rely on a sharp function/implementation distinction in their critique of connectionism; in 'Connectionism and Cognitive Architecture' (1988) they come perilously close to asserting methodological and epistemic independence of psychology.

Section 9.2

Patricia Churchland's most important attack on autonomy is *Neurophilosophy* (1986), especially chapter 9, but a good deal of what she says there is prefigured in earlier papers, particularly 'A Perspective on Mind-Brain Research' (1980). The book was the subject of a special issue of *Inquiry* (vol. 29, no. 2), both the discussion and her response is worth looking at. The

Churchlands demonstrate their ideas on the reconfiguration of folk psychology in their papers on consciousness and qualia, for they are not eliminativist about the experiential states of the mind. Particularly good are 'Consciousness: The Transmutation of a Concept' (P. S. Churchland, 1983), 'Reduction, Qualia and the Direct Introspection of Brain States' (P. M. Churchland, 1985), and 'Functionalism, Qualia and Intentionality' (Churchland and Churchland, 1981). The case studies detailed in Sachs' *The Man Who Mistook his Wife for a Hat* (1985) demonstrate the significance of neurology for psychology; unfortunately the case studies are accompanied by a good deal of 'humanistic' moralizing that is a bit hard to take. Dennett's 'The Logical Geography of Computational Approaches: The View from the East Pole' (1986) entertainingly maps the terrain of views on the relations between psychology and implementation, and argues that differences have been overplayed.

Section 9.3

Reduction is an extremely murky issue in the philosophy of science; there is no generally accepted view of its nature or consequences. Churchland relies heavily on the account defended in a three-part paper by Hooker; 'Towards a General Theory of Reduction, Parts I–III' (1981). But this is technical and difficult. Philip Kitcher gives a philosophically and biologically acute account of the relations between population and molecular genetics in two papers, 'Genes' (1982) and '1953 and All That' (1984). Dawkins in *The Extended Phenotype* (1982) emphasizes the importance of the gene as the unit of inheritance; genes are identified functionally, not biochemically.

Section 9.4

Fodor defends his distinction between rule governed and lawlike response in 'Why Paramecia Don't Have Mental Representations' (1986). There are two collections on, in effect, the biological mechanisms underlying modular processes, Caplan's *Biological Studies of Mental Processes* (1980) and Walker's *Explorations in the Biology of Language* (1978). Part IV of Garfield's *Modularity in Knowledge Representation and Natural Language Understanding* (1987) covers only vision, but is much more up to date. A recent, reasonably accessible text on the biology of memory is Squire's *Memory and Brain* (1987).

Section 9.5

Three good sources on reasoning are Kahneman, Slovic and Tversky's collection *Judgment Under Uncertainty* (1982), Johnson-Laird and Wason's collection *Thinking* (1977), and Johnson-Laird's *Mental Models* (1983). These studies are lucidly, though pessimistically, summarized in Stich's 'Could Man be an Irrational Animal?' (1985).

10

Explaining Intelligence

10.1 Computation and Intelligence

In the preceding chapters I have both elaborated and defended a theory of cognition. According to that theory, cognitive states are representations, often representations in a language of thought. Cognitive processing is the transformation of those representations. Computation, as I have used the term, is the rule-governed transformation of representations where those rules apply, or fail to apply, in virtue of the structural features of a representation. The rules of a natural deduction system are paradigms of the kind of rule I have in mind. I have not claimed that *all* cognitive processing is computation. I think it likely that at least some perceptual processing is not; the same may be true of output systems. Moreover I have left open the possibility that rule-governed transformations are implemented by processes that are still cognitive, but are not in this sense computations. It may be that connected networks, for instance, implement the processing of structurally complex representations. Moreover, there are important noncomputational questions to be asked about even those representations that are input to computations, questions about ecological function and implementation.

None the less, it is clear that an important part of my story is computational. As I explained in section 2.4, the representational theory of mind rests heavily on the computational theory of mind. I have explained the serious challenges this theory faces. I have discussed internal problems; in particular, the need for, and the difficulty of finding, a decent account of representation. I have discussed the sceptical challenge of those who allege that an account of cognition based on a language of thought is unnecessarily and debilitatingly extracted from a theory of the biological basis of cognition. No one could think that these issues are settled, but I claim that nothing like a knock-out blow has been landed on the representational theory of mind.

I have seen the computational theory of mind as a theory of the implementation of representational capacities. Some have seen it as a theory of general intelligence. In section 2.1, I argued that the distinctive features of intelligence are the adaptability, flexibility and informational sensitivity of the behaviour that it guides. Some theorists, perhaps most explicitly Newell, have identified this characteristic of on-the-hoof intelligence with a particular property of computer programs (see Newell, 1980). A function is a relation between two sets such that, given a member of the first set as input, there is an unambiguous member of the second that is the value of the function. So if the first set is the set of men, the second, women, the relation wife-of is not a function. For many men have had more than one wife. But the relation mother-of is a function. Not all functions are computable, that is, there is no routine sequence of operations that will, given an arbitrary member of the first set, tell you its match in the second. But many are computable: e.g. the truth table method of the propositional calculus is a mechanical procedure for checking the validity of an argument. If the lines in the table in which all the premises are true are also lines in which the conclusion is true, the argument is valid, not otherwise.

It turns out that there are 'universal machines'; an appropriately programmed Turing machine can compute all the functions any Turing machine can compute. Rather strikingly, it turns out that the same class of functions is computable by the universal machine of other architectures. Most computers in routine use have a 'von Neumann' architecture. These differ from Turing machines in a number of ways, most importantly in their access to memory. A Turing machine's memory is its tape, and it has access to a square on that tape *relatively*; as sequences of left and right scans from the square it is currently considering. There are no output instructions on a machine table that say anything like 'go into state 7 and scan square 47002 from the beginning of the tape'. 'Square 47002' is an absolute, not a relative memory address. Von Neumann machines can access their memory *absolutely*, a fact that enables them to make much easier use of a store of subroutines for standard problems that recur. There would be no point in having a subroutine for, say, determining whether castling was legal in a chess machine, if the program could not find the subroutine when needed. It is much clumsier to find these subroutines if they are not locateable absolutely.

Just as there are universal Turing machines, so too there are universal von Neumann machines. Furthermore, the class of functions universal Turing machines can evaluate is the same class that universal von Neumann machines can evaluate. The same goes for all the other known basic ways of organizing computational devices. All universal machines, no matter what their organization, have in this sense the same power. Newell proposes to identify being an intelligent being with being a universal machine. For its characteristic flexibility is a consequence of its having this computational universality. If so, AI would be vindicated indeed. But I rather doubt it. Universal programs are very psychologically unrealistic. For constraints both of time and capacity are ignored. Natural minds have to make intelligent decisions 'in real time'; problems have to be solved quickly enough to guide behaviour. Universal machines solve their problems eventually, but they are notoriously slow. Natural minds, unlike universal machines, have finite (and fallible) memories. In general, resource limits are crucial to biological intelligence. Any theory that idealizes away from that fact idealizes away not from messy but noncentral detail, but from a fundamental fact, as we shall see in our discussion of the frame problem.

I intend to conclude this book with a discussion of two sceptical challenges aimed particularly at a computational theory of general intelligence. In section 10.2, I deal with Searle's well-known challenge. He argues, in my view unconvincingly, that understanding is not a computational process. The crucial example bears directly on language understanding, but if it were any good it would apply much more generally. In sections 10.3–10.5, I discuss a class of problems collectively known as the 'frame problem'. Here, I have not even a solution sketch to offer. The aim of these sections is to bring out the difficulty and dimension of the problem. The frame problems are very important, but an inability to solve them is not a refutation of a computational theory of cognitive process. I say that not just for the usual reason, namely that nobody else is better off. It is rather that if the frame problems are unsolvable, then we have no general computational problem solver. We will turn out to be intelligent in virtue of having a large stock of efficient domain specific capacities.

10.2 Searle's Chinese Room

Searle, in a much reprinted paper (1980) and a follow-up book (1984), argued that neither a computational nor even a functionalist account of intelligence can succeed. Searle focused on the notion of understanding, trying to show that no computational theory captures the essence of understanding. It's an argument by counterexample. Searle constructs a scenario which (he thinks) (a) includes all the features a defender of the computational theory is entitled to, and (b) manifestly fails to exhibit understanding. Searle thus follows Block in charging functionalists of the computational stripe with liberalism: their theory mistakenly claims that nonsentient entities are sentient.

The example goes as follows. Imagine a windowless room with two slits in the walls. Inside the room is a monolingual English speaker, Mr Thatcher. There is no other person in the room, but it is not empty. There is a vast collection of curiously organized data; long lists of squiggles and squoggles, looking something like this:

$$\%_{0} \ \# \ ^{*} \ z^{*} \ \bullet \ \parallel \ \wedge \ , \ < \ ——$$

There is as well some blank paper, and some simple instructions written on the lists. The instructions say 'when a piece of paper with squiggles on it gets pushed through slit A, look through your lists until you find those squiggles on the right-hand side in one of your books. Write on a new piece of paper what's on the left-hand side, and push that paper out of slit B'.

Now, unbeknownst to Thatcher, who is deeply and aggressively monoglot, the squiggles are ideograms of Chinese. The inputs are questions, and the lists are drawn up with such care and insight that the outputs from slit B are idiomatic and sensible Chinese answers to the questions. Further, Thatcher is extremely good, and extremely fast at carrying out these operations. So it looks for all the world as though there is someone in the room who writes and understands Chinese. But we can see that that is not so. Thatcher, *ex hypothesi*, understands not a single word of Chinese.

Searle is doing more than making the antibehaviourist point that something could mimic the behaviour of a Chinese speaker without being able to understand Chinese. He wants to make an antifunctionalist, anticomputationalist point too. For he claims that the resources exhibited in the Chinese room exhaust the resources to which a functionalist can licitly appeal. According to the computational theory of the mind, linguistic processing consists of the manipulation of symbols according to rules that apply, or fail to apply, to the symbols in virtue of their formal properties. Whether we map a '*' onto a '<' depends only on the syntax and orthography of those symbols. Computational theory is an individualist theory; the processes are formally specified. So too is the linguistic processing in the Chinese room. A formal theory is the right theory of Thatcher's activities in the room. He, the central processor, manipulates symbols: he looks them up in his lists, matches, copies, and outputs symbols in virtue of their formal properties alone. Thatcher is executing a program. That is why he does not understand Chinese. Indeed, it is not just that in Searle's view following a program is not sufficient for understanding, it is not necessary either. Computational theories of the mind – 'strong AI', as Searle calls it – have nothing interesting to say about understanding or intentionality.

> There is so far no reason at all to suppose that my understanding has anything interesting to do with computer programs, that is, with computational operations on purely formally specified elements. As long as the program is defined on purely formally specified elements, what the example suggests is that these by themselves have no interesting connection with understanding. (1980, p. 418)

There are a number of responses to Searle's example. First, note that it is no part of functionalism to say that *any* functional, computational system that behaves the same way as an intentional system is itself an intentional system. Turing, in proposing the Turing test, advocated a behavioural test of intelligence and hence of understanding. If you cannot tell which of two hidden interlocutors (one person, one machine) is human, both are intentional systems (Turing, 1950).

In a fine paper, Block (1981b) showed that the Turing test is too weak. Any test of finite complexity and length could be passed by a very dumb machine provided that machine had a large memory and fast access to that memory. In effect, that is the situation inside the Chinese room. These conditions met, a machine that can look up and print out can pass the Turing test.

So perhaps what is going wrong in the Chinese room is not that the operations are specified formally. Rather, the room has the wrong kind of functional organization to qualify as a Chinese understander. This is how Searle himself describes the Chinese room, identifying himself as Thatcher.

> Suppose that I'm locked in a room and given a large batch of Chinese writing ... To me, Chinese writing is just so many meaningless squiggles. Now

suppose further that after this first batch of Chinese writing I am given a second batch of Chinese script together with a set of rules for correlating the second batch with the first batch. The rules are in English, and I understand these rules as well as any other native speaker of English. They enable me to correlate one set of formal symbols with another set of formal symbols, and all that 'formal' means here is that I can identify the symbols entirely by their shapes ... I get so good at following the instructions for manipulating the Chinese symbols and the programmers get so good at writing the programs that from the external point of view – that is, from the point of view of somebody outside the room in which I am locked – my answers ... are absolutely indistinguishable from those of native Chinese speakers. Nobody just looking at my answers can tell that I don't speak a word of Chinese. (1980, p. 418)

Once we see this, differences in organization leap off the page. Fodor and Pylyshyn, for example, in defending the computational model of the mind, defend a 'classical architecture'. To be a Chinese understander, the inner system of representation must be productive and systematic, and guaranteed so in virtue of its basic architecture. The symbols manipulated inside the room are not part of a systematic and productive system, for Thatcher has no means of generating new symbols of arbitrary complexity. Nor is there any guarantee that, if the Chinese translation of 'China will invade Poland' is on the list, so too will be the translation of 'Poland will invade China'.

The functional organization of the Chinese room is odd in other ways as well. For it does not consist of a system of interacting homunculi, but instead a super-fast homunculus and a collection of inert data stores. Further, the one homunculus in the Chinese room is *only* fast; it is not required to be smart or versatile. It just performs look-up and copying, even though it is physically realized by a very smart homunculus. Thatcher is over-qualified for his job.

So one response to the Chinese room is to insist that it only refutes the idea that behavioural identity with a Chinese speaker is sufficient for understanding Chinese. Searle tells only what we already know.

This response suggests a second. We might agree that *Thatcher* does not understand Chinese, yet argue that the example makes not even a prima facie case against a computational theory of understanding. For such theories do not attribute understanding to an 'understanding centre' within a black box; rather, it is attributed to the organization as a whole. The Chinese room understands Chinese, even though no proper part of it does. Searle considers and dismisses this reply (the 'systems reply'). First, he considers it staggeringly implausible; he thinks it could be offered only by someone in the grip of ideology. Second, he gives the following argument against it:

My response to the systems reply is quite simple: let the individual internalize all of these elements of the system. He memorizes the rules in the ledger and the data banks of Chinese symbols, and he does all the calculations in his head. The individual then incorporates the entire system. There isn't anything at all to the system he doesn't encompass. We can even get rid of the room and suppose he works out doors. All the same, he understands nothing of Chinese, and *a fortiori* neither does the system, because there isn't anything in the system that isn't in him. (1980, p. 419)

This reply fails for two reasons. First, notice that it is only coherent because of the very peculiar functional structure of the room, namely that only one component *does anything*. That is why we can imagine it all inside Thatcher. If Thatcher first passed the incoming message to Kinnock, the ledger keeper, who passed it to Winston, the copier, who gives the output back to Thatcher, we cannot so easily imagine this whole system internal to Thatcher. So, first, this antidote to the systems reply depends on a feature of the example that is already objectionable.

Second, Searle is wrong in supposing that any property of a system *in* Thatcher is a property *of* Thatchers. Grant that the system (input, look-up/checker, data banks, copier, output) is all in Thatcher. It may be that this whole organization understands Chinese, but that Thatcher does not. Consider an analogy with colour vision. According to Land's well-supported retinex theory of colour vision, perceived colour is a function of three distinct sampling processes. One samples long wavelengths, one samples medium, and a third short. Perceived colour is based on integrating information from three retinal sources. Now the colour vision system is something inside us, and it is an information processing system. But it is not information we have. The information available to, and processed by, the retinex system is not that available to the agent who houses that system.

So Searle's response to the systems reply is no good. None the less, though that reply is part of the right response to Searle, it is only part of it. For Searle is right in thinking that the manipulation of symbols, no matter how sophisticated, is not sufficient for understanding, for it is not sufficient for intentionality. Nothing can understand Chinese unless it has thoughts, for the room has got to rightly believe (say) that the last input was a question about Beijing. Sophisticated internal processing is consistent with the thoughts being about Twin Beijing, or about nothing at all. For thought to have content it must be appropriately connected with the thinker's environment. So I am inclined to run the systems reply jointly with the so-called 'robot reply'.

The robot reply envisages placing a computer inside a robot that can both perceive and act upon the world. Under those circumstances, the computer really does understand Chinese. Searle does not like the robot reply either, for the man inside the room does not know the sources of the symbols he gets. The room is now equipped with sensors, but the TV eye and the electronic ear convert their input to symbolic form, and pass it into the room, where it is still squiggles and nothing more to Thatcher.

All I am doing is manipulating formal symbols ... I am receiving 'information' from the robot's 'perceptual' apparatus, and I am giving out 'instructions' to its motor apparatus without knowing either of these facts. (1980, p. 420)

The knowledge of the homunculus inside the room is irrelevant. The symbols are given content by their causal connections with the world, not by the homunculus' recognition of those connections (see chapter 6).

In effect, the robot reply is a version of the system reply. Understanding Chinese, like the capacity to have other intentional states, does not reside in a single place in the system. The system as a whole, where that includes perceptual organs registering the environment, understands Chinese. It does so in part in virtue of its location in its environment and in part in virtue of its internal organization. Notice that this version of the reply is immune to Searle's comeback: we cannot coherently think of all these goings on, *including the connections to the environment*, as wholly inside Thatcher.

Thatcher does not understand Chinese. But not because of facts that undermine a functionalist or computational theory of the mind.

10.3 The 'Frame Problem'

What are the cognitive requirements for a modestly intelligent system? In particular, a system whose basic means of representing the world is a language of thought, and whose basic mental operation is inference. The 'frame problem' names a cluster of problems that arise in the design of such a creature, and which arise for those who think we are such creatures. I will follow Dennett, Fodor and Haugeland in taking 'the frame problem' to name a broad area of concern about the prospects for reconstructing intelligence as mechanizable reasoning. I have not the beginnings of an idea how these difficulties should be solved. So the purpose of these sections is to explain the problems, and to explain why they are hard.

In a delightful paper, Dennett (1984) has introduced these problems by illustrating the design difficulties facing the creator of a robot able to act in the world. He has in mind not the problems of mechanizing genius; no one expects a chrome Newton or Napoleon to come rolling out of MIT. Merely getting through the day alive is all we ask of this robot. So we construct our first prototype, R1. R1 had better be able to work out how to achieve its essential life-preserving goals from its information about the current state of the world, otherwise it will never be able to find the power point for a feed. So we equip R1 with the capacity to, in effect, prove theorems from the basis of its current information store. When it needs to do something, say, replenish power, it proves the theorem Pluginto (power-point, socket) from its data base; the intermediate steps in that proof will describe actions it needs to perform to meet its need. Clearly, R1 is a sophisticated guy, equipped with a means of both representing the world and its own goals and with the capacity to draw complex and directed inferences from that world representation. But sadly, it seems that R1 is not sophisticated enough. For Dennett confronts R1 with the task of collecting its power source from a room with a bomb in it. R1 does just that, extracting the battery by pulling out the wagon on which it, providentially, was resting. But providence is quirky; the bomb was on the wagon too, and R1 failed the survival test. R1 was able to construct a plan, but was unable to pick up the side-effects of its actions.

So R1 is replaced by R1D1; R1D1 is constructed to check for the side-effects of its plans, for clearly these side effects can frustrate the plan, or can have consequences that render the plan pointless. R1D1 is confronted by the test that doomed its ancestor, and does not fall into the same trap, or any other. For R1D1 is an Italian government; it does nothing at all. R1D1 faces two problems. It needs to know what it needs to think about, and it needs to know when it has thought enough. First, there are indefinitely many consequences of any act; nearly all are utterly trivial. Taking the battery out of the room changes the number of objects in the room, the total mass of the objects in the room, the surface area of the objects in the room and so on. You do not want to know about most of the changes your behaviour causes. But in addition to the changes, there are all the states of affairs that did not change, but which might have. Removing a battery does not cause the colour of the walls to change. But that is not true of all actions; exploding the bomb will change the colour of the walls. Moreover, though our robot does not usually care about mass or surface area, there are times when it will. When the room is in a rocket, R1D1 needs to worry about mass. So what does not matter, and what does not change, must be settled on a case-by-case basis rather than once and for all. So R1D1 needs to know what matters in *these circumstances* if it performs this action. Change circumstance or action, and you can change what matters.

So R1D1 needed to be directed in its thoughts; when you must rescue your battery from a bomb you should not spend hours proving theorems about the independence of motion and colour. In the favoured terminology, R1D1 needs improved mechanisms of control, so that its thoughts are tailored to its intended deeds. But it also needs to know when to stop. It needs a 'halting criterion'. Even if our robot is thinking about the right issues, about (say) the chances of its vibrations, or its magnetic field, detonating the bomb, there comes a time when R1D1 simply has to go for it. Creatures with finite resources of time, computational power and information can never be certain that their plans will not be frustrated by some foreseeable but unforeseen effect of their behaviour. In the jargon of economics, we must satisfice; near enough is good enough. So our device needs to know when it has thought enough, even though at that point the very next deduction may be crucial. Here, too, contextual effects are crucial. We can not just tell R1D1 to think for ten minutes and only ten minutes about everything. The sensible expenditure of resources will depend on at least: the importance of the act, the availability of information and the pressure of time. It is clear that there is no simple rule of when enough is enough.

Could we solve the relevance problem, at least, by developing some test of which effects (including 'no change' effects) of its actions a robot needs to care about? Apparently not; such a test would only make matters worse. For then our improved robot, R2D1, would not only have to prove all the junk theorems; it would have to apply the test to them, label the junk as 'irrelevant' and then proceed to the next member of its endless list. So R2D1 would suffer even more severe deductive diarrhoea than its ancestor. We need some way of getting R?D? to genuinely ignore most but not all of the consequences of its explicit representation of the world as it is and is about to change.

Thus those who think that intelligence is based on language of thought representation, and inferences from those representations, are faced with nasty problems. We need to know (a) the exact nature of these problems; (b) the prospects for their solution, and (c) the extent to which these problems are derived from one particular view of cognition.

10.4 Problem or Problems?

Essentially, we are faced with two types of problems. We need to solve a problem of *representation*. Which aspects of its world must the robot model? And we need to solve a problem of *transition*. How are the models transformed? These issues interact. In the final section, Fodor (1983) expresses a good deal of pessimism about the prospects for a good theory of central processing. The problems that I have discussed above, Fodor takes to be a special case of a more general problem, the rational fixation of belief. R1D1 needs to come to fix its beliefs about what will happen when it goes into the room for its battery. R1D1's beliefs had better be arrived at rationally, else it is likely to suffer from recalcitrant experience. But much human reasoning is nondemonstrative. We reason by analogy and from symmetry considerations. We use inductions of various kinds. Even our most routine planned behaviour involves much reasoning of this kind. Think of all you must know in planning your route home from your university. Most of this is utterly banal: that sticking the key in the lock in the car might open it. But if you did not know facts of this kind you could not go home.

Nondeductive inference must surely be a feature of any intelligent action in a natural environment. In those environments we must repeatedly form beliefs about what's on the other side of the door, beliefs based on information always limited and perhaps even unreliable. Rational belief will rarely be the result of proofs from what has been proven. But this is bad news for a theory of intelligent action, for we are a good way from a theory of nondemonstrative reasoning. Moreover, we need not just any theory. The project is to reduce intelligence to inference, and inference to formal symbol manipulation. That is, inferences are transformations of complex symbols in virtue of facts about their structure. That is a reasonably plausible view of deduction; systems of natural deduction are collections of rules for just such transformations. But there is no current prospect of a theory that represents a good nondeductive inference in terms of the structure of the premises and conclusion.

Why is it so hard to find a nondeductive analogue of deductive logic? Fodor emphasizes the global nature of assessments of inductive reasoning. In part, this just means that everything you know is potentially relevant to the assessment of an inductive inference. The first 18 people to walk into room X are fit young men over six feet tall. Should I bet that the next person to walk in will probably be the same? That depends on the rest of my information; if I know that those 18 are the complete Australian Rules football team I would be a fool to think so. One can draw the conclusion from an inductive inference only if the premises include all your evidence; there is a 'total evidence' requirement on sound inductive inference. Deductive inference is not global in this sense, for adding a premise never turns a good inference into a bad one.

The global nature of inductive inference is more than the potential relevance of everything you know. Global properties of the belief system are relevant to the assessment of nondemonstrative inference. Why is it irrational to believe that the universe was created five minutes ago, looking just like a 20 billion year old one? That hypothesis is not inconsistent with the observational data, nor is it self-contradictory or incoherent. Some have argued, in my view very implausibly, that the hypothesis is really meaningless. I think it is perfectly meaningful, but it would be very silly to accept it, or even to seriously consider it. It violates canons of plausibility, simplicity and testability. But these are features of one's overall belief structure, or at least large chunks of that structure. These canons do, and ought to, play a very large role in determining which inferences we accept. The apparent age of the universe shows that it really is very old; it does not show that the universe has been prefaded by God. But no one has much idea how to formalize the ideas of simplicity, or plausibility, and the attempts to formalize testability have not been markedly successful.

A second problem is the problem of complexity, of the combinatorial explosion of tasks faced by a computer. R2D1 needs, in the course of planning and acting, both to have an effective model of its environment and to continually update that model, because of the changes it effects in the world, because of its changing position in the world, and because of R2D1–unrelated causal processes. Suppose, for example, that the robot represents the distance and direction from it of objects in its environment by a list of sentences; by discrete chunks of information in some form. It certainly needs egocentric representation if it is to actually manipulate anything, for it needs to know, as Paul Churchland has emphasized, the direction and distance it needs to grasp. But every time it moves, every single member on that list needs to be recomputed, and continuously so. R2D1 must incessantly deduce, to keep its egocentric world model in repair. But this of course massively understates the potential explosion of tasks the RnDns face.

For one thing, it is not merely its egocentrically specified relations to its environment that the robot must update. For the robot will cause many other changes to its world, both directly and indirectly, and its model must be updated to include these. Further, no real robot will be the only agent of change in its world. If it is to survive, it must be able to deduce the consequences of the processes it knows of, not just those it initiates. These tasks are demanding enough (as we shall see) even if we can somehow engineer the robot so that it only needs to worry about real changes. We somehow need to get R1D1 to ignore pseudochanges. (Congratulations! You have just become the first robot in the universe to have recharged on Ex-O-Energy batteries 50 times ...), and normally *not* to have to deduce no change.

If our robot can avoid thinking about nonchange and pseudochange, it still has problems enough. For we are taking update to be an *inferential* process. That raises problems. For some deductions will take a very long time. Many algorithms make exponential demands on the resources of the device executing it. Calculating sequences of moves in chess is an obvious example. In an average chess position, there are about 20 legal moves. So the number of one-move sequences is only 20, but the tree gets very bushy very quickly: 400 2–move sequences, 8000 3–move sequences, and so. Theorem-proving tasks are also typically exponential if there is an algorithm that can execute the task at all. The number of steps required to solve the problem goes up as a power of the number of independent premises in the base. Checking for consistency is a problem like this. It is not always this bad; these measures of the computatational difficulty of a problem are 'worst case' measures. You may find inconsistency in the first line. But the number of independent elements in R1D1's picture of its environment is bound to be large even if we can eliminate the junk (see Cherniak, 1986, especially chapter 4). Furthermore, if nondeductive inference really does have a 'total evidence' condition, its addition to the picture is bound to make things worse. For nondeductive inferences will be inferences over large bodies of information that depend on consistency and coherence within those bodies.

Complexity is important; not all procedures that are in principle possible are feasible. A solution to the update problem does not have to be perfect. R1D1 can make mistakes. Presumably, that is where the hope of a solution lies, in theorem-proving strategies that are not guaranteed to solve a target problem, but will solve it, if they succeed at all, in reasonable time. There is a good deal of work already exploring this option. But the solution must be usable by a creature with finite resources.

A third problem, or problem area, is relevance. It is a characteristic of the various aspects of the frame problem that each makes the others worse. We have just seen how the combinatorial explosion of tasks is aggravated by nondemonstrative inference. That problem is also aggravated by the relevance problem; unless we can exclude the junk even otherwise reasonable heuristics are going to be overrun by the size of their task. But as we have seen, that task is very hard. What might change varies with context. Within unclear limits, what is important also varies with context. There are contexts in which the number of recharges matters; contexts in which R1D1 has actively tried to be the first to 50. There could even be contexts in which sensitivity to fleebees is desirable (section 6.6); if, for example, R1D1 can metabolize only flies or airgun pellets, then a fleebee detector is just what it wants. So we probably cannot exclude pseudochange once and for all by declaring certain predications of change bogus. Even if we could, Fodor emphasizes that we are in the business of explaining natural intelligence. So we cannot stipulate our way to a solution of the relevance problem. We need to explain how natural intelligences acquire the appropriate concepts for representing change, and how they avoid the junk (Fodor, 1987).

So a solution to the relevance problem requires a solution to the problems of control: R1D1 must think about the appropriate facts. It requires solving the 'halting problem'; the robot must have a criterion for moving from thought to action. Both seem to require a prior distinction, amongst all that R1D1 knows and can find out, between important and ignorable information. What makes information ignorable is far from clear, and it may not be one distinction but many. I have distinguished between no change and pseudochange; doubtless there is lots more to be said. But we need more than just an account of the distinction; we need a feasible means of applying it. Yet the finiteness of resources and the potential infinity of junk precludes significant resources being devoted to case-by-case testing for junk. We must mark the examine/ignore boundary while not searching the other side; a mere glance must suffice. Well, hardly anyone thinks the frame problems are easy to solve (though see the papers by McDermott, and Dreyfus and Dreyfus in Pylyshyn, 1987). But you haven't seen anything yet.

10.5 Why the Frame Problem is Hard

The 'frame problem' names an area, not a point. The last two sections list technical problems within AI of formidable difficulty. Yet in addition to each of these particular thorns, there is an overarching issue as well. Put briefly, attempts to solve the frame problem threaten to decompose our general intelligence into a myriad of specialist subabilities. For many have thought that these problems are generated by our representational hypothesis; they arise because the robot's model of the world is formulated in a language of thought.

It is no great surprise that sceptics about computational models of cognition think this. So Dreyfus and Dreyfus argue that the frame problems have their roots in the analysis of skill. They think the problems are generated by attempting to explain knowing how in terms of knowing that. They think this could not be more mistaken; learning how to do something is not the move from particular cases to the abstraction of general rules, but the converse. Skilful behaviour, from cooking to chess and bridge, is the grounding of a skill in a large number of key examples. Knowing when to add the garlic to the curry paste is not the unconscious application of a rule: add the garlic when the paste looks like thus and smells like so. It is having cooked, successfully and unsuccessfully, many pastes in the past and having thus become sensitive to the key features of *this* paste's pattern. Perhaps a connectionist network, or something like it, might realize an ability of this sort. For they write:

When things are going well experts do not solve problems or make inferences or figure out anything at all; they simply do what normally works and it normally works. (Dreyfus and Dreyfus, (1987), p. 102)

There is an air of 'with one bound Ralph was free' about all this. But that is really the wrong objection, for it is important to see the attraction of an anti-sententialist view of representation here. Haugeland brings this out nicely in his musings on Dennett's robots. Wouldn't it be lovely if R1D1 had inside it a little scale model of the room, with a pigmy battery and bomb on a tiny wagon. R1D1 could then try out its proposed course of action, namely pulling out the wagon, and would see that this was not a good idea. Of course, this requires our robot to have some moderately fancy perceptual tools. But they were needed for looking outside anyway. Why not have another set inside? Internal models would solve many problems. In particular, the complexity problem and the problems to do with nondemonstrative inference disappear. For if the internal model is a real scale model, the robot does not need to know how and why one state of the world changes to another state. The same laws and mechanisms that operate in the target case operate in the scale model. But the individual who exploits that parallel does not need to know the nature of those processes. I can find out the aerodynamic efficiency of a car design by testing a model in a wind tunnel even though I have no good theory of the nature of air flow; that is why models and wind tunnels are useful. So scale models in R1D1 are not an alternative representation of the world's dynamics, but are a way of avoiding having to know how the world will change. Scale models inside finesse much of the frame problem. You do not have to work out how the world changes in interesting ways, and distinguish these from pseudo-change and nonchange. For you do not have to work out how it changes at all. For the same reason you do not have to make a complex nondeductive inference to the underlying causal order of your fragment of the world; you do not need to know about that order.

Scale models inside reduce inference to observation. For they are an example of *intrinsic* representational media. Intrinsic representational media are those in which features in the represented domain are represented not in virtue of convention or use but as a matter of nomic law (Palmer, 1978). For example, in a system in which the length of objects in the represented domain is modelled by the mass of objects in the representing domain, we need no further structure to ensure that the transitivity of 'is longer than' is represented. Suppose the room with the bomb in it has two doors, and the wagon is further from one than the other. R?D?, equipped with its scale model, discovers that it takes less time to extract the wagon through the closer door. The model intrinsically represents spatial relations and their temporal derivatives. It intrinsically represents the fact that it takes more time to traverse more space. The robot does not need to infer this fact, nor does it need to work out which features of spatial relations it needs to represent.

No one has ever thought the mind contains scale models of the objects of thought. But some cognitive psychologists, for example Johnson-Laird (1983) and Kosslyn (1983), have proposed non-language-like systems of mental representation, in part because they doubt that problem solving is typically an inferential process. Johnson-Laird is responsible for some of the most interesting data suggesting that our inferential capacities are limited and fallible, and Kosslyn for much of the recent work within cognitive psychology on mental imagery. But I do not think that they are proposing intrinsic systems of representation. Kosslyn, for instance, thinks that we can scan mental images: we can form an image and survey it to find the features on it of representational interest. It turns out that scanning time increases with distance on the image. But is 'distance' here distance on the image itself, or distance in the situation represented? If images are intrinsic representations of spatial relations, then it is both. Image distance represents world distance. That is why it takes longer to scan greater distance. But images are not intrinsic representations of spatial relations and movement in space, for we can image the nomically impossible. You can image instantaneous changes in position, impossible distortions and the like. So mental images (and, for similar reasons, mental models) do not escape the frame problems. The agent has to know the dynamics of the world they confront; the physical properties of the representing medium will not absolve them of the problem by exemplifying the very same dynamics.

There may well be intrinsic representational systems in the mind. There seem to be a number of 'topological maps' in the brain; areas of the cortex in which the organization of the cells preserves the organization of their input. So, for example, in the visual cortex the connections from the retina preserve the spatial relations (though not distances) on the retinal image. So if B is between A and C on the retinal image the chunk in the visual cortex that registers B will be between those registering A and C. The retinal image, in turn, preserves some of the spatial relations of the scene in view. The other sense modalities make similar arrangements (see Nadel et al., 1986).

Paul Churchland has made intriguing and ingenious suggestions about the use of such maps (1986). He points out that an agent must often translate between them. He makes his points through a simplified example, a crab faced with a cut-down frame problem, sensorimotor coordination. The crab has a visual map of the terrain in front of its eyes. To live, it must seize the occasional edible titbit and gobble it. To do so, it must translate from its visual map to its muscle map. For each place within the crab's reach, there is a setting of the muscles controlling the crab's pincer arm that directs it to that place. Churchland imagines that there are only two such muscles. So two muscular coordinates will determine a unique position of grasp; the place of the pincer. The crab spots something edible. So it must go from a place on its visual map to a muscle setting that will guide the arm to the right spot. Now Churchland points out that, even if we make the simplifying assumption that only two muscles control the pincer, this is a computationally ugly task. But he also shows how to avoid the computation. For the cortex is arranged in layers. So if the eye map is on top of the muscle map, we can drop a line from each place on the visual map to the corresponding place on the muscle map. Connecting the maps avoids a complex computation.

The crab has to act, but does not suffer a frame problem. Why not? The crab does not just represent the world as it is; the translation from the visual to the muscular is a plan of action. So the crab is a dynamic agent. But first, the crab is not faced with a decision of what to think about. It suffers from no version of the relevance problem, and, second, wiring the maps together avoids the inference problem.

The crab is, of course, a much oversimplified version of the sensorimotor coordination of even simple creatures. Does it nevertheless offer an insight into the way real agents act successfully? One might think that it suggests how real creatures might use intrinsic representation to side-step the problems of inference. It would be foolish to be dogmatic, especially given the paucity of alternatives. But there are certainly reasons for caution. (a) The crab avoids the relevance problem by having a hard-wired cut-down world representation. The crab's design embodies a once and for all decision governing what the crab is to think about. I have already argued that for genuinely intelligent creatures the control problem cannot be solved that way. (b) Intrinsic representation avoids entirely, or massively simplifies, the transition problem. But intrinsic representations are special purpose representational devices, for their physical medium exemplifies some of the very same laws of the domain they represent. So they are tailored to a particular domain.

Patricia Churchland suspects that the frame problem is generated by a 'linguaform model' of mental representation (section 7.4). She must be at least partly right, for the frame problem is partly a problem of inference, and inference is paradigmatically a relation between sentences. But jettisoning the language of thought is not a free option. Languages, unlike images, maps and other intrinsic representations, are domain general. Languages enable us to think and talk about anything. Being able to think about anything is a necessary condition of general intelligence, of being able to solve problems in domains for which we have no special purpose mechanism. There are surely many such domains. I am sure most could figure out how to find the Sydney Opera House, or how to start a tractor; even those innocent of Sydney or farms. Perhaps this appearance of flexibility is an illusion. We may be just bundles of special purpose devices, though it is hard to see how experience could install special purpose devices without enlisting some much more general capacity. Attempts to solve, or avoid, the frame problem by proposing special, context specific representational systems in effect make the proposal that we are without general intelligence. Minsky's original paper (from which the name of the problem comes) is a suggestion of just this kind; frames are a domain specific representation aiming to cut down the inferential load of the transition problem by building stable features of the particular domains into the representation. As far as I know, so are all the other suggestions. They are suggestions not about how a domain general capacity might work but about how we might be getting by without one. This is why these problems are so very hard. We seem to have a general capacity, but we can explain only the possession of lots of particular capacities. Oh well, no one ever said that working out how the mind works would be easy.

Suggested Reading

Section 10.2

Searle's argument is given in his 'Minds, Brains and Programs' (1980); that was published with commentaries and a reply. That paper was reprinted, again with comments, in Dennett and Hofstadter's *The Mind's I* (1981). It is restated in *Minds, Brains and Science* (Searle, 1984) and also in 'Minds and Brains without Programs' (Searle, 1987). For a critical response similar to mine, see Rey's 'What's Really Going On In Searle's "Chinese Room"' (1986). For a relatively sympathetic discussion of Searle see Cummins' *The Nature of Psychological Explanation* (1983, section III.8). Cummins has his own, rather similar, doubts about the computational theory of the mind, but it is hard to work out exactly what these are; his is a rather obscure work.

Sections 10.3–10.5

Pylyshyn's collection, *The Robot's Dilemma* (1987), is excellent. It contains a good paper by Dennett and excellent surveys by Glymour, Haugeland and Hayes. It also includes a fractious exchange between McDermott and Fodor, and Dreyfus and Dreyfus' nonsolution. Haugeland's collection, *Mind Design* (1981) is slightly older, but still good. Chapters 1 through to 6 touch on various aspects of these problems, and Haugeland's own contribution 'The Nature and Plausibility of Cognitivism' is well worth reading. Dreyfus' sceptical outlook on AI, *What Computer's Can't Do* (1979) is less dated than it ought to be. Dreyfus updates that scepticism, and returns to his theme that intelligence is founded in skill in 'Misrepresenting Human Intelligence' (1987). For a very readable scepticism of current heuristic approaches to the problem of intelligence, see Manning's 'Why Sherlock Holmes Can't be Replaced by an Expert System' (1987). Levesque's 'Logic and the Complexity of Reasoning' (1988) is a good discussion of complexity and its bearing on an empirically plausible theory of reasoning. Fodor (1983, part IV) presents a gloomy picture of the prospects for an account of nondemonstrative inference; for a less pessimistic assessment see Holland et al. *Induction* (1986), or Johnson-Laird's *Mental Models* (1983).

Glossary

Antirealism   *See* realism.

Belief-desire psychology   The explanation of an agent's mental states or behaviour by appeal to the agent's beliefs and desires. These explanations normally work by showing the behaviour to be rational given those beliefs and desires. So, for example, we explain Toadface's robbing the bank by citing his desire to be rich, his belief that the robbery will make him rich, and his belief that no more important desire will be frustrated by the robbery.

Content   Short for 'semantic content', i.e. how a thought represents the world.

Dualism   Dualist theories are those that hold that some aspect or part of the mind is not physical.

Epistemology   The theory of the nature, acquisition, or growth of knowledge.

Folk psychology   In this book, folk psychology is used as a synonym for belief-desire psychology. It has a broader use encompassing the whole of commonsense concepts of our mental life. This broader use involves not just intentional states, but moods, emotions, character traits and experiences as well.

Functionalism   Functionalist theories of mind claim that the essential or defining conditions of mental states are their causal interactions with inputs, other inner states and outputs.

Homunculus A homunculus is a device within the mind whose states and operations are characterized in representational terms. A face recognizer, for example, is a homunculus because its basic job, face recognition, is representationally specified and because our account of its operations will talk about matching inputs with information held in memory and the like.

Implementation A functional device, or a state of that device, must be implemented or realized by some structure whose operation we can explain. So, for example, a mouse trap can be implemented by a base plate with a spring, trigger and bait attached.

Individualism Individualism is a doctrine about the natural kinds of psychology, the doctrine that the psychology of an organism depends only on features internal to it. A creature's skin contains a well-defined and integrated system, so the natural kinds of psychology are defined by properties internal to that system.

Intentional psychology *See* belief-desire psychology.

Intentional states An agent's thoughts, i.e. mental representations whose content can be, at least roughly, specified sententially and to which the agent takes some kind of 'attitude' – fear, belief, hope, desire and the like.

Intentional systems Any creature or device whose behaviour has a belief-desire explanation.

Module A mechanism within the mind that can operate with at least relative independence from others, in particular it needs little direction or information from the centres of conscious deliberative thought.

Narrow functionalism Narrow functionalist theories define psychological kinds by appeal to their causal interactions with inputs, outputs and other psychological kinds, but the inputs and outputs determining a causal role are internal to the mind. Hence it is a species of individualism. *See* wide functionalism.

Naturalism Philosophers who (a) are physicalists and (b) claim that philosophy is continuous with the natural sciences are naturalists.

Physicalism Physicalism is the doctrine that there is nothing but physical entities, and that ultimately physical laws explain everything.

Propositional attitude psychology *See* belief-desire psychology.

Realism Realism about a domain is the doctrine that the entities in that domain exist, and do so independently of any observer. Realists about, for example, the past hold that what went on in the past is mind-independent; it depends in no way on what we can observe, believe or find out. Antirealists, about a domain, either deny that the entities of that domain exist or that they are mind independent.

Realization *See* implementation.

Reduction   Reduction is a relationship between the kinds and laws of one scientific domain, and the kinds and laws of a more fundamental domain. Derivatively, it is also the relation between theories of the two domains. A reduced theory is shown to be a special case of the reducing theory, so a reduced theory can be replaced without loss of explanatory power.

Supervenience   One domain supervenes on another if there can be no difference in the supervening domain without difference in the base domain. Individualists think that psychology supervenes on neurophysiology; they think that there can be no psychological difference without difference in the intrinsic properties of brain states.

Syntax   The set of rules governing allowable combinations of a language's lexical items. It's a language's instruction manual. It tells how to combine words into larger units, phrases, and how these larger units are combined into sentences. So a language's syntax shows how its sentences are organized into phrases, and how phrases are organized into smaller phrases and words.

Teleology   Teleological claims are claims about a device's purpose or function. In biological contexts, these are cashed by appeal to natural selection. For the function of a device within a biological system is its effect(s) that have been favoured by natural selection, and which are thus responsible for its existence.

Transducers   Transducers are the interface between the mind and the world. Their function is to detect a particular kind of physical stimulus, and to produce an elementary symbolic representation of that stimulus.

Turing machine   Turing machines are a type of computer with an extremely simple basic organization, consisting only of a tape divided into sections and a reader through which the tape passes. Despite their simple organization, Turing machines are, in principle, as powerful as any other mode of organizing computing systems.

Wide functionalism   A variety of functionalism (sometimes also called broad functionalism) in which the inputs and outputs that specify mental states are environmentally defined. A typical input might be given as 'seeing a ripe apple', a typical output might be 'grasping a ripe apple'. By contrast, a narrow functionalist would define the same input in terms of the retinal stimulation it caused, and would specify the output as motor commands to the muscles of hand and eye.

References

Alcock, J. 1989: *Animal Behavior: An Evolutionary Approach*, 4th edn. Sinauer Associates, Massachusetts.

Anderson, J. A. and Rosenfeld, E. (eds) 1988: *Neurocomputing: Foundations of Research.* MIT Press, Cambridge, Mass.

Anderson, J. R. 1978: 'The Argument Concerning Representations for Mental Imagery'. *Psychological Review* 85, pp. 249–77.

Arbib, M. 1972: *The Metaphorical Brain.* Wiley Neuroscience, New York.

Armstrong, D. M. 1968: *A Materialist Theory of the Mind.* Routledge and Kegan Paul, London.

Armstrong, D. M. 1983: *What is a Law of Nature.* CUP, Cambridge.

Baker, L. R. 1987: *Saving Belief: A Critique of Physicalism.* Princeton University Press, Princeton, New Jersey.

Berwick, R. C. and Weinberg, A. S. 1986: *The Grammatical Basis of Linguistic Performance.* MIT Press, Cambridge, Mass.

Bigelow, J. and Pargetter, R. 1987: 'Functions'. *Journal of Philosophy* 84, pp. 181–96.

Block, N. J. 1978: 'Troubles with Functionalism' In W. Savage (ed.), *Perception and Cognition: Minnesota Studies in the Philosophy of Science, IX.* University of Minnesota Press, Minneapolis.

Block, N. 1980: *Readings in the Philosophy of Psychology, vol. 1.* MIT Press, Cambridge, Mass.

Block, N. 1981a: *Readings in the Philosophy of Psychology,* vol. II. MIT Press, Cambridge, Mass.

Block, N. 1981b: 'Psychologism and Behaviorism'. *Philosophical Review* 90, pp. 5–43.

Block, N. 1986: 'Advertisement for a Semantics for Psychology'. *Midwest Studies in Philosophy* 10, pp. 615–78.

Block, N. and Fodor, J. A. 1972: 'What Psychological States Are Not'. *Philosophical Review* 81, pp. 159–81. Reprinted in Block (1980).

Boden, M. 1977: *Artificial Intelligence and Natural Man*. Basic Books, New York.

Boden, M. 1981: *Minds and Mechanisms*. Cornell University Press, Ithaca.

Boghossian, P. (forthcoming) 'The Status of Content'. *Philosophical Review*.

Braddon-Mitchell, D. and Fitzpatrick, J. (forthcoming) 'Explanation and the Language of Thought'. *Synthese*.

Brandon, R. S. and Hornstein, N. 1986: 'From Icons to Symbols: Some Speculations on the Origins of Language'. *Biology and Philosophy* 1, pp. 169–90.

Broadbent, D. 1985: 'A Question of Levels: Comment on McClelland and Rumelhart'. *Journal of Experimental Psychology: General* 114, pp. 189–97 (includes a reply).

Burge, T. 1979: 'Individualism and the Mental'. *Midwest Studies in Philosophy* 5, pp. 73–122.

Burge, T. 1986: 'Individualism and Psychology'. *Philosophical Review* 95, pp. 3–46.

Byrne, R. and Whitten, A. 1988: *Machiavellian Intelligence*. Clarendon Press, Oxford.

Camhi, J. 1984: *Neuroethology*. Sinauer, Massachusetts.

Campbell, K. 1970: *Body and Mind*. MacMillan, London. (2nd edn, 1984, University of Notre Dame Press, Notre Dame, Indiana.

Caplan, D. (ed.) 1980: *Biological Studies of Mental Processes*. MIT Press, Cambridge.

Changeux, J-P. 1986: *Neuronal Man: the Biology of Mind*. OUP, Oxford.

Cherniak, C. 1986: *Minimal Rationality*. Bradford/MIT Press, Cambridge, Mass.

Churchland, P. M. 1979: *Scientific Realism and the Plasticity of Mind*. CUP, Cambridge.

Churchland, P. M. 1981: 'Eliminative Materialism and the Propositional Attitudes'. *Journal of Philosophy* 78, pp. 67–90.

Churchland, P. M. 1985: 'Reduction, Qualia and the Direct Introspection of Brain States'. *Journal of Philosophy* 82, pp. 8–28.

Churchland, P. M. 1986: 'Some Reductive Strategies in Cognitive Neurobiology'. *Mind* 95, pp. 279–309.

Churchland, P. M. 1988a: *Matter and Consciousness*, 2nd edn. MIT Press, Cambridge, Mass.

Churchland, P. M. 1988b: 'Perceptual Plasticity and Theoretical Neutrality: A Reply To Jerry Fodor'. *Philosophy of Science* 55, pp. 167–87.

Churchland, P. M. 1990: 'On The Nature of Theories: A Neurocomputational Perspective'. In P. M. Churchland, *A Neurocomputational Perspective: The Nature of Mind and the Structure of Science*, MIT Press, Cambridge Mass.

Churchland, P. M. and Churchland, P. S. 1981: 'Functionalism, Qualia and Intentionality'. *Philosophical Topics* 12, pp. 121–45.

Churchland, P. S. 1980: 'A Perspective on Mind-Brain Research'. *Journal of Philosophy* 77, pp. 185–207.

Churchland, P. S. 1981: 'Language, Thought and Information Processing'. *Nous* 14, pp. 147–70.

Churchland, P. S. 1983: 'Consciousness: The Transmutation of a Concept'. *Pacific Philosophical Quarterly* 64, pp. 80–95.

Churchland, P. S. 1986: *Neurophilosophy.* Bradford/MIT Press, Cambridge, Mass.

Churchland, P. S. and Churchland, P. M. 1983: 'Stalking the Wild Epistemic Engine'. *Nous* 17, pp. 5–18.

Clark, A. 1989: *Microcognition.* Bradford/MIT Press, Cambridge, Mass.

Cohen, L. J. 1981: 'Can Human Irrationality be Experimentally Demonstrated?'. *Behavioral and Brain Sciences* 4, pp. 317–370.

Cowie, F. (forthcoming) *Three Kinds of Meaning Holism.*

Cummins, R. 1983: *The Nature of Psychological Explanation.* Bradford/MIT Press, Cambridge, Mass.

Dawkins, R. 1982: *The Extended Phenotype.* OUP, Oxford.

Dawkins, R. and Krebs, J. R. 1984: 'Animal Signals: Mind-reading and Manipulation'. In J. R. Krebs and N. B. Davies (eds), *Behavioural Ecology: An Evolutionary Approach.* Blackwell Scientific Publications, Oxford.

Dennett, D. C. 1971: 'Intentional Systems'. *Journal of Philosophy* 68, pp. 87–106. Reprinted in Dennett (1978).

Dennett, D. C. 1978: *Brainstorms.* Bradford Books, Montgomery.

Dennett, D. C. 1981a: 'True Believers: The Intentional Strategy and Why It Works'. In A. F. Heath (ed.), *Scientific Explanation.* OUP, Oxford. Reprinted in Dennett (1987).

Dennett, D. C. 1981b: 'Three kinds of Intentional Psychology'. In R. Healy (ed.), *Reduction, Time and Reality.* CUP Cambridge. Reprinted in Dennett (1987).

Dennett, D. C. 1982: 'Beyond Belief'. In A. Woodfield (ed.), *Thought and Object.* Clarendon Press, Oxford. Reprinted in Dennett (1987).

Dennett, D. C. 1983: 'Intentional Systems in Cognitive Ethology: The "Panglossian Paradigm" Defended'. *Behavioral and Brain Sciences* 6, pp. 343–90. Reprinted in Dennett (1987).

Dennett, D. C. 1984: 'Cognitive wheels: the frame problem of AI'. In C. Hookway (ed.), *Minds, Machines and Evolution.* CUP, Cambridge. Reprinted in Pylyshyn (1987).

Dennett, D. C. 1986: 'The Logical Geography of Computational Approaches: The View from the East Pole'. In R. Harnish and M. Brand (eds), *Problems in the Representation of Knowledge.* University of Arizona Press, Tucson.

Dennett, D. C. 1987: *The Intentional Stance.* Bradford/MIT Press, Cambridge, Mass.

Dennett, D. C. (forthcoming) 'Mother Nature versus the Walking

Encyclopedia: A Western Drama'. In W. Ramsey, D. Rumelhart and S. Stich (eds), *Philosophy and Connectionist Theory*.

Dennett, D. C. and Hofstadter, D. R. (eds) 1981: *The Mind's I*. Harvester, Brighton, Sussex.

Devitt, M. 1981: *Designation*. Columbia University Press, New York.

Devitt, M. 1984a: *Realism and Truth*. Basil Blackwell, Oxford.

Devitt, M. 1984b: 'Thoughts and Their Ascription'. *Midwest Studies in Philosophy* 9, pp. 385–420.

Devitt, M. 1989: 'A Narrow Representational Theory of the Mind'. In S. Silvers (ed.), *Representation: Readings in the Philosophy of Mental Representation*. Reidel, Dordrecht.

Devitt, M. (forthcoming a) 'Why Fodor Can't Have It Both Ways'. In B. Loewer and G. Rey (eds), *Meaning in Mind: Fodor and His Critics*.

Devitt, M. (forthcoming b) 'Meaning Localism'. (Devitt forthcoming b)

Devitt, M. (forthcoming c) 'Transcendentalism about Content'.

Devitt, M and Sterelny, K. 1987: *Language and Reality*. Blackwell/MIT Press, Oxford.

Dretske, F. I. 1981: *Knowledge and The Flow of Information*. Blackwell, Oxford.

Dretske, F. I. 1986a: 'Misrepresentation'. In R. Bogdan (ed.), *Belief*. OUP, Oxford.

Dretske, F. I. 1986b: 'Aspects of Cognitive Representation'. In M. Brand and R. M. Harnish (eds), *The Representation of Knowledge and Belief*. University of Arizona Press, Tucson.

Dretske, F. I. 1988: *Explaining Behavior: Reasons in a World of Causes*. Bradford/MIT Press, Cambridge, Mass.

Dreyfus, H. L. 1979: *What Computers Can't Do*, revised edn. Harper and Row, New York.

Dreyfus, H. 1987: 'Misrepresenting Human Intelligence'. In R. Born, (ed.) *Artificial Intelligence: The Case Against*. Croom Helm, London.

Dreyfus, H. L. and Dreyfus, R. 1987: 'The Frame Problem'. In Pylyshyn (1987).

Eckardt, B. von 1984: 'Congnitive Psychology and Principled Scepticism.' *Journal of Philosophy* 81, pp. 67–88.

Feldman, J. A. and Ballard, D. H. 1982: 'Connectionist Models and their Properties'. *Cognitive Science* 6, pp. 205–54.

Feyerabend, P. 1975: *Against Method*. New Left Books, London.

Field, H. 1978: 'Mental Representations'. *Erkenntnis*, 13, pp. 9–61. Reprinted in Block (1981a).

Field, H. 1986: 'The Deflationary Conception of Truth' In G. MacDonald and C. Wright (eds), *Fact, Science and Morality*. Basil Blackwell, Oxford.

Fodor, J. A. 1968: *Psychological Explanation*. Random House, New York.

Fodor, J. A. 1975: *The Language of Thought*. Thomas Crowell, New York.

Fodor, J. A. 1978: 'Propositional Attitudes' *The Monist* 61, pp. 501–23. Reprinted in Block (1981a).

Fodor, J. A. 1980: 'Methodological Solipsism Considered as a Research

Strategy in Cognitive Psychology'. *Behavioral and Brain Sciences*, 3, pp. 63–110.

Fodor, J. A. 1981: *Representations*. Bradford/MIT Press, Cambridge, Mass.

Fodor, J. A. 1983: *The Modularity of Mind*. Bradford/MIT Press, Cambridge, Mass.

Fodor, J. A. 1984a: 'Observation Reconsidered'. *Philosophy of Science* 51, pp. 23–43.

Fodor, J. A. 1984b: 'Semantics, Wisconsin Style'. *Synthese*, 59, pp. 1–20.

Fodor, J. A. 1985a: 'Precis of The Modularity of Mind'. *Behavioral and Brain Sciences* 8, pp. 1–42.

Fodor, J. A. 1985b: 'Fodor's Guide to Mental Representation'. *Mind* 94, pp. 76– 100.

Fodor, J. A. 1986: 'Why Paramecia Don't Have Mental Representations'. *Midwest Studies in Philosophy* 10, pp. 3–24.

Fodor, J. A. 1987: 'Modules, Frames, Fridgeons, Sleeping Dogs, and the Music of the Spheres'. In Garfield (1987).

Fodor, J. A. 1988a: *Psychosemantics*. Bradford/MIT Press, Cambridge, Mass.

Fodor, J. A. 1988b: 'A Reply to Churchland's "Perceptual Plasticity and Theoretical Neutrality"'. *Philosophy of Science* 55, pp. 188–98.

Fodor, J. A. (forthcoming) *A Theory of Content I & II*.

Fodor, J. A. and McClaughlin, T. (forthcoming) 'The Rutgers Chainsaw Massacre II', *Cognition*.

Fodor, J. A. and Pylyshyn, Z. 1981: 'How Direct Is Visual Perception: Some Reflections on Gibson's "Ecological Approach"'. *Cognition* 9, pp. 139–96.

Fodor, J. A. and Pylyshyn, Z. 1988: 'Connectionism and Cognitive Architecture: A Critical Analysis'. *Cognition* 28, pp. 3–71.

Gardner, H. 1985: *The Mind's New Science: A History of the Cognitive Revolution*. Basic Books, New York.

Garfield, J. L. (ed) 1987: *Modularity in Knowledge Representation and Natural Language Understanding*. Bradford/MIT Press, Cambridge, Mass.

Gibson, J. J. 1979: *The Ecological Approach to Visual Perception*. Houghton Mifflin, Boston

Godfrey-Smith P. 1986: 'Why Semantic Properties Won't Earn Their Keep'. *Philosophical Studies* 50, pp. 223–36.

Godfrey-Smith, P. 1989: 'Misinformation'. *Canadian Journal of Philosophy* 19, pp. 553–50.

Godfrey-Smith, P. (forthcoming) *Indication and Adaptation*.

Goodman, N. 1969: *Languages of Art*. OUP, London.

Gould, S. J. 1980: 'A Biological Homage to Mickey Mouse'. In S. J. Gould, *The Panda's Thumb*. W. W. Norton, New York.

Harman, G. 1975: *Thought*. Princeton University Press, Princeton, New Jersey.

Hatfield, G. 1988: 'Representation and Content in some (Actual) Theories of Perception'. *Studies in the History and Philosophy of Science* 19, pp. 175–214.

Hatfield, G and Kosslyn, S. 1984: 'Representation without Symbol Systems'. *Social Research* 51, pp. 1019–45.

Haugeland, J. 1981: (ed.) *Mind Design: Philosophy, Psychology, Artificial Intelligence.* Bradford Books, Vermont.

Haugeland, J. 1985: *Artificial Intelligence: The Very Idea.* Bradford/MIT Press, Cambridge, Mass.

Hinton, G. E., McClelland, J. L. and Rumelhart, D. E. 1986: 'Distributed Representations'. In McClelland et al. (1986).

Holland, J. H., Holyoak, K. J., Nisbett, R. E. and Thagard, P. R. 1986: *Induction.* MIT Press, Cambridge, Mass.

Hooker, C. A. 1981: 'Towards a General Theory of Reduction, Parts I–III'. *Dialogue* 20, pp. 38–59, 201–36, 496–529.

Horgan, T. and Tienson, J. 1988: 'Settling into a New Paradigm'. *Southern Journal of Philosophy* 26, Supplement, pp. 97–114.

Horgan, T. and Woodward, J. 1985: 'Folk Psychology is Here to Stay'. *Philosophical Review* 94, pp. 197–226.

Hubel, D. 1988: *Eye, Brain and Vision.* Sinauer Press, New Jersey.

Jackson, F. 1982: 'Epiphenomenal Qualia'. *Philosophical Quarterly* 32, pp. 127–36. Reprinted in Lycan (1990).

Jackson, F. and Pettit, P. 1988: 'Functionalism and Broad Content'. *Mind* 107, pp. 381–400.

Jackson, F. and Pettit, P. (forthcoming) 'In Defence of Folk Psychology'.

Johnson-Laird, P. N. 1983: *Mental Models.* Harvard University Press, Cambridge, Mass.

Johnson-Laird, P. N. and Wason, P. C. (eds) 1977: *Thinking.* CUP, Cambridge.

Kahneman, D., Slovic, P. and Tversky, A. (eds) 1982: *Judgment under Uncertainty: Heuristics and Biases.* CUP, Cambridge.

Kirsh, D. 1988: 'Putting a Price on Cognition'. *Southern Journal of Philosophy* 28, Supplement, pp. 119–36.

Kitcher, Patricia 1984: 'In Defense of Intentional Psychology' *Journal of Philosophy* 81, pp. 89–106.

Kitcher, Patricia 1988: 'Marr's Computational Theory of Vision'. *Philosophy of Science* 55, pp. 1–24.

Kitcher, Philip 1982: 'Genes'. *British Journal for the Philosophy of Science* 33, pp. 337–59.

Kitcher, Philip 1984: '1953 and All That'. *Philosophical Review* 93, pp. 335–73.

Kosslyn, S. M. 1980: *Image and Mind.* Harvard University Press, Cambridge, Mass.

Kosslyn, S. M. 1983: *Ghosts in the Mind's Machine.* W. W. Norton, New York.

Kripke, S. 1980: *Naming and Necessity.* Harvard University Press, Cambridge, Mass.

Kuhn, T. 1970: *The Structure Of Scientific Revolutions,* 2nd edn. Chicago University Press, Chicago.

Levesque, H. J. 1988: 'Logic and the Complexity of Reasoning'. *Journal of Philosophical Logic* 17, pp. 355–90.

Lloyd, D. 1989: *Simple Minds.* Bradford/MIT, Cambridge, Mass.

Lycan, W. G. 1981a: 'Form, Function, and Feel'. *Journal of Philosophy* 78, pp. 24–50. Reprinted in Lycan (1990).

Lycan, W. G. 1981b: 'Towards a Homuncular Theory of Believing'. *Cognition and Brain Theory* 4, pp. 139–59.

Lycan, W. G. 1987: *Consciousness*. Bradford/MIT Press, Cambridge, Mass.

Lycan, W. G. (ed.) 1990: *Mind and Cognition*. Blackwell, Oxford.

Maloney, J. C. 1984: 'The Mundane Mental Language: How To Do Words With Things'. *Synthese* 59, pp. 251–94.

Maloney, J. C. 1985: 'Methodological Solipsism Reconsidered as a Research Strategy in Cognitive Psychology'. *Philosophy of Science* 52, pp. 451–69.

Manning, R. T. 1987: 'Why Sherlock Holmes Can't Be Replaced by an Expert System'. *Philosophical Studies* 51, pp. 19–28.

Marr, D. 1982: *Vision*. W. H. Freeman, New York.

Matthen M. 1988: 'Biological Functions and Perceptual Content'. *Journal of Philosophy* 85, pp. 5–27.

Maudlin, T. 1989: 'Computation and Consciousness'. *Journal of Philosophy* 86, pp. 407–32.

McClelland, J. L., Rumelhart, D. E. and the PDP Research Group 1986: *Parallel Distributed Processing: Explorations in the Microstructure of Cognition, Volume II Psychological and Biological Models*. Bradford/MIT Press, Cambridge, Mass.

McGinn, C. 1982: 'The Structure of Content' in A.Woodfield ed. *Thought and Object*; Clarendon Press, Oxford.

McGinn, C. 1983: *The Character of Mind*. OUP, Oxford.

Millikan, R. G. 1984: *Language, Thought and Other Biological Categories*. Bradford/MIT Press, Cambridge, Mass.

Millikan, R. G. 1986: 'Thoughts Without Laws; Cognitive Science With Content'. *Philosophical Review* 95, pp. 47–80.

Millikan, R. G. 1989a: 'Biosemantics'. *Journal of Philosophy* 86, pp. 281–97.

Millikan, R. G. 1989b 'In Defense of Proper Functions'. *Philosophy of Science* 56, pp. 288–302.

Millikan, R. G. (forthcoming a) 'Truth Rules, Hoverflies, and the Kripke–Wittgenstein Paradox'. *Philosophical Review*.

Millikan, R. G. (forthcoming b) 'Speaking Up For Darwin'. In G. Rey and B. Loewer (eds), *Meaning and Mind: Fodor and his Critics*. Blackwell.

Millikan, R. G. (forthcoming c) *What Is Behaviour? Or Why Narrow Ethology Is Impossible*.

Nadel, L., Willner, J. and Kurz, E. 1986: 'The Neurobiology of Mental Representation'. In M. Brand and R. M. Harnish (eds), *The Representation of Knowledge and Belief*. University of Arizona Press, Tucson.

Nagel, T. 1979: 'What is it Like to be a Bat?' In T. Nagel, *Mortal Questions*. CUP, Cambridge.

Neander, K. (forthcoming) 'Functions as Selected Effects'. *Philosophy of Science*.

Newell, A. 1980: 'Physical Symbol Systems'. *Cognitive Science* 4, pp. 135–83.

Newell, A. 1982: 'The Knowledge Level'. *Artificial Intelligence* 18, pp. 87–127.

Palmer, S. E. 1978: 'Fundamental Aspects of Cognitive Representation'. In E. Rosch and B. B. Lloyd (eds), *Cognition and Categorization*. Erlbaum, New Jersey.

Papineau, D. 1984: 'Representation and Explanation'. *Philosophy of Science* 51, pp. 550–72.

Papineau, D. 1987: *Reality and Representation*. Blackwell, Oxford.

Peacocke, C. 1986: 'Explanation in Computational Psychology: Language, Perception and Level 1.5'. *Mind and Language* 1, pp. 101–23.

Piattelli-Palmarini, M. 1989: 'Evolution, Selection and Cognition: From "Learning" to Parameter Setting in Biology and the Study of Language'. *Cognition* 31, pp. 1–44.

Pinker, S. (ed.) 1985: *Visual Cognition*. MIT Press, Cambridge, Mass.

Pinker, S. and Prince, A. 1988: 'On Language and Connectionism: Analysis of a Parallel Distributed Model of Language Acquisition'. *Cognition* 28, pp. 73–193.

Premack, D. 1986: *Gavagai! Or the Future History of the Animal Language Controversy*. Bradford/MIT Press, Cambridge, Mass.

Premack, D. and Woodruff, G. 1978: 'Does the Chimpanzee Have a Theory of Mind?' *The Behavioral and Brain Sciences* 1, pp. 515–26.

Putnam, H. 1975a: *Mind, Language and Reality: Philosophical Papers Volume 2*. CUP, Cambridge.

Putnam, H. 1975b: 'The Meaning of "Meaning"'. In K. Gunderson (ed.), *Minnesota Studies in the Philosophy of Science*, vol. 7. University of Minnesota Press, Minneapolis. Reprinted in Putnam (1975a).

Putnam, H. 1981a: *Reason, Truth and History*. CUP, Cambridge.

Putnam, H. 1981b: 'Brains in Vats'. In Putnam (1981a).

Putnam, H. 1988: *Representation and Reality*. Bradford/MIT Press, Cambridge, Mass.

Pylyshyn, Z. 1980: 'Cognition and Computation'. *Behavioral and Brain Sciences* 3, pp. 111–32.

Pylyshyn, Z. 1984: *Computation and Cognition*. Bradford/MIT Press, Cambridge, Mass.

Pylyshyn, Z. (ed.) 1987: *The Robot's Dilemma*. Ablex, New Jersey.

Quine, W. V. 1970: *Philosophy of Logic*. Prentice-Hall, New Jersey.

Ramsey, W., Stich, S. and Garon, J. (forthcoming) 'Connectionism, Eliminativism, and the Future of Folk Psychology'. *Philosophical Perspectives*.

Rey, G. 1986: 'What's Really Going On In Searle's "Chinese Room"?' *Philosophical Studies* 50, pp. 169–85.

Rock, I. 1983: *The Logic of Perception*. Bradford/MIT Press, Cambridge, Mass.

Rumelhart, D. E., McClelland, J. E. and the PDP Research Group 1986a: *Parallel Distributed Processing: Explorations in the Microstructure of Cognition, Volume I Foundations*. Bradford/MIT Press, Cambridge, Mass.

Rumelhart, D. E., Smolensky, P., McClelland, J. L. and Hinton, G. E. 1986b: 'Schemata and Sequential Thought Processes in PDP Models'. In Rumelhart et al. (1986).

Sachs, O. 1985: *The Man Who Mistook his Wife for a Hat*. Pan Books, London, England.

Schiffer, S. 1987: *Remnants of Meaning*. Bradford/MIT Press, Cambridge, Mass.

Searle, J. R. 1980: 'Minds, Brains and Programs'. *Behavioral and Brain Sciences* 3, pp. 417–57.

Searle, J. R. 1983: *Intentionality: An Essay in the Philosophy of Mind*. CUP, Cambridge.

Searle, J. R. 1984: *Minds, Brains and Science*. Harvard University Press, Cambridge, Mass.

Searle, J. R. 1987: 'Minds and Brains without Programs'. In C. Blakemore and S. Greenfield (eds), *Mindwaves*. Basil Blackwell, Oxford.

Segal, G. 1989: 'Seeing What Is Not There'. *Philosophical Review* 98, pp. 189–214.

Sejnowski, T. J. and Rosenberg, C. R. 1988 'NETtalk: a parallel network that learns to read aloud'. In Anderson and Rosenfeld (1988).

Simon, H. A. 1981: *The Sciences of the Artificial*, 2nd edn. MIT Press, Cambridge, Mass.

Smolensky, P. 1988a: 'On the Proper Treatment of Connectionism'. *Behavioral and Brain Sciences* 11, pp. 1–74.

Smolensky, P. 1988b: 'The Constituent Structure of Connectionist Mental States: A Reply to Fodor and Pylyshyn'. *Southern Journal of Philosophy* 26, Supplement, pp. 137–62.

Sober, E. 1984: *The Nature of Selection*. Bradford/MIT Press Cambridge, Mass.

Squire, L. R. 1987: *Memory and Brain*. OUP, Oxford.

Stabler, E. P. 1983: 'How are Grammars Represented?' *Behavioral and Brain Sciences* 6, pp. 391–421.

Stalnaker, R. C. 1984: *Inquiry*. Bradford/MIT Press, Cambridge, Mass.

Stampe, D. 1979: 'Towards a Causal Theory of Linguistic Representation'. *Midwest Studies in Philosophy* 2, pp. 81–102.

Stampe, D. 1986: 'Verification and a Causal Account of Meaning'. *Synthese* 69, pp. 107–137.

Sterelny, K. 1981: 'Critical Notice of D. C. Dennett's "Brainstorms"'. *Australasian Journal of Philosophy* 59, pp. 442–53.

Sterelny, K. 1983: 'Natural Kind Terms'. *Pacific Philosophical Quarterly* 64, pp. 110–25.

Sterelny, K. 1989: 'Fodor's Nativism'. *Philosophical Studies* 55, pp. 119–41.

Sterelny, K. 1990: 'Animals and Individualism'. *Vancouver Studies in Cognitive Science* 1, pp. 323–39. This paper was originally written jointly with Godfrey-Smith.

Sterelny, K. (forthcoming) 'Learning, Selection, Species'. *Behavioral and Brain Sciences*.

Sterelny, K. and Kitcher, P. 1988: 'The Return of the Gene'. *Journal of Philosophy* 85, pp. 339–61.

Stich, S. P. 1978a: 'Autonomous Psychology and the Belief-Desire Thesis'. *The Monist* 61, pp. 573–91.

Stich, S. P. 1978b: 'Beliefs and Subdoxastic States'. *Philosophy of Science* 45, pp. 499–518.

Stich, S. P. 1982: 'On the Ascription of Content'. In A. Woodfield (ed.), *Thought and Object.* Clarendon Press, Oxford.

Stich, S. P. 1983: *From Folk Psychology to Cognitive Science.* Bradford/MIT Press, Cambridge, Mass.

Stich, S. P. 1985: 'Could Man Be An Irrational Animal?' In H. Kornblith (ed.), *Naturalizing Epistemology.* Bradford/MIT Press, Cambridge, Mass.

Stillings, N. A., Feinstein, M., Garfield, J. L., Rissland, E. L., Rosenbaum, D. A., Weisler, S. E., and Baker-Ward, L. 1987: *Cognitive Science: An Introduction.* Bradford/MIT Press, Cambridge, Mass.

Tienson, J. 1988: 'Introduction to Connectionism'. *Southern Journal of Philosophy* 28, Supplement, pp. 1–16.

Trivers, R. 1985: *Social Evolution.* Benjamin/Cummings, Merlo Park, California.

Turing, A. M. 1950: 'Computing Machinery and Intelligence'. *Mind* 59, pp. 433–60. Reprinted in Dennett and Hofstadter (1981).

Ullman, S. 1979: *The Interpretation of Visual Motion.* MIT Press, Cambridge, Mass.

Ullman, S. 1980: 'Against Direct Perception'. *Behavioral and Brain Sciences* 3, pp. 373–415.

Waal, F. de 1982: *Chimpanzee Politics: Power and Sex Amongst Apes.* Harper and Row, New York.

Walker, E. (ed.) 1978: *Explorations in the Biology of Language.* Bradford Books, Vermont.

Index